Bryan Sparrow

with grateful thanks
from Royal Botanical Gardens
Hamilton

January 87.

Rhetoric and Roses

Edwinna von Baeyer

We at Royal Botanical Gardens are delighted to be associated with Edwinna von Baeyer's work. Our Centre for Canadian Historical Horticultural Studies, endowed by the Dunington Grubb Foundation in 1979, is committed to documenting Canada's gardening history. Rhetoric and Roses *is a major acquisition.*

Rhetoric and Roses

A History of Canadian Gardening 1900–1930

Edwinna von Baeyer

Fitzhenry & Whiteside

Fitzhenry & Whiteside Limited
195 Allstate Parkway
Markham, Ontario L3R 4T8

Editor *Peg McKelvey*
Designer *Sandi Meland*
Typesetting by *Jay Tee Graphics Ltd.*
Printed and bound in Canada by *John Deyell Company*

Canadian Cataloguing in Publication Data

von Baeyer, Edwinna, 1946-
Rhetoric and roses

Bibliography: p.
Includes index.
ISBN 0-88902-983-0

1. Gardening - Canada - History. 2. Horticulture - Canada - History. 3. Canada - Social conditions - 1918-1930.* 4. Canada - Social conditions -1867-1918.* I. Title.

SB451.36.C3V64 1984 635'.0971 C84-099542-3

Contents

Preface

Rhetoric and Roses is the history of how and why we gardened during the first thirty years of the twentieth century; as such it is not a full treatment of professional landscape design. These first thirty years were an exciting era, characterized by a variety of horticultural innovations as well as an abundant rhetoric, frequently forceful, sometimes moralistic, which influenced the creation of our ornamental gardens in railway stations, school grounds, vacant lots and our own back yards.

I came upon this fascinating tale indirectly. While reading through the extensive literature of British gardening histories, I began to wonder what had happened in Canada. Were we totally bereft of a noteworthy horticultural past, or were our efforts just weak reflections of the dominating British (or American) landscape theory and garden movements? Preliminary research did not turn up anything significant. It was not until I found myself compiling a bibliography of Canadian garden history for Parks Canada that I began to discover where our horticultural writings were to be found and to gather an inkling of what a rich horticultural history we have.

During forays into card catalogues and periodical indexes, I did not find any book-length histories of our gardening past — certainly no one had focused on the twentieth century. I discovered that the majority of our horticultural writings were in periodicals, ranging from the horticultural, to the agricultural, to the general. In my research I concentrated on examining, issue by issue, a great variety of magazines and journals, branching out into provincial sessional reports, horticultural society reports, and a selection of histories on related topics.

It is likely, however, that manuscript archives and personal papers across Canada contain material relating to gardening and landscaping which could enrich the story as it is known so far. We should exploit these resources and promote more studies of the personalities and landscapes important to our horticultural past. Then perhaps a complete history from the very beginnings will be written. A rose is a rose . . ., but the story behind it is sometimes more than one might imagine.

I would like to express my appreciation to the many people who helped me find my way down the garden path. Susan Buggey (Historical Research, Parks Canada) not only placed my feet there, but she has also contributed a lively afterword on historic garden preservation issues. She has continually supported this project with information and suggestions and a critical reading of several chapters. Pleasance Crawford has contributed generous helpings of her own detailed garden research, moral support and a fine reading of five chapters. Daniel Francis not only provided invaluable contacts, but also offered suggestions on the text, and on the publishing world in general.

Ina Vrugtman, Librarian at the Royal Botanical Gardens Library in Hamilton, Ontario, supplied needed information and kindly brought the manuscript to the attention of officials at the Royal Botanical Gardens. Its Director, Allen Paterson, has provided the foreword. He and the Royal Botanical Gardens deserve special thanks.

Bryan Evans has my heartfelt gratitude for his painstaking patience in photographing the many pictures from period journals and books which enhance this history. I would also like to thank G. Ross Hodgins (Agriculture Canada Libraries Division) for generously allowing access to their material, Omar Lavalee (CP Archives, Montreal), George Smellie (CP Winnipeg), Vivian Hysop and H.W. Paar, as well as the helpful staff at the many libraries I haunted, and the many, many people who supplied bits of information or hints of an interesting lead to follow.

Many thanks to Peg McKelvey, my editor, for her astute comments and suggestions which have improved the book so much. And more than thanks to my husband Cornelius. His helpful comments and editing (much appreciated even when it caused rewriting), and his support all along the course of the project have added immeasurably to the final form and content of the book.

I would also like to acknowledge gratefully the Canada Council Explorations Program which supported six months of the research, and the Ontario Arts Council for further financial support.

Although many friends and relations have read portions of the manuscript and offered suggestions and corrections, any errors or omissions can, alas, only be attributed to me.

Edwinna von Baeyer
Ottawa 1984

Foreword

In examining the history of gardeners and gardening it is usual to quote patrician writers of times past who were able, with Biblical authority, to claim not only the Deity as an enthusiastic gardener but, following His example, all the most enlightened princes of the earth. Thus have Francis Bacon's rolling seventeenth-century phrases become familiar:

> God Almightie first planted a Garden. And, indeed it is the Purest of Human pleasures. It is the Greatest Refreshment to the Spirits of Man; without which Buildings and Palaces are but Grosse Handy-works: And a Man shall ever see, that when Ages grow to Civility and Elegancie, Men come to Build Stately, sooner than to Garden Finely: As if Gardening were the Greatest Perfection.

Gardening is seen here, and with subsequent authorities, as being morally uplifting as well as epitomizing taste among the cognoscenti of an established civilization.

Edwinna von Baeyer's account of Canadian gardening in the first three decades of this century might seem an unlikely extension to Bacon's expectations of Civility and Elegancie preceding fine gardens. For, paradoxically, we see a still emergent nation being exhorted at many levels to attain Baconian ideals *through* gardening.

The motives were many; some coming from highminded dogooders to others that appear positively devious. Much reflects the prevalent attitudes of the ruling groups in nineteenth-century Europe towards their lower classes. The poor who looked after their little plots of ground were considered less likely to indulge in wife-beating; neither did they neglect their children. These were the sort of settlers required in a new land for, by extension, those who owned and maintained a garden would have a vested interest in the political status quo.

From the encouragement of adults to the bringing of such ideals into the schools was but a short step. The rise of school gardening in the early 1900s (as in Europe) is shown as significant in inculcating desirable standards in the children of Canadians as well as helping to "Canadianize the foreign-born." It is easy to be cynical about such attitudes which, with hindsight, appear so transparently condescending. Yet they hold a truth which is just as valid in today's softer society: where man makes his home and puts down metaphorical roots there too does he (more traditionally she) put down actual roots in back-yard or window box. It seems that we need plants, and regardless of moral worth and economic advantage we take satisfaction in their cultivation "for use and for delight."

Garden history is a new discipline, yet one which relates to all sorts and conditions of men: it can be seen also as an inevitable part of the social history of a nation. Gardening, as Edwinna von Baeyer shows, touches everyone. Here at Royal Botanical Gardens, a Centre of Canadian Historical Horticultural Studies (*CCHHS*) has been in existence for five years: *Rhetoric and Roses* makes a major contribution to its holdings.

Allen Paterson, Director
Royal Botanical Gardens
Hamilton, Ontario

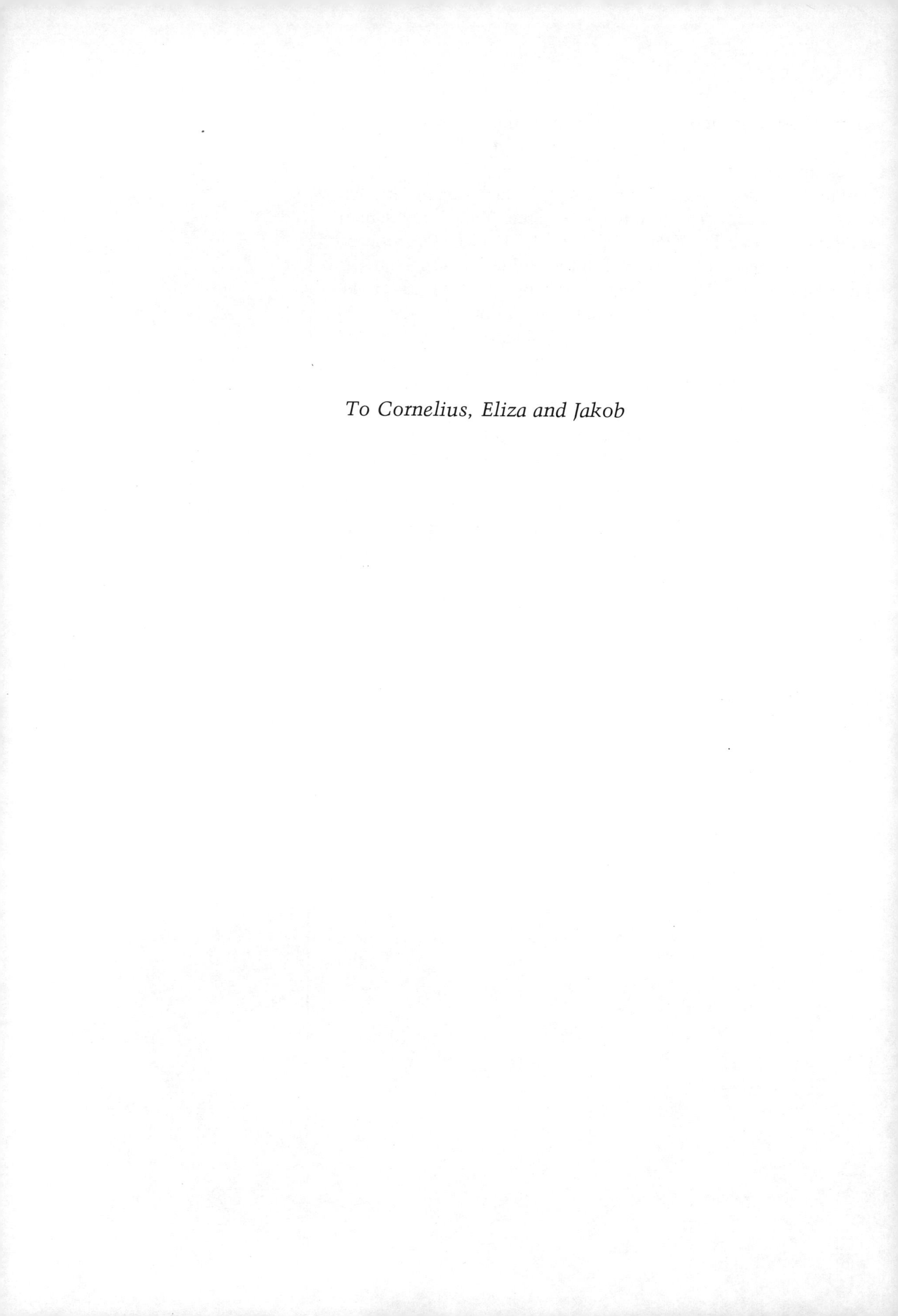

To Cornelius, Eliza and Jakob

The Background

1 The Moral Garden:

Gardening and Reform In Canada

A GLIMPSE OF THE VIRTUOUS TWENTIETH-CENTURY GARDENER

The early twentieth-century Canadian garden was not created solely for aesthetic reasons. A reforming zeal, evident throughout society in the actions of prohibitionists, suffragettes, evangelists and others, provided the impetus for our first great movement to improve our surroundings, that is, to garden.

Yet, Canadians in the early 1900s were not allowed to just putter around the back-yard, deciding whether to replace those straggly hollyhocks with a clump of orange day lilies. They were told to clean up their back-yards, creating gardens for moral and spiritual welfare, and ridding the grounds of pest-filled eyesores. After the back-yard, the front was to be ornamented by judicious tree planting, lawn care, even a corner rockery — all contributing to Civic Beautification. Right-thinking Canadians were not to stop at the front step; they were to join civic improvement societies and plan public parks, and execute public plantings near civic centres, railway lines, school houses and post offices. They were encouraged to support nature study and school gardening on the school curriculum — by which children (both urban and rural) would learn to love nature, to garden, to think for themselves, and to become good Canadian citizens.

Never has the craft of gardening had to bear such heavy psychological, social and moral burdens. Beauty ceased to be the

main goal; it now struggled for a place alongside good citizenship, improvement, social remedy, morality and material progress. For example, the railway garden, popularized in Canada by the CPR, was not promoted for its beauty alone, but rather for demonstrating the fertility of the land to potential settlers and the progressiveness and worth of towns. Parks functioned as local beauty spots, but were promoted rather as urban breathing spaces offsetting the adverse psychological effects of ugly crowded cities in the throes of industrialization. Parks also raised nearby real estate values. Worker housing was to incorporate gardens — reformers stated that anyone who owned his own land would not endanger the nation by agitating, striking, drinking or turning to communism. Vacant-lot gardening was initially promoted as a form of welfare for the poor, then as a beautifying measure, and finally as a patriotic duty during World War I. Foreigners were to be Canadianized through a love of gardening. Slums were to be brightened and cleansed through gifts of cuttings, pots of geraniums, and seed packets of annual asters. The Canadian gardener not only laboured to weed his own garden, but society's as well.

The majority of the gardening promoters were solidly middle-class and mostly urban, holding dear the values of property, family, profit, social status and the status quo. Gardening was seen to incorporate and express many of these values. Also, ornamental gardening had been long accepted as a pursuit worthy of people of means and distinction. Because those who garden are the "right sort," it followed that others introduced to the *real* values of gardening would naturally adopt a way of life which did not include strikes, Bolshevism, foreign ideals, or unhygienic and unaesthetic surroundings. A person who owned and maintained a garden would have a vested interest in the status quo. Gardening in Canada from 1900 to 1930 carried many cultural messages. Canadians were to garden for the benefit of home, city and nation.

Entrance to Prince's Lodge, Bedford Basin, Halifax. Park-like entrance grounds were typical of the Picturesque landscape style.

THE RISE OF ORNAMENTAL GARDENING IN CANADA

The emphasis was new, but the practice of gardening in Canada certainly was not. Our horticultural past extends back into the seventeenth century. Samuel de Champlain planted food crops as early as 1605 at St. Croix.[1] Monastery gardens were established as early as 1653.[2] In that year Marie de l'Incarnation of the Ursuline convent wrote friends in France asking for French flower seeds. There were "none here that are either very rare or very beautiful. Everything is wild, flowers as well as men."[3]

There were landscaped gardens as early as the 1790s. Prince's

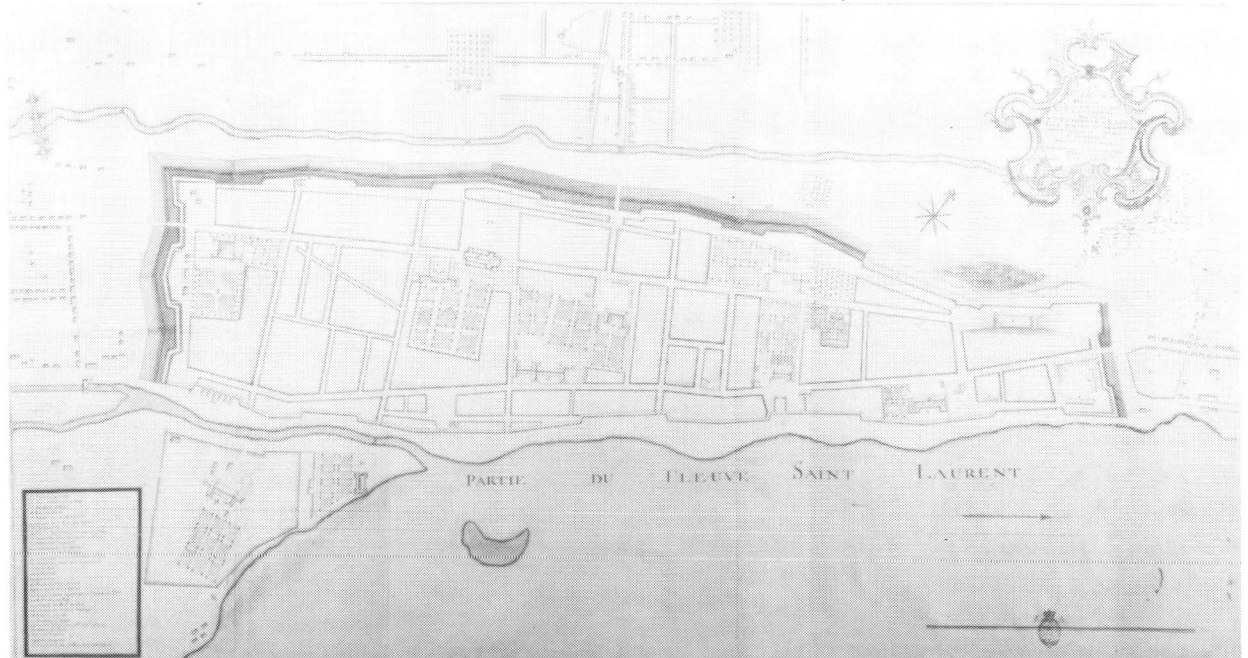

Eighteenth century Montreal. Seven seminary gardens laid out according to the medieval pattern.

Lodge, Bedford Basin (Halifax) was the site of Canada's oldest example of the English Picturesque landscape style. Laid out by Queen Victoria's father, the Duke of Kent, for his mistress Julie de St. Laurent (while he was commander-in-chief of the garrison), the design incorporated a heart-shaped pool, a meandering path which spelled out "Julie," a miniature lake and waterfall and secluded grottoes.[4]

Many landscaped estate gardens were created in Upper and Lower Canada in the nineteenth century, which reflected British landscape styles. J.M. LeMoine, in 1865, describes thirty-five "country seats" around Montreal and Quebec.[5] These substantial gardens, owned by wealthy merchants and government officials, were managed by professional British gardeners. LeMoine's description of Ravenswood, home of a wealthy Montreal businessman, demonstrates the park-like ideal of contemporary British landscaping:

> No sylvan spot could have been procured, had all the woods around Quebec been ransacked, of wilder beauty. In the centre a pretty cottage; to the east, trees; to the west, trees; to the north and south, trees — stately trees all around you. Within a few rods from the hall door a limpid little brook oozes from under an old plantation, and forms, under a thorn tree of extraordinary size and most fantastically shaped limbs, a reservoir of clear water, round which, from a rustic seat, you notice speckled trout roaming fearlessly. Here was, for a man familiar with the park-like scenery of England, a store of materials to work into shape. That dense forest must be thinned; that indispensable adjunct of every Sillery home, a velvety lawn, must be had; a peep through the trees, on the

Belvedere Lodge (above) and Rosewood (right) were two mid-nineteenth century estate gardens along the St. Lawrence River in Lower Canada, which reflected prevailing British style.

> surrounding country obtained; the stream dammed up as to produce a sheet of water, on which a birch canoe will be launched; more air let in round the house; more of the forest cut away; and some fine beach, birch, maple, and pine trees grouped. The lawn would look better with a graceful and leafy elm in the centre, and a few smaller ones added to the perspective.[6]

The most common form of gardening in the 1800s was, however, occurring on a much smaller scale. Both urban and rural gardens reflected economic concerns rather than ornamental ones — although flowers were never completely absent. Most early nineteenth-century gardens were unplanned with clumps of flowers planted wherever they would grow best.[7] However, by 1834, Canada's first horticultural society was founded in Toronto, and by the 1880s there were horticultural societies in most Canadian cities, although these early societies primarily served the more affluent citizens.

As the century progressed and more communities evolved out of a predominately pioneer life-style, more land was cleared and smaller home lots took on a designed and ornamental look. By the late 1860s, the Victorian landscape style (which included carpet bedding and geometrical layouts) was becoming prevalent in Canada. Many rural gardens, however, continued in the style of former years.

Public parks were few. In the early 1800s, cemeteries were the first landscaped areas to be enjoyed by the public, where "graves

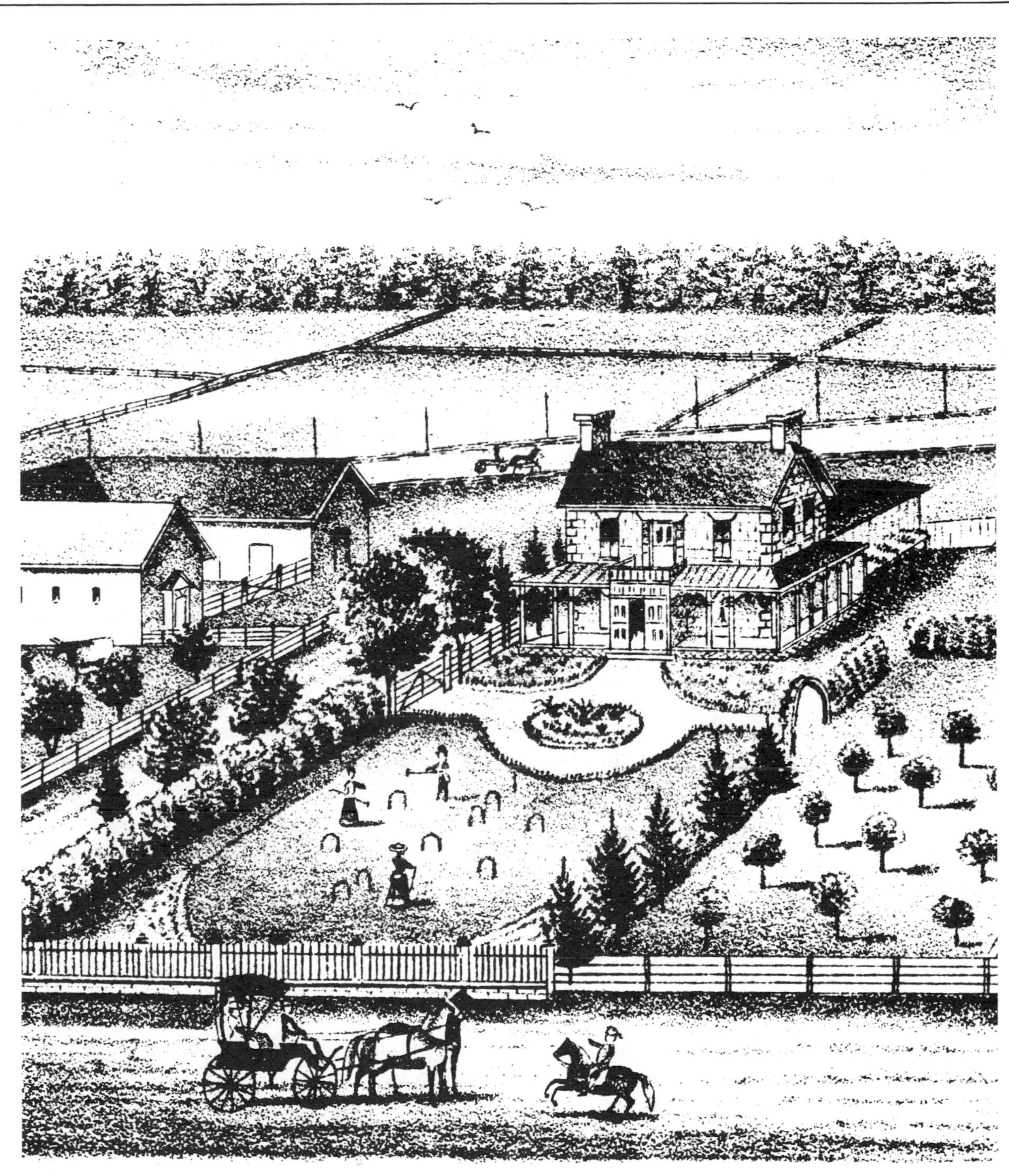

Fitzroy Harbour, Ontario, about 1879. The late 1800s saw Victorian landscape ideals transposed into the Canadian scene.

A pioneer garden. Adam Ferguson (founder of Fergus, Ontario) noted in 1851 that "Canadians and Americans are deficient in . . . 'dressing up their doors,' they are, in fact, so much engaged in heavier and more important work that the period for training roses and honeysuckles has not yet arrived."

were set in natural scenery with open spaces, plantings and path systems."[8] One of the oldest parks is the Halifax Public Gardens, founded in 1867.

By the 1800s British gardening books and magazines were available in Canada in private collections as well as libraries.[9] In 1878 the *Canadian Horticulturist*, a monthly periodical, began publication, and some gardening books written especially for Canadian conditions began to appear.

To furnish domestic and public gardens, seeds and plant material were brought directly from American and British nurseries, as well as being traded among friends and imported by settlers. Some Canadian nurseries were already in operation by the early 1800s. William Custead of York ran an orchard nursery from 1811. In 1827 he issued a catalogue which listed fruit and ornamental trees, flowering shrubs, garden seeds, greenhouse plants and bulbous roots.[10]

By 1900, the conditions required to promote Canadianized ornamental gardening were well in place:

- House yards in our older towns and cities were well cleared of stumps and trees; more people had the leisure and money to devote to pleasure gardening rather than "survival" planting.
- Garden design philosophy had been and continued to be imported from the United States and Britain through immigrants and the media; the imported designs provided numerous models which stimulated our horticultural thinking.
- Support institutions, such as the Dominion Experimental Farm System (established in 1886), nurseries, seed companies, horticultural societies, and horticultural media were in their

infancy, but were already exerting influence on the Canadian garden.

- The burgeoning science of plant breeding was influencing amateurs as well as professionals in Canada to hybridize hardier plants for our climate.

When the active ingredient of the contemporary reform spirit was added to the horticultural mix, many varied gardening movements were produced.

Horticulturally, the nation benefited from some of the upheavals in society. The great influx of settlers into the west prompted increased plant breeding, creating hardier and more varied plant material for Canadian conditions. An increased need for Canadian horticultural information motivated greater publishing efforts — more handbooks, bulletins, newspaper articles and horticultural periodicals began to appear. In turn, expanded gardening efforts prompted the growth of the Canadian nursery and seed industry, and "city beautiful" improvements (parks, greenbelts, parkways) strengthened the influence of landscape architects and town planners. As we shall see in the following chapters, these horticultural events played a unique part in our social history. The following brief, general examination of the reform spirit will provide a background for the horticultural reforms that came after.

REFORM IN CANADA, 1890-1930

From the late 1800s until the late 1920s, Canadian society was characterized by a reforming zeal which, especially before World War I, was buoyed up by a spirit of optimism.[11] This would be Canada's century!

By the turn of the century, Canada was just emerging from the effects of a world-wide depression, new lands and markets were opening in the west as a result of massive immigration, technological advances were resulting from the rapid rise of industrialization, and for some the standard of living was improving. The resulting changes unsettled many Canadians, who then sought to redesign existing institutions to conform to a new, unfamiliar society.[12] Yet not all Canadians shared in the good times. Rapid industrialization and urbanization coupled with waves of immigration inflicted misery on many, especially lower class workers — low-paid, ill-housed and ill-educated.[13] Between 1900 and 1910, the urban population increased by sixty-two per cent.[14] Existing welfare institutions (charitable organizations, religious orders, and government agencies) were unable to cope with the resulting social ills: poverty, disease, intemperance, crime, prostitution, child abuse, and political unrest.[15] The problems were not new but they had multiplied to such an extent that they could not longer be so easily ignored.

Quebec City, 1890s. The urban landscape offered many challenges for the horticultural reformer. However, street planters and tree plantings did not always solve every aesthetic problem.

Many reform organizations were already well established by 1900. The leaders and their followers were mainly drawn from an urban middle class which was intent on stabilizing and improving society in accordance with their own middle-class values. The reformers were a mixture of humanitarians, temperance workers, business promoters, evangelists, suffragettes and professionals of many types (such as architects, city planners, doctors, journalists, educators, clergy). The number of supporting voluntary associations was so great in 1895 that it was remarked that "people had been seized by some inexplicable urge to save mankind."[16] Yet they were not united in a single movement or creed, nor were they all motivated solely by altruistic intentions. They saw themselves as reformers, but posterity, with hindsight, sees many of them in a less generous light, as promoters rather than saviours.

The problems confronting the reformers were challenging and diverse. The rural problem (the migration of rural people into the city and the stagnation of rural life) was spoken of as one of the major problems of the century. The city was characterized as godless, evil, dirty and unaesthetic. Slum conditions were aggravated by an increasing number of immigrants electing to stay in the city rather than face the rigours of homesteading. Temperance workers attempted to lessen the influence of the saloon on family and civic life. Municipal reformers sought to reorganize "inefficient" local governments. City planners decried the ugliness of our cities — citing comparisons with beautiful, old European cities. The social gospelers promoted a society based on Christian brotherhood. World War I gave more impetus to reform, as reformers urged support for their programs so that "our boys won't have died in vain."

After the war, reform movements became much more compartmentalized and bureaucratized. The urge to change society remained, but during the twenties, it was steadily diminished by worsening economic conditions. The overwhelming optimism with which reformers armed themselves to effect change efficiently and rapidly was also waning. By 1930, many reform movements had either died out or become the wards of a government agency.[17]

This was the context in which horticultural offshoots of the reform movements were produced. We shall see how they developed and thrived as morality, class values and commercialism entered the Canadian garden.

The Movements

2 Corporate Paradise:

The Canadian Pacific Railway Company Gardens

THE VOLUNTARY ERA, 1890-1907

For nearly seventy years, the Canadian Pacific Railway Company was involved in garden design, maintenance and plant selection. The company became Canada's head gardener, at one point overseeing gardens dotted along 25 749 kilometres of track, from coast to coast, through every climatic condition possible in Canada. The company's interest in the merits of petunias versus pansies was motivated and sustained through these years by a combination of economics, public relations, European railway traditions and the contemporary spirit of reform.

Economically, the CPR had a great need to "fill up" the west — it needed the revenue generated by increased passenger rail traffic, by the sale of railway land to settlers, by shipping manufactured goods from eastern to western settlements, and by shipping western agricultural produce all over Canada. To reach this goal, the CPR invested heavily in a campaign (through the media, excursion trains, and an active immigration policy) promoting the richness of prairie land. Station gardens could be good advertisements for prairie fertility.

In the east, the rail companies were under some pressure from city beautification groups to clean up storage yards, waste places, and the right-of-way. American examples of landscaped railway station gardens were cited as examples of what could be done. Elsewhere, many CPR employees lived in isolated spots, far from

(Opposite) Broadview, Saskatchewan, about 1920. The majority of CPR gardens were geometrical, balanced and regular. It was also usual to fence them off from the public.

BROADVIEW

David Hysop (above) of Killarney, Manitoba and N. Stewart Dunlop (below) of Montreal co-founded the CPR garden idea in the late 1800s. "The planting of a little garden at a station, especially in certain bleak, treeless areas, was a conspicuous feature and added some little beauty to the surroundings."

towns or villages. Gardening was seen as a pleasant recreation and the garden as a paradise in the wilderness — a place to maintain mental and physical health.

The town railway station, especially in the west, had become the focus of the community and its major link with the outside world. Civic boosters said the only evidence of a town's worth to passengers was given by the condition of its railway station. These factors together made the CPR ripe for a horticultural "take-over."

The specific origin of the CPR garden movement is clouded by contradictory evidence. CPR accounts and some outside sources (in journals such as the *Canadian Municipal Journal* and the *Canadian Horticulturist*) claim N. Stewart Dunlop as the originator of the garden idea. However, a recent article by Aileen Garland offers evidence that David Hysop began the gardening movement. There is parallel evidence supporting each man: both began working for the CPR in the 1890s, both at that time were insurance claims adjusters, and both had the ear of important officials on the matter. Whether the two men wrote one another to further railway gardening is unfortunately not known.

David Hysop immigrated from Ireland in 1847, and found a job as a conductor on the CPR Toronto-Montreal run. By 1882, he and his sons were homesteading in Manitoba, where he continued working for the CPR as well as dabbling in real estate. William Whyte, superintendent of the western lines (from Fort William to Victoria) promoted Hysop to the position of claims adjuster. Hysop reported on damage caused by sparks from the locomotives to farmers' homes and livestock along the tracks.

By that point, Hysop had become one of the most influential men in the Killarney District — he had even persuaded Sir John A. Macdonald of the area's need for a connecting railway line.[1] When Hysop learned of the CPR's financial need to sell surplus land, he suggested:

> If you want to show how good the soil is, why not have gardens at the railway stations in which flowers and vegetables can be grown. The company can supply the seeds, the station agents and the section foreman can look after the gardens, and, if water is needed, the locomotives can supply it, and it can be kept in barrels along the track. The vegetables and flowers can be used in the dining cars and shown at fairs far and wide.[2]

Aileen Garland says William Whyte accepted the idea wholeheartedly, later appointing Hysop as superintendent of forty-four gardens from Brandon to Golden.

In the east, N. Stewart Dunlop entered the CPR service in 1888, and soon became head of the claims department based in Montreal.[3] At some point between 1880 and 1897, when Dunlop was tax and insurance commissioner, he began sending out seeds from his home garden to various station agents.[4] What prompted Dunlop to distribute flower seeds is not clear. In 1925, the magazine writer E.L. Chicanot described what he felt to be the reason:

> Along the more than three thousand miles of main line there were naturally a good many men, station agents, section foremen, and others, who were garden lovers, and who with the limited means at their command, and to the best of their ability, cultivated little pieces of ground about the scenes of their activities. . . . This gave to a higher official of the company, about thirty-five years ago, the idea of expanding the work of beautifying station grounds by aiding agents and others in the work.[5]

This is certainly plausible, for many CPR employees had immigrated from Europe where railway gardens were already known. (Hysop, born in Ireland, could also have drawn on his background.)

By 1901 when Dunlop was manager of the tax and insurance department, he was well known throughout the CPR system as "the flower man."[6] He is said to have defended station gardens to Sir William Van Horne, president of the CPR, by stating: "The agent with a nice garden is the agent who has a clean and tidy station; has a flower in his buttonhole; wears his coat; has a clean collar and well-brushed boots."[7] Whether it was the thought of all those gleaming boots and starched collars, or the appeal to the reform spirit of the times, Van Horne was said to support the idea.

In time, Dunlop expanded the seed distribution by including small gardening instruction booklets filled with hearty aphorisms:

> You can have flowers if you want them hard enough.
> Grow flowers and keep on the sunny side of life.
> Busy people always grow flowers.[8]

In return, grateful employees sent Dunlop letters and snapshots detailing their garden work. One rather poignant letter to him was reprinted in the *Canadian Municipal Journal* (a monthly for municipal officials):

> Just a few lines to tell you that we have moved from ____ to ____ Section House. We came here in November and there has never been any garden here, so we set to work to make one. . . . We have named the baby Pansy Verbena. All my girls are named after flowers, so if you have anything you can send to help make this place pretty, I shall be thankful . . . I have now nine children living and one dead, making ten in all, so you see I am kept busy, but I love my garden and often when I feel tired and out of sorts, I go into my garden and work for a while and it soon passes off. . . . I do not do it all myself, I am teaching my boys and girls to help in the garden

too, as I think it is so nice to see children caring and taking an interest in flowers.[9]

Dunlop also wrote letters. To an agent who refused the offer of bulbs because of poor soil and the neighbouring cows' appetites, he replied predicting that if the agent once saw the beauty of tulips in spring, he "would wheel the soil for a mile to make a bed, then sit up all night with a gun to keep off the cows."[10] Result — the agent hauled in topsoil and became an enthusiastic gardener.

The CPR had large reserves of labour to draw on, but in the early part of the century the movement was still largely voluntary. There were of course "grumblers" — those who criticized the company for trying to get them to do extra work without pay in their leisure time, but they seemed to be in the minority.[11] The majority of men who lived in company housing were eager to brighten up their surroundings as seen in pictures of section foremen's small entrance gardens. A "friendly rivalry" sprang up between railway gardeners, but at this time actual competitions were not held.[12] Dunlop believed that flowers were to be grown for themselves and "not for a paltry prize."[13]

Thus, the movement had an unofficial leadership which kept it in motion. Mr. Dunlop was popular and trusted. An informal communication system was in place: seed orders were sent to Dunlop who then sent them to their destinations on the trains. The first distributions seemed to take the "shotgun" approach — seed was sent out indiscriminately. Later this was changed and seed was only sent to those who asked for it.

An early railway garden in Markdale, Ontario, 1906. This was a more elaborate version of the usual railway garden layout.

There was outside support as well. Magazines such as the *Canadian Horticulturist* and the *Canadian Municipal Journal* as well as various newspapers carried laudatory articles on the work so far accomplished. In some cases, especially in eastern Canada, horticultural societies supported railway beautification in their towns by voting money for plants or labour to further the work.

Enthusiasm, opportunity and means: everything was in place. In the words of the editor of the *Canadian Municipal Journal*, the CPR was to be commended highly for its beautification projects which "are made object lessons to the towns" and "reveal the true value of this movement in the uplifting of humanity." He added that the United States was still behind Canada in railway beautification: "we felt . . . Canadians might reasonably be proud to think that we . . . had already solved the problem, at all events as far as one railway is concerned . . ."[14]

THE HORTICULTURAL ERA, 1907-1917

By 1907, the gardening urge had become so widespread that the CPR decided more could be accomplished if the work was handled systematically. Economic benefits had already resulted from the beautification program, as small pieces of usable equipment had been salvaged during clean-ups.[15] Accordingly, a Forestry Department was formed to take control of existing garden work and to establish permanent gardens. The departmental duties included management of company nurseries and greenhouses, distribution of trees, shrubs, perennials and bedding plants to employees, design and planting of station grounds and planting of trees along the right-of-way for windbreaks.[16] A few paid local gardeners were already employed, laying out and maintaining various gardens.[17]

To further the departmental directives, Dr. Gustaf A. Bosson-Krook was appointed chief horticulturist for the western lines. He had formerly been manager of the CPR tree and shrub nursery at Wolseley, Saskatchewan, which supplied windbreak material. The other officials in the forestry department oversaw work on the eastern lines.

The CPR was at this time under attack for its garden design. From an aesthetic viewpoint, a critic complained:

> Much of the work so far executed . . . belongs to the geometrical rather than to landscape gardening. While the lawns are pretty and well kept, the beds well planted and pretty, not the slightest effort has yet been made in any case that we have noticed toward unity of design or the making of the whole to harmonize into a picture. No attempt has been made to hide ugly views by appropriate grouping of trees, nor to add picturesqueness to the lawns by carefully disposed clumps of choice shrubbery; nor in any case have we noticed any effort made to make the place inviting to the waiting traveller by rustic or other seats in shady spots.[18]

Critics stressed that the work should not continue in a haphazard manner, that a landscape architect should be hired to design the gardens, and professional gardeners hired to do the planting and maintenance. This stress on unity of design, and on making use of professional overseers, was commonplace in town planning philosophy, as we shall see in a later chapter on "The City Beautiful."

Most of the existing station gardens were small patches attended only by the agent or section foreman when they had the time or inclination for it. Many relied on the "star-shaped beds with whitewashed stone edging" variety of garden, with few, if any, trees or shrubs in the design. Another aesthetic problem was the fencing: "the places are to be seen and not touched; they are guarded by ugly and forbidding palings, and woe betide the passenger who would dare to set a foot inside."[19]

Evidently, the only type of fencing permissible along the right-of-way at this time was a woven wirefence, 1.37 metres high, with ordinary rough white-washed cedar posts, with the tops painted black. There were ordinary wooden picket fences around station gardens.

The small garden at the Orford Lake, Quebec, station was an example of a rudimentary garden, featuring white-washed stones and a few flowers.

Hamilton, Ontario. Railway garden sites generally were determined by the horizontal lines of track and adjoining roads.

Despite these criticisms, the CPR was acknowledged to be fostering a sense of beauty and responsibility among its employees, with important social benefits for the country as a whole. The editor of the *Canadian Municipal Journal* reflected:

> The man who has a nice garden is not the man who spends his leisure time at the nearest saloon, or in lounging idly with a pipe in his mouth, doing nothing, till some mischief turns up. The man with a nice garden is not the man who has to be discharged for beating his wife and neglecting his children. The man with a nice garden is a decent industrious man, who will bring up his children to be the best kind of citizens.[20]

The CPR, after 1908, strongly promoted station gardens, incorporating the movement into company policy. If a station agent desired promotion or a favourable recommendation, he was wise to establish a garden. Circulars, catalogues and advice began to circulate around the system. Forms had to be filled out and sent in by a fixed date, flower beds laid out just so, and gardens were now to be inspected by travelling inspectors. The movement remained voluntary, it seems, only in respect to employee's homes.

By 1912, design criteria were well in place. When a new station garden was to be planted, a Forestry Department official traveled to the location. After studying the station site and taking measurements, the approximate size of the garden was decided. These measurements and descriptions of the site were given to the company's landscape gardener back at the department. When drawing up the plan, he was to consider the following conveniences: sidewalks must follow the most direct route into town, access for teamsters must allow for loading and freight, and garden placement must be sited for the best view from the platform or train.

Each locality offered its own challenges — whether of site conditions, climate, or labour availability. For example, the station at Schreiber (north of Lake Superior) had only a very thin soil cover. More soil had to be hauled in on temporary track laid especially for this purpose.

The company began to change its fencing styles. Where wire fences were in use, a lighter fencing was recommended, only 1.07 metres high instead of 1.37 metres, and supported by smaller square or rounded painted posts. Picket fences, on the other hand, were being replaced by iron piping fences, (three lines of pipe supported by wooden or cement posts). These styles were much less obstructive, letting the view dominate rather than the enclosure.[21]

The establishment of a central horticultural authority had the effect of standardizing the railway station garden, so much so that by 1912, the railway garden was a recognizable entity. The site was generally squeezed between two horizontals: the track on

Red Deer, Alberta, about 1912. An example of the few park-sized gardens on the CPR line.

one side and the access road on the other, creating a long narrow site, sometimes broken into two sections by a station entry road. Usually the design was no more than a border of trees, shrubs, perennials and bedding plants along one or more sides of a lawn. Many gardens also contained "island" beds (usually circular), full of clumps of perennials and annuals graduated by height, dotted along the length of the site. The feeling was still formal, although some naturally landscaped sites were designed as well.

Two park-like gardens were planned for the stations at Red Deer and Macleod in Alberta. The Macleod plan was a mixture of natural and formal plantings. The focus of the plan was a central circular garden. The centre of the garden was dominated by a 4.5 metre hill with a bandstand on top.[22] The Red Deer plan was much more formal with fewer park-like strolling areas. In the centre of this wedge-shaped garden was placed "a handsome and elaborate fountain basin."[23] To hide the ugly scene in front of the station, a circular flower bed with a central rockery was planned.

A fine example of a station garden planned at headquarters was situated at Herbert, Saskatchewan. Laid out in 1912, it was a large garden (90.8 metres by 36.6 metres) — about eight average city lots long and two lots deep. The garden was a combination of natural and formal elements: a circular shrub planting dominated the central section, around which curved the station drive. The two side sections were treated more naturally by long sweeps of

A portion of the extensive Calgary station garden — one of the largest on the line.

shrub groupings — these sections were planned to be viewed from the platform. It was unusual in that neither annuals nor perennials were used widely; rather, 499 trees and flowering shrubs were called for. It was a hardy, colourful, low-maintenance garden.[24]

The Herbert station garden was unlike the majority of CPR gardens, which were geometrical, balanced and regular. For example, the Regina station garden was a formal composition dominated by a large circular bed, ringed by a concrete path, with four paths radiating out from the circle. The garden at Smiths Falls, Ontario, was an example of another, less enterprising type. Here large circular beds were dotted along the long, narrow lawn, and a hedge of shrubs and flowers followed the outer boundary. All beds were edged with the ever-popular white sweet alyssum. (The popularity of this flower which grows in small white mounds may be due to its resemblance to the favoured whitewashed stones used earlier for edging gardens and for spelling out station names on the right-of-way.)

Front gardens of employee houses also reflected a preoccupation with regularity. Basically, the main path leading to the front door was flanked on each side by a strip of garden, and the lawn was balanced by matching flower beds, or specimen shrubs or trees. The beds could be circular, star, scroll or diamond-shaped. With some exceptions, the designs of the increasing number of gardens were nearly interchangeable.

To supply its many gardens, the CPR established company greenhouses and expanded its nurseries. By 1908, the nursery at Wolseley, Saskatchewan had a permanent plantation of 22 000 tamarac trees and 8000 perennials.[25] The complex also included seedbeds for ornamental shrubs and conifers. The nursery at Wolseley was originally established in the mid-1880s after the completion of the western line, mainly to supply trees and shrubs for windbreaks along the right-of-way, around CPR experimental farms and around private farmland. Windbreaks were needed in places where snow was likely to drift onto the tracks.[26] At one point, the Wolseley nursery supplied 464 200 trees for windbreaks and ornamentation.

After the establishment of the Forestry Department in 1907, another nursery was begun in Springfield, Manitoba, which supplied the bulk of the bedding plants and perennials. And by 1912, greenhouses were operating in Fort William, Kenora, Winnipeg, Moose Jaw, Calgary, Revelstoke and Vancouver. From these points, plant material was distributed up and down the line.[27] The material had to pass two tests to be used in the railway garden and windbreaks: survival under winter conditions and under an almost constant rain of cinders.[28]

Members of the Forestry Department were also kept busy during the spring and summer on numerous garden inspection trips, offering suggestions and instructions to both the amateur gardeners and the increasing number of labourers being hired for garden maintenance. Skilled garden labour was difficult to find, especially in the west. The company's unwillingness to hire permanent skilled gardeners (who were only needed in the summer) aggravated the situation. Some large centres supported their own part-time gardener, other smaller stations would share a gardener who would travel between them.

A garden could take up to three years to be properly designed, prepared and planted. After the design was made, the site was disc-ploughed and harrowed to prepare the soil and eradicate the weeds. Any necessary grading was done that summer, followed by installation of water pipes. These pipes were only laid down in large stations having a water tank. Otherwise, all water had to be carried into the garden by bucket. Then the fencing would be installed. Tree and shrub positions were pegged out, and planting could begin. Perennials were introduced the second year, followed by a lawn.

As the company became more directly involved, garden competitions were included in the attempts to encourage the movement. Cash prizes were awarded for top gardens in district and divisional categories with fifty dollars the top prize. The awards were fiercely contested. Up into the 1940s, prizes were even won by gardens where the gardeners, despite drought and other calamities, had to carry in the daily water supply.[29]

By 1912, the CPR was said to be supporting 1500 gardens along the right-of-way — many of which were permanent. Not only were the products of the company's gardens efforts becoming highly visible, CPR employees were also becoming prominent in local horticultural society activities for town and city improvement.

In turn, town councils, horticultural societies and boards of trade were asking the company to establish gardens in their respective towns.[30] The granting bodies would sometimes vote money to purchase additional plants for existing railway gardens. In some cases, a town would plant and maintain its own railway garden. The CPR evidently began supporting these types of permanent gardens in 1908. J.S. Pearce, Parks Superintendent for London, Ontario, reported to the local horticultural society that after two years of suggestions the CPR had finally given him permission to plant tulips followed by annuals (supplied by the company) at the passenger station. J. Lockie Wilson in a speech before the Ontario Horticultural Society in 1913 stated:

> The influence of our members with the railway companies and station agents in such localities, if properly applied, will remove the grievance [ugly stations]. In England, Scotland and Ireland great pride is taken by railway corporations and their employees in beautifying not only the station and grounds but the homes of the employees as well. Let us follow the example of the Motherland in this regard, and the inaugurators of similar improvements here will not have lived in vain.[31]

One of the most elaborate railway gardens of all was in Kenora, Ontario. It contained not only flower beds and a fountain, but also a large rock garden.

But the CPR had problems with some of the municipally-run railway gardens. From the railway's point of view, many of these gardens were poorly designed. Trees were planted along the railway side of the garden, blocking the view from the train. When the company took the garden over and tried to remove the trees, opposition would arise. Usually, these were the only trees in town, so a compromise was generally reached: a few trees would be eliminated each year, while the company rearranged the garden layout.[32]

To counter the neglect that sometimes occurred when enthusiasm declined for a municipally-run garden, the CPR would make an agreement with a town: in return for plant material supplied by the CPR, the town would agree to company supervision of all planting and maintenance.[33] In many locations the railway garden became the only spot of colour in a dull landscape.

World War I did not cause cessation of CPR support for its railway gardens, it only changed the focus a bit. Complying with federal pleas for greater food production, many railway employees planted war gardens. In many cases this meant plowing up the ornamental gardens in order to plant vegetables. The CPR granted more land to its employees, supplied detailed vegetable gardening instructions, and provided free fertilizer. The estimates vary, but at one point in the war, over a thousand war gardens were in cultivation. One-third of the land was devoted to potatoes, the remainder to mixed vegetables.

The largest lawn at the Saskatoon station was ploughed up and planted with potatoes, which were used in the CPR dining cars. The station lawn at Broadview, Saskatchewan was also ploughed up and planted with vegetables. The word "produce" was spelled out in mammoth letters (formed by lettuce plants) near the station.

The majority of gardeners kept some part of their flower gardens in addition to the vegetable patch, for the war did not stop station beautification. In Ontario alone, sixty stations were "improved."[34] To aid in the work, the CPR had been hiring students from Macdonald College (near Montreal) and the Ontario Agricultural College (at Guelph) even before World War I. The students designed station gardens and supervised the planting, which the company felt would serve two purposes: the CPR benefited from the students' years of study, and the students benefited from the work experience.[35] One student summed up his experience as having the "satisfaction of knowing you are a small factor in an organization which has as its object making the world more beautiful."[36]

By 1917, railway beautification was a CPR watchword and an established policy. The next step was to consolidate its position as the largest "garden" in the world.

ERA OF CONSOLIDATION, 1917-1930

The prospering railway gardens acted as an incentive for the CPR to undertake even further efforts. A Floral Committee was formed to promote the movement as well as to consolidate past garden endeavours and policies. Dr. G.A. Bosson-Krook was made consulting horticulturist for the entire railway. (This position took him along a remarkable 48 279 kilometres to 64 372 kilometres of CPR line every year.[37]) The head forester of the eastern lines (B.M. Winegar) was also a member, as well as F.J. Curtis. The three men continued the work of the Forestry Department, and in 1917, tried to initiate a major change: substituting more permanent low-maintenance gardens.

By eliminating annuals, the Committee felt they could drastically reduce the amounts expended on material and labour. Aesthetically, the Committee promoted perennial gardens in order to provide a floral display from spring until the fall frosts. They reasoned that annual flower beds, which looked fairly sparse until they had filled out later in the season, were really only at their best for short periods during the summer.[38]

Now only perennials would be supplied on request and bulbs distributed solely to the larger divisional points, eliminating the yearly expense of planting and lifting them.[39] Annuals in the future would be selectively supplied for colour until the newly planted perennials were established and for stations north of Lake Superior (the coldest section on the line).[40] After years of experimenting, the official in charge of the north-of-Superior line had discovered that pansy beds in the lawn not only gave the best display in that region from spring until fall, but that they were still blooming after light snowfalls in late autumn.

The new policy of distributing perennials to underplant shrubs (giving colour close to the ground) and to form exclusive perennial borders stimulated a fresh outpouring of instructions, circulars, bulletins, forms, personal letters and personal contact — all to ensure the success of the "new style" in the ever-increasing number of station and employee gardens. The Committee stated there was always enough land for a perennial border, so the employees really should take advantage of available plots.[41] To counter outmoded garden designs, the Committee stated it was in bad taste to cut up the lawn with paths, too many flower beds or specimen trees: "In making beds in lawns avoid fancy designs such as stars, crosses, etc. A good sized circular or oval bed is far more effective than a lot of small beds dotted all over the lawn."[42]

The Floral Committee was trying to modernize the railway garden, away from formal and rigid Victorian designs and into a more natural, less regular planting scheme. To further their aims, the Committee also kept in touch with other horticultural

Greenhouse and perennial borders adjacent to the T&NO railway station at Englehart, Ontario, 1917. Such greenhouses supplied the annuals so necessary for the typical railway garden.

experts "including agricultural college staffs and horticultural societies, so that everything is done to keep the work up to modern standards."[43] Additional support to the Committee's efforts was given by the *Staff Bulletin*, which in 1917, began running a monthly column of photos and descriptions of employee gardening efforts.

The Committee was really fighting on two fronts as they simultaneously encouraged employees to change not only the content, but the form of their gardens as well. Despite the flurry of departmental activity and advice, the change-over policy did not proceed smoothly. Employees were seemingly indifferent towards efforts to re-orient their garden sensibilities, and, by the evidence of the garden photographs in the *Staff Bulletin* up to 1930, they continued to plant traditional railway gardens. The linear garden sites did lend themselves nicely to Victorian planting designs. The CPR's new style of natural plant groupings favoured less rigid, subtler designs which were best appreciated when strolled through, but since most of their gardens were still fenced off from the public, such an active contemplation was not possible. In fact, the stylized geometrical plantings were probably quite suitable for a quick view from a speeding train or a lazy gaze over the garden fence while waiting on the platform.

During the Floral Committee's early years there was a marked increase in the choice of plant material available from the CPR.[44] In garden history it is sometimes the case that an infusion of new plant varieties initiates new garden design theories and practices, but this did not occur along the CPR lines. The gardens retained their formal, clipped look as if they were frozen in time.

An indication of what the Committee was up against was shown in an 1918 award-winning garden, designed in the best Victorian manner. At the Markdale, Ontario station, the agent (Mr. Caesar) made a lawn and garden where once there was a siding, cinder path and dumping ground for ties. A border (38 m by 1.2 m) was planted with mixed annuals, edged with the usual sweet alyssum. In the centre of the border was a rockery, built of broken stones. In the centre of the rockery was the station name in floral design, with letters of golden feverfew, filled in with tan hemlock bark. In the centre of the lawn was a circular bed (5.5 metres in diameter) filled with nineteenth-century favourites: King Herbert cannas, scarlet geraniums, and sweet alyssum. Two other star-shaped beds were filled with cannas, geraniums and edging lobelia.[45]

Not only was the attempt to change the style of gardens unsuccessful, but the attempt to change the content of the gardens was also proving to be a failure. A 1924 report stated that while 150 000 annuals, and 60 000 pansies were distributed, only 2000 perennials were sent out.[46] A 1938 report further supports this notion of failure: that year 115 000 bedding plants (composed of forty different varieties, the most popular being snapdragons, sweet alyssum, geraniums, marigolds, petunias, phlox, zinnia and verbena), 20 000 pansies, 78 000 tulips, 96 000 seed packets and 227 kilograms of grass seed were distributed.[47]

Its policies in ruins, the Floral Committee began in 1923 to retrench in some areas. The CPR nurseries were sold, and the horticultural staff headed by Bosson-Krook was consolidated in Winnipeg. The reason for this measure was delicately stated by Mr. Winegar: "The loyalty and support shown by the railway employees, in the beautification of the waste ground around depots and shunting yards, has resulted in a far bigger outlay of money than was first thought of."[48]

By 1925, the CPR was still promoting permanent plantings, but they found it more economical to purchase trees, shrubs and perennials from commercial nurseries.[49] The greenhouses however were kept for the production of annuals and even expanded somewhat as a few small greenhouses were established at the Western Shops, Ogden, Kamloops and in Montreal.[50] The flow — "several car loads each spring" — of annual bedding plants never stopped.

The twenties were a high-profile time for the CPR gardens as the company continually received compliments from travellers and in the popular press — even from past critics. Floral Committee members were active on the lecture circuit and as contributors to newspapers and journals. The CPR garden "panorama"

The Grand Trunk Railway sponsored a few railway gardens in the nineteenth century, such as this station garden in Brockville, Ontario.

had acquired an international reputation — one that officials were extremely proud of and endeavoured to uphold.

These were also times of reassessment, as CPR officials began explaining why they were promoting this horticultural venture — both retrospectively and currently. The philosophical explanations became codified as the CPR repeatedly listed the familiar justifications, namely, beautification, exhibiting soil fertility and encouraging social reforms among their employees.[51] Even when these motives were no longer relevant, the CPR continued the gardens as promotions of community spirit and as "first class advertising at a reasonable cost."[52]

Although not generally publicized, another strong motive for the continuing company support for the gardens was competition with other railways. The 1920s were a time of a visible increase in many other companies' gardening efforts — the gardens were good business. Other companies' efforts closely mirrored the CPR garden movement, both in style and content. Before 1920, many smaller companies beautified selected stations, usually under pressure from civic promoters. The Grand Trunk Railway had a few station gardens as early as the 1860s. But the most extensive garden program among the other competing railways was pursued by the Canadian National Railway Company. In 1916 the CN began an intensive gardening program which strongly reflected what the CPR had already established along its lines. In 1921, the work began in earnest when the gardening efforts were turned over to the CN Forestry Department.

EPILOGUE: THE DEMISE OF THE RAILWAY GARDEN, CA. 1960

The CPR garden movement continued throughout the 1930s, and up into the 1950s with little innovation, but with a continuation

Smithers, British Columbia. The CN gardens, created after 1916, greatly resembled the CPR's in style and plant material.

of garden competitions, distribution of annuals, and unceasing company promotion — all augmented by over fifty years of tradition and many employees' genuine love of gardening.

In the post-World War II period, however, the function of railways in Canadian society changed drastically as airplanes, private cars and buses provided rapid, flexible, alternative transportation. Rural settlement of the west was finished, and there was no longer a need to advertise prairie fertility. Railway passenger traffic drastically declined. As the railways became increasingly freight-oriented, the era of the railway garden also declined and has finally perished. In many places where station gardens bloomed, there are now only parking lots.

3 Hoe a Straight Row:

The School Garden

(Opposite)
Manitoba, 1912. Nature study programs advocated the opposite of rote learning and encouraged direct investigation of the environment.

THE MILIEU

On an average June day before 1930, thousands of Canadian school children were weeding a government-sponsored school or home garden, oblivious of the numerous forces which had placed them there. In fact, probably few adults were aware of the many disparate theories, ideals and promotions which converged to form the foundation and the motivation for the Canadian school garden movement.

The school garden gained support from educational change, new child welfare programs, and rural reconstruction schemes. The interplay of these social movements with traditional values and factors of social change gradually produced a favourable reception for the school garden. Yet, there was a long row to hoe before the school garden flourished and became the symbol of the resurrection of rural life and its economy.

Even though the school garden eventually influenced urban education and secondary school curricula, this chapter will focus only on the response of the rural primary school to this movement. In fact, the main thrust of the movement's leaders and their philosophy was towards bettering rural society through an improved rural schooling beginning at the primary level.

Canadian society, by the turn of the century, underwent many, often disturbing, changes as industrialization and urbanization increasingly challenged traditional beliefs. Rural society

was especially affected, particularly in what was known as "the rural problem," that is, ever-increasing migration to the cities. Many commentators feared the collapse of rural society and the weakening of the nation due to the deterioration of what they saw as its major industry, agriculture. Abandoned farm houses had become mute symbols of rural malaise. Men and women were leaving the rural areas in large numbers for many reasons: among them were social isolation, unprofitable returns from farming, the decreased farm labour market due to mechanization, the lure of "city lights," and for eastern Canadians especially, cheaper farm land in the West.[1]

The problem's cure was increasingly portrayed as educational, and rural schooling as inadequate for the task. Urban commentators reasoned that if new, scientific farming methods could be taught effectively to the rural population, the countryside would be revitalized. Country children should receive a more relevant curriculum, tailored to their needs, rather than a weak reflection of urban education.

Traditionally, primary education had been viewed as religious and moral, based on rote memorization of the "3 Rs," Latin and Greek, and character development.[2] Opposition to this curriculum, and the one-room school in which it was taught, began to assert itself by the 1890s. Yet, traditionalists continued to successfully limit many proposed innovations by a mixture of denunciations of educational secularization, financial resistance and sentimental appeals to the "good old days."

Urban educators had been advocating the addition of technical courses to the school curriculum to make education more relevant for city children. "Save the Children" campaigns centred on education as a cure for society's ills: properly-educated children were "tomorrow's hope for a better society."[3] New educational theories from Europe were another major impetus to the promotion of rural curriculum reform. The "new education" (as it was dubbed) promoted a shift from traditional book-centred education to a child-centred one, a philosophy which tried to make the schools "more humane . . . more responsive to the way in which children grew."[4] European innovations stressed the individuality of every child and the right to an education designed to suit the child's own nature, needs, aspirations and interests. Learning was to be interesting, even exciting, as the child "learned by doing"; the traditional method of passive recitation of facts was considered obsolete, if not harmful. The "doing" must be related to the world outside the classroom. The natural world was considered to be one of the more relevant teaching aids, because of its closeness to the child's own experiences.

Educators were also working within the system to effect change. Teacher qualifications were raised, teacher training was improved, and steadier school attendance was promoted. On the surface, the advocated changes seemed radical, but the educational goals had not really changed. Children were now to be gently led into an acceptance of traditional moral values rather than having these values imposed upon them by adult society. The means were changing, not the end.[5]

All these factors prepared the foundation of the school garden in Canada. The remainder of this chapter will trace the development of the movement from its origins in the nature study movement and the "pilot-program" of a private philanthropist, through provincial and federal support programs, to its demise by 1930.

THE BEGINNINGS: THE NATURE STUDY ERA, 1890-1904

One of the major proposals for curriculum change, especially in Ontario, was agricultural education in the rural school. "Book farming" had been successfully opposed until the 1890s when it was revived in more receptive educational circles influenced by the "new education" and the demands for relevant courses in the public schools. Even though opposition continued, a new American movement, nature study, begun in the late nineteenth century, provided a more palatable means of introducing agricultural teaching, and curriculum change. Nature study, in fact, laid the foundation of the path into the school garden.

The movement's main promoter and architect was Liberty Hyde Bailey, a professor at Cornell University, who was firmly in the "new education" camp. Nature study, according to him, was a natural, informal, spontaneous and free method of teaching. It was designed to "teach by doing." That is, to study the life cycle of a grasshopper, the child actually studied a real insect, not just diagrams in a book. The child was then to be led into discoveries from the observations made.

Education was to make people happy, and nature study was the best way to create a happy, satisfied and educated population. Spirit counted for more than mere recitation of facts, memorized without proper understanding. The rural child would benefit by gaining a greater understanding of the world and a happiness of spirit. Through the study of nature, the child (it was hoped) would realize that country life offered the best possible way of living.[6]

By 1900, nature study was being discussed in Canadian educational circles. Ecstatic descriptions became common whenever a true believer described the movement: if everyone adopted this teaching method, the promised land would be well within reach.

Nature study soon had its own vocal Canadian promoters. The Ontario Agricultural College (OAC) was well in the forefront of the movement, and issued a few pamphlets to aid the primary school teacher with the method. Professor William Lochhead,

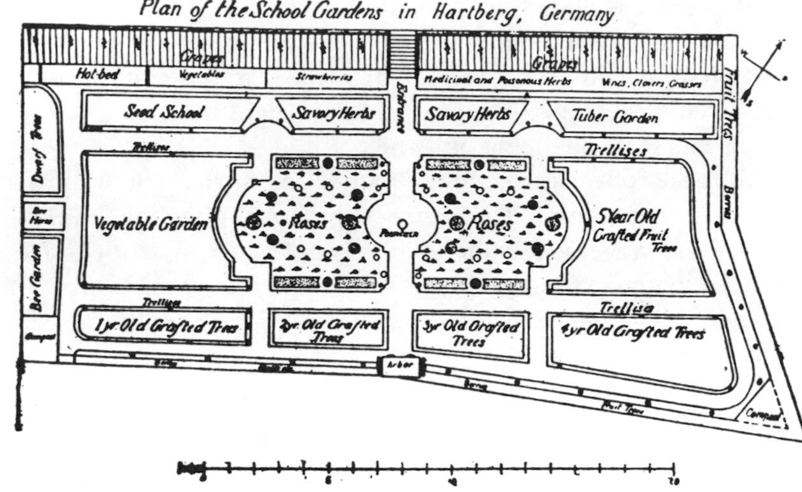

Plan of a school garden in Hartberg, Germany. School gardens were often part of technical education programs in Europe.

professor of biology and geology, journeyed to the United States to observe the nature study movement first hand, and afterwards wrote a long article in the *Canadian Horticulturist* explaining the movement and its teaching method.

The method was vague and depended on a quasi-religious belief in nature. The teacher had to know intuitively how to lead the student spontaneously into "discoveries" and then relate them to the rest of the curriculum — all without the aid of a textbook. Textbooks were frowned upon because they led to rote learning. For a teacher trained in the traditional manner, the nature study method was disconcerting. Although Professor Lochhead wrote and lectured with the true zeal of the converted, progress was slow.

This uneasy state of affairs continued until nature study enthusiasts began highlighting school gardening, a component of the movement. Before its importation into Canada, school gardens had flourished in Europe, in some cases from early in the nineteenth century. Germany, Belgium, France, Sweden, Russia, Austria and England all had either state-supported or privately financed school gardens.[7] North American commentators noted that these gardens, dedicated to teaching rural children an occupation, were purely economic or "industrial" in intent.[8] The Canadian school garden was to be primarily educational, producing well-educated, patriotic citizens.

Here was a way out of a dilemma caused by the nature study method. A garden was a concrete entity, governed by well-known rules, facilitating (it was hoped) greater teacher acceptance. For many educators, the school garden fulfilled prevailing educational and social ideals and concerns.

Professor Lochhead also celebrated the virtues of school gardening in articles in the *Canadian Horticulturist* in 1903. He urged an acceptance of this miracle cure for our educational and social ills: "The children are crying out for gardens; the home demands a garden; the state should insist upon gardens; and civilization will revert without gardens."[9]

The Ontario government responded to the new movement's publicity by offering small grants and equipment to schools undertaking school gardening. However, the response was so slight that the Department of Education concluded "that neither the country nor the teaching profession were ready for this course."[10]

Meanwhile, various horticultural societies in Ontario and Quebec were advancing the cause of horticultural education. As early as 1895, the Montreal Horticultural Society distributed plants and flower seeds to selected school children.[11] Ontario horticultural societies were also active in seed distribution. The results varied and the enthusiasm varied. One happy little gardener in Woodstock, Ontario described her experience: "Flowered like something awful!"[12]

The Paris, Ontario, Horticultural Society in 1902, to further nature study in their community, planted the grounds of the South Ward School with various Canadian trees and shrubs, labelled them, and "handed them over to the Board of Education to remain for all time an object lesson to the young."[13]

However, by no means all schools or horticultural societies or communities participated in promoting nature study and school gardening. The appearance of school gardens was sporadic. Nova Scotia led the nation with fifty-two school gardens in 1903. A widely admired and publicized school garden was established in Toronto at the Broadview Boys Institute in 1901. But the response remained sketchy until 1904. Only then did another,

(Above)
Ontario, 1906. Ontario horticultural societies were especially active in promoting children's gardening programs.

(Below)
Broadview Boy's garden, Toronto, 1903. The students organized, planted and maintained the garden, and then marketed the produce.

William C. Macdonald (above) financed educational programs designed to improve rural life and learning. James W. Robertson (below) put the programs into motion. He was also a major force in the changeover of Ontario agriculture from a cash crop basis to a reliance on dairying.

more widespread, school garden movement begin to gather momentum and to establish itself closer to the mainstream of Canadian educational programs.

THE MACDONALD MOVEMENT, 1904-1907

In 1904, the Montreal philanthropist, Sir William Macdonald, funded a unique and ambitious educational experiment. In the 1890s he met James W. Robertson, then Dominion Commissioner of Agriculture and Dairying. Macdonald knew Robertson had effected a series of successful agricultural reforms in eastern Canada. Here was a man who shared Macdonald's concerns over the quality of rural life, who had effectively changed a group of farmers' lives for the better, and who had pronounced ideas on rural education. The two men successfully collaborated on a "seed grain contest," in which farm children won money prizes for selecting the best head of grain, and a privately-funded pilot program promoting manual-training education in selected schools.[14]

The third phase in this collaboration, the Macdonald Rural Schools Fund, focused directly on rural education. The Fund was to introduce and demonstrate the beneficial aspects of school gardening and nature study. The cost of maintaining the gardens, fencing, buying tools and garden sheds, purchasing additional land when needed, and the salaries of three travelling inspectors for three years were covered by the Fund. At the end of the funding period, it was hoped that the local school boards would take over the program.

Under the energetic directorship of Robertson, the Fund's program rapidly proceeded along highly organized lines and five schools were selected in each of Ontario, Quebec, New Brunswick, Nova Scotia and Prince Edward Island.*

Negotiations were conducted with school boards, and meetings were held with provincial education departments. Robertson successfully lobbied to have the scheme placed under the education departments' jurisdiction rather than the agricultural departments', so the school gardens would be on a broader educational base. The Fund soon had a "recognized place in the

---

* *Ontario*: all five schools were in Carleton County: Carp, Galetta, Richmond, North Gower, Bowesville; *Quebec*: Knowlton, West Brome, Iron Hill, Brome, West Bolton; *New Brunswick*: Woodstock Grammar School, Broadway School, Woodstock, Hartland Superior School, Florenceville Superior School, Andover Grammar School; *Nova Scotia*: Brookfield, Old Barns, Belmont, Bible Hill, Great Village; *P.E.I.*: Kensington, Bedeque, Searletown, Tryon, Emerald.[15]

The school garden in North Gower, Ontario, 1905, was one of the original Macdonald program gardens where children were taught the ideals of living harmoniously with nature.

provincial systems of education . . . conducted under the authority of the school trustees and the express approval of the ratepayers."[10]

Selected teachers (funded by Macdonald) were sent on a year's study program to previously evaluated programs at the University of Chicago, Cornell, Columbia, Clark and the Ontario Agricultural College. During the year, the teachers underwent advanced training in nature study and school gardening. To support future teacher training, Macdonald donated $175 000 to the province of Ontario to build what became known as the Macdonald Institute at OAC.

By the fall of 1904, the program began a successful three-year term, marked by a steady stream of enthusiastic progress reports. The promoters always claimed that the school garden was not an incongruity, but an organic part of the school program.

Academically, the curriculum was enhanced by the interrelation of school garden activities and daily lessons. The garden created reality out of unreality in the best nature study tradition. The students benefited from such "exciting" learning:

> Where gardens have been in operation a few years, the school authorities report that the pupils are decidedly superior to others of their age in general education. A problem in surface

> measurement worked out practically in the garden is educationally worth many such exercises in the school where the pupil has to imagine the conditions.[17]

Garden activities served as a concrete basis for mathematics, reading, composition, drawing and spelling. As a result of using garden topics for compositions, the development of language skills, according to E.G. Worley, principal of Carp School, Ontario, was said to be remarkable:

> The children seem to be in an environment adapted to them. They have thoughts about something familiar which they can express. The work frees them from that artificial expression so common among children when they are trying to express something they do not understand clearly.[18]

The school garden, in a favourite image which persisted in later writings as well, was the outer classroom with the plots as its blackboards where lessons could be erased and new ones begun.[19]

Absenteeism, always the bane of the rural school, decreased as the students rushed to school to see if their beans were up yet. The students were also learning skills that it was said would serve them through subsequent schooling and into adult life. The skills included the principle of cause and effect, the habits of close observation, thoughtfulness and carefulness, the technique of combining thought and action, the "power of initiative," and the habit of taking responsibility for one's own work.[20] Physically, the child's development was being properly stimulated by outdoor exercise. Spiritually and morally, the school garden, according to George D. Fuller, director of the school in Brome County, Quebec, had a salubrious effect on the "moral tone of the school" because of the new objects of the children's attention which was "turned to a consideration of the beautiful to the exclusion of many baser thoughts. . ."[21]

More docile, well-behaved students were welcomed by-products of the school garden program. But one can imagine the bewilderment or the amusement of parents and trustees when viewing the neat rows of carrots, beans and zinnias. What exactly was all the fuss about, they may have wondered. How could this well-tended little plot save rural society?

Generally, the economic motive was underplayed during the Macdonald era in favour of cultural and philosophical ideals: "The garden is the means, the pupil is the end."[22] However, Robertson did admit that the best rural education not only infused the students with a love of rural life, but also made such a life profitable: "the best way to make a worker like his work is to make him understand it."[23]

As the movement proceeded, the disparate benefits were slowly packaged into *the* solution to the rural problem. Through school gardening a generation of intelligent, prosperous country folk could be created. This generation, raised in the belief of the nobility of farming, would be so in harmony with their surroundings that they would never want to leave the countryside. The school garden movement ultimately would strengthen the nation by supporting its "fundamental industry," sustaining life in the expanding urban centres, and maintaining the right order of society by creating citizens who knew their place.

Behind the rhetoric and the theorizing lay twenty-five well-organized and aesthetically pleasing school gardens — the realized ideal which subsequent provincial and federal programs attempted to attain.

Although the Macdonald school gardens varied according to soil, surface conditions and location, a physical description of the school garden in Bowesville, Ontario, demonstrates the ideal:

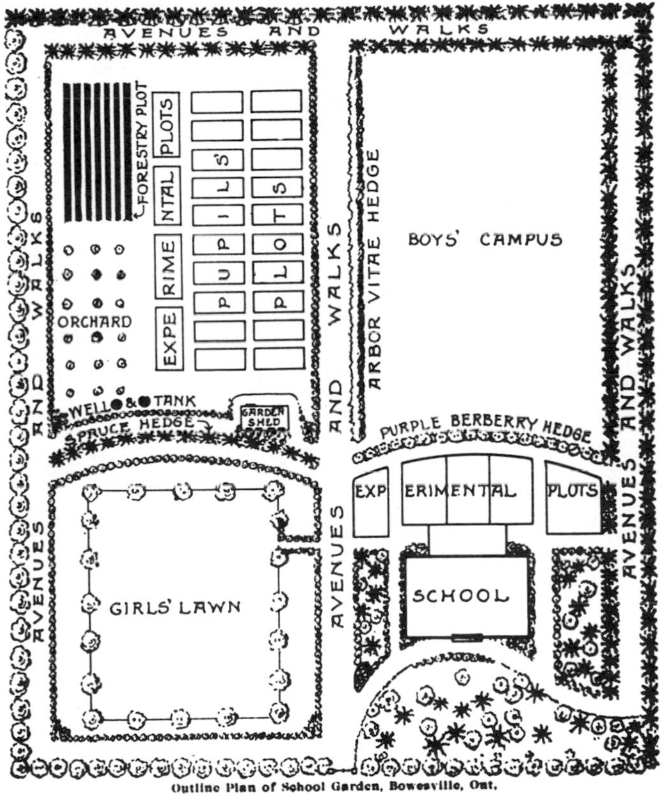

Plan of the school garden in Bowesville, Ontario, 1905.

> . . . a belt of ornamental native trees and shrubs surrounding the grounds; two walks, each about one hundred yards long, between rows of trees; a playground about half an acre in area for the boys; a lawn of about a quarter of an acre for the girls, bordered with some light and graceful shade, such as the cut-leaf birch; a small orchard, in which are grown a few varieties of the fruit trees most profitable to the district; a forest plot, in which the most important Canadian trees will be grown from seed and by transplanting; a plot for cultivating the wild

> herbs, vines and shrubs of the district; space for individual plots and special experimental plots; an attractive approach to the school, including open lawn, large flowering plants, foliage, rockery, ornamental plants, etc.[24]

The experimental plots, varying from 18.5 square metres to 186 square metres, were used to study crop rotation, the value of fertilizers, the effects of spraying, seed selection processes, soil types and performance, and productiveness of different crop varieties — a mini-experimental farm, in fact.

Each student had a small plot, managed "on the basis of individual ownership, individual effort and individual responsibility."[25] The size of the plot depended on the age and strength of the child. At some schools, students had two plots: one for flowers, and one for vegetables. The gardens usually covered about 8094 square metres.

Garden sheds varied in size, the most popular one measuring about 3 x 6 metres with a 1.5 metre extension on one side which, with its glassed-in roof, served as a greenhouse. The shed housed tools (hoes, rakes, hand weeders, spades, shovels, wheelbarrow) numbered corresponding to each individual plot. The well-lit shed also provided room to prepare plant labels, analyze soil, sort seeds, transplant seedlings and conduct other garden work that was done outside the school room.

Every school garden was visited weekly by a specially trained inspector, who checked to see if the garden and school work were proceeding smoothly. Most schools maintained their gardens on a two-hour-a-week schedule which the teachers did not find burdensome. One school reported that the students were so enthusiastic about the garden that they did all their garden work outside regular school hours.[26]

The problem of summer upkeep was not yet recognized. Either the children gardened an hour a week during the holidays, or they did not. The example of a well-tended plot was thought to be an incentive for a negligent gardener.

In fact, the Macdonald Rural School program was considered an incentive for all rural schools. The school garden promoters did not recognize that the program had been nurtured and protected like a hot-house plant by monetary infusions and highly-trained personnel. They truly felt the ideal rural education was at hand. The promoters' enthusiasm seemed to be infectious. When Macdonald's support ended in 1907, four of the five provinces (all except Quebec, where Macdonald continued to fund the programme) assumed funding responsibility for those schools continuing school gardening. Canadian children were firmly placed on the garden path.

ONTARIO LEADERSHIP, 1907-1913

The educational climate had become increasingly favourable

towards school gardening, especially in Ontario. This was due not only to the Macdonald school garden program but also to the growing civic beautification movement and to the horticultural societies' efforts to interest children in horticulture:

> If you can get a boy or girl really interested in growing flowers, you are doing him or her a great benefit. There is nothing that tends more to keep a boy or girl out of mischief, out of bad habits and bad company, than the care of a garden of his own and one in which an interest is taken.[27]

The Ontario Department of Education remained in the forefront of the movement for many years. By 1907, the department, with the active assistance of OAC, began regularizing the school garden movement. Circular 13 (*Elementary Agriculture and Horticulture and School Gardens in Village and Rural Schools — Explanatory and Descriptive Circular*) was sent to all Ontario school boards in an attempt to popularize school gardening and to counter rural reluctance to educational spending. The regulations provided an initial grant of $100, followed by annual $20 grants for any rural school maintaining an acceptable school garden. This was defined as a garden adjacent to the school grounds, large enough to accommodate the required number of student plots, and supervised by a qualified teacher. The teacher either had to have a certificate from an approved institution or had to be judged competent to teach the subject. An annual grant of $30 was given to these teachers. (Teacher training in nature study had already started at the Macdonald Institute in 1904, under the leadership of S.B. McCready.) Early on, the Department of Education and OAC, recognizing that school gardening and nature study were not a priority in urban education, concentrated all their energy, influence and available funds on improving rural education through this medium. There were urban school gardens, but they were not heavily promoted.

The circular also contained teaching aides: how the teacher could help students make a garden plan, keep a garden notebook, lay out a garden, prepare the plots, and relate all the work to the daily curriculum. Crop selection was also considered crucial:

> To allow the pupils as much freedom as possible in choosing their own plants and at the same time safeguard them from possible failure and consequent disappointment may become one of the most difficult school garden problems.[28]

Communal produce "might be sold by the pupils, the salesman in each case to get a commission of say 10 per cent on his sales, and the balance to be placed in a general garden fund and used to defray expenses or to purchase tools, pictures, apparatus, etc."[29] Summer care followed the Macdonald program dictum: if the student was enthusiastic, the garden will be maintained.[30]

Citizenship was another potential school garden product to be carefully cultivated. Where traditional educators had emphasized individual character development as a major educational goal, the "new educationalists" promoted the social virtues of citizenship. School garden spokesmen soon followed suit, claiming that the school garden fostered "the qualities that make for good citizenship, such as the responsibility of ownership, respect for public property, consideration for the rights of others and the principle of co-operation in seeking the common good. . ."[31]

This aspect of school gardening, as an instrument of social control, promoted middle-class social and moral values. Moulding rural children into idealized, hierarchical roles in society and channeling their choice of occupation were the unstated, but underlying intentions of the developing school garden movement.

Originally, the cultural and intellectual goals of nature study had dominated, with the nature study method and the school garden as props for the "new education" movement. However, as these two props combined, forming an independent movement — in which the school garden dominated — the objectives became more complex. Influenced by fears over the rural problem, the school garden movement espoused social and economic goals in addition to educational ones. By 1907, school garden spokesmen were claiming that these disparate goals were in fact being achieved.[32]

S.B. McCready, professor of nature study at OAC, tried to downplay the growing occupational emphasis: "The garden and the products are secondary; the results to the child's character are of prime importance. So we may have poor school gardens but good school gardening."[33] But the efforts of McCready and others succeeded only in the short run. This seemingly innocent conjunction of vocational and intellectual concerns surfaced again later in a conflict which plagued the school garden movement in every province up into the 1930s. In 1907, however, the conflict was not yet visible, as members of the school garden movement worked urgently to solve the countryside's problems. The rural problem had not abated; migration to the city continued in a steady flow.

Even though battles between proponents of classical education and "new education" still raged, "new education" was gaining influence. Men and women who espoused these ideals were judged to be forward-looking, reformist and right-thinking people who through sheer righteous energy would transform Canadian rural society. "New education" promoters now proclaimed the school garden *the* gospel to believe in and to disseminate by intensive "missionary" work. The school garden had become the answer for the educational shortcomings of the hundreds of one-room rural schools.

During the early years of the movement, a school garden ap-

The beautifully landscaped Rittenhouse school yard was originally maintained by a professional gardener until parents and trustees decided it would be more beneficial for the children to do the work themselves.

peared which was the spiritual heir of the Macdonald era school garden. This widely-publicized garden was a "classical" example of the pre-1914 government-sponsored style school garden, with all its various sections in harmony with one another. Built in 1890, Rittenhouse School in Jordan Harbour, Ontario, was partially funded by a former resident, Moses F. Rittenhouse. He donated land and buildings to the town residents, and in 1892, hired a landscape gardener to beautify the 8094 square metre school grounds. He thereafter provided for continuing maintenance by hiring a full-time gardener and providing a home for him. This professional gardening continued until 1907, when the trustees authorized a school garden to be managed by the children.[34] Girls in white dresses and hair bows and boys in knickers and caps populated this little paradise, happily hoeing in the garden, next to weedless flower beds overflowing with well-tended flowers.

Provincial grants supported the entire enterprise. The principal proudly stated that any school could accomplish the same — the provincial grants were still in force, and the maintenance of the garden only took forty-five minutes of work on Tuesdays and Thursdays. All the latest equipment was in use, from cold frames to budding knives to transplanting tables. Flowering shrubs were propagated from cuttings, fruit trees were budded, and nature study projects (insect collections, for example) were pursued. The older students were allowed to plant whatever they liked, with sometimes surprising results:

> A few years ago they [the boys] wished to grow vegetables exclusively — things that represented money and their living appealed to them. To-day the same boys are cultivating the larger area in flowers, which shows the aesthetic is on the ascendant.[35]

Summer holidays were not a problem as the children were said to willingly care for the garden themselves.

The Rittenhouse school garden (1911) was held up by school garden promoters as an ideal to be emulated.

Rittenhouse School also sponsored garden projects in which the entire community was involved. (One year the school sponsored a co-operative experiment with tomatoes.) This, according to provincial standards, was agricultural education at its best.

In other regions, especially in eastern Canada, school gardening was becoming more popular. The "gospel" was being spread through teacher's institutes, educational journals, the popular press, government bulletins, and the horticultural media.

OAC continued to sponsor provincially accredited teacher-training courses in elementary agriculture, nature study and school gardening. The government offered scholarships to deserving teachers, especially those already teaching in a rural or village school. After successfully completing the course, a teacher would be granted a certificate in Elementary Agriculture and Horticulture. Summer school courses were also offered, usually taking three summers to earn a certificate. To further help teachers along the garden path, the Ontario Department of Education also published, in 1913, a suggested course outline of agricultural education. Teacher training in nature study and school gardening in a few other provinces was becoming more popular and more subsidized. Plant material and seeds were being readily supplied by government and private sources.

Because of the growing number of school gardens in Ontario, Circular 13 was updated in 1909 and 1913. Instructions were expanded; less was left up to the teacher. Experimental plot pro-

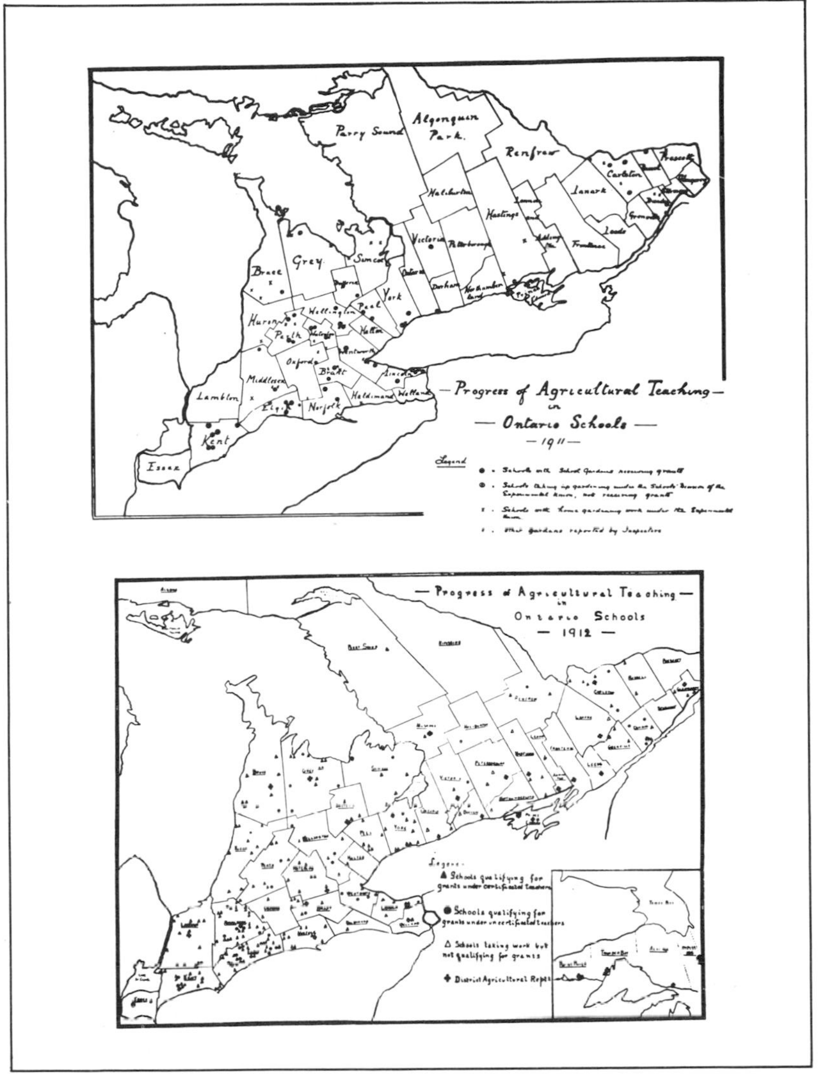

The increase in school gardening was dramatic in Ontario between 1911 and 1912.

jects were detailed, perennial border plants were listed, forest tree nursery cultivation charts were noted and lists of garden and carpentry tools (with prices) were included. The circular had become a comprehensive handbook detailing all a teacher needed for a successful school garden.

The 1913 revision aggressively promoted the school garden and advised the garden teacher. The "Country Boy's Creed" ("I believe that the country which God made is more beautiful than the city which man made. . .") led off the booklet. After this bit of moral bracing, the teacher was given a list of dos ("Use opportunities of better equipping yourself as a rural school teacher; join forces with your local horticultural society; aim to have your school attractive and the people proud of it") and don'ts (Don't remain isolated in your work; don't make the garden merely a school affair; don't commence the work without patience and perseverance."). One of the more interesting don'ts was: "Don't think that teaching agriculture and school gardening are one and the same thing: a school garden is simply a *means* to an end, and the end is teaching agriculture."[36]

In spite of the growing awareness of and participation in the garden movement, by 1912 it was encountering opposition from some teachers, parents, trustees and school administrators. Teachers complained about already full daily schedules. Many of them did not want to or did not know how to co-ordinate the garden work into the ordinary curriculum. Many lacked the support of their inspectors or the parents. Some parents opposed the idea from a variety of stances: other studies would suffer, young girls could not teach agriculture, it was an American-inspired whim,[37] it would cost too much, and (a peculiar reason) if the work became widespread, professional gardeners might suffer.[38]

Summer holiday care was a problem — many gardens declined into masses of unsightly weeds. And there were problems with the great turn-over of rural teachers, which seriously weakened the continuity of garden efforts. The opposition never really addressed the issue of winter — that basic condition in our Canadian lives. Sustaining interest in a "paper" garden through the bottled sunshine of nature studies for a good six months of the year required not only imagination but the teacher's absolute dedication to the movement. The gardening season in most schools was limited from mid-May to the end of June, and harvest-time in September if the garden had survived the sum-

Staking out the garden, Indian Head, Saskatchewan, 1916. One observer compared the school garden in its early stages to a dog's cemetery she had once seen in London.

mer. All was not well in the garden, but the spirit of reforming optimism continued to override the dissident voices.

THE AGRICULTURAL INSTRUCTION ACT — SUBSIDIZING UTOPIA

> It is not necessary in this day and hour to defend or justify generous assistance to agriculture. We all recognize the soundness of such a doctrine. To increase the farmers' output; to improve the conditions of rural life; to swell the numbers of those who till the fields, — to do these things, even in the very attempting of them, we are doing something to solve the greatest problems and avert many of the manifest evils that face us in modern life.[39]

On January 17, 1913, the Federal Minister of Agriculture, Martin Burrell, rose in the House to announce the Agricultural Instruction Act which would subsidize a grand effort to create order and prosperity in the rural areas through agricultural education. The act alloted $10 000 000 to the provinces over a ten-year period for the promotion of agricultural education, of which school gardening was a part. The public school subsidy covered the salary of a supervisor for agricultural teaching, expenses of agricultural teachers, the printing and distribution of pertinent literature, expenses for maintaining school gardens, and teaching nature study or agricultural instruction. The act was to produce future farmers who farmed efficiently:

> Too often the spectacle is witnessed, pathetic and pitiful, of ceaseless, honest laborious toil, bringing distress of mind and body, and even after long years, bringing no reward, solely and simply from lack of knowledge and misdirected energy.[40]

The act secured approval in both Houses. James Duff (Ontario Minister of Agriculture) commented in a letter to Martin Burrell: "The almost complete absence of any real criticism is in itself the best tribute to the conception of the idea and to the manner in which it has been worked out in legislation."[41] The new educationalists could now afford to launch their educational theories on a large scale.

There was an economic aspect to the promotion and acceptance of the act. In 1912, a depression began to be felt in the country. At the same time, retail food prices were rising, credit was tightening in the rural areas, and farmers were leaving the land they could not afford to farm and joining the urban unemployed.[42] Farmers' groups were agitating for fiscal reform. Politicians and social commentators were fearful of the effects which might result from these unsettled conditions and the rising cost of living. There was a current sentiment, promoted especially by non-farmers, that food prices would decrease if farming was efficiently pursued with scientific agricultural practices. The act

The school garden run by the Children's Aid School in Victoria, B.C., 1917, was used by the teacher as a "means of helping these little lads upward into better ideals of citizenship."

was not merely a gift to the agricultural community, it was insurance against the breakdown of society and the diminishing of supplies for the urban centres — where the middle classes were relentlessly pursuing their own form of efficient progress.

The urban élite may have promoted the idea that in every city-dweller's heart there lurked a desire to be a farmer, in harmony with the natural world and God's handiwork:

> Every farmer boy wants to be a school-teacher, every school-teacher hopes to be an editor, every editor hopes to be a banker, every banker hopes to be a trust magnate, and every trust magnate hopes some day to own a farm and have chickens and cows and pigs and horses to look after.
> We end where we begin.[43]

But closer to reality was the feeling that although the ideal life was led in the country, someone had to pursue material, industrial goals in the benighted city for the benefit of the nation. If anyone was to live in this rural paradise it might as well be those who farmed already.

At the time when the Agricultural Instruction Act was under consideration, the state of agricultural education and school gardening was unorganized and uneven across the nation. Some provinces forged ahead, while others lagged behind. In British Columbia, few school gardens existed and nature study was the main source of agricultural education. The school garden movement in the prairie provinces was hampered by climate and distance, but mostly by the immense numbers of immigrants pouring into the west, causing a school shortage. During the early years of the movement, western efforts were deflected by the necessity of building hundreds of schools. There was some nature study and school gardening, but efforts were sporadic. Quebec's gardens were split along language/religious lines — the English Protestants were aided by the Macdonald College Staff, and the

French Catholics by the Oka Agricultural Institute and the agricultural school at Ste. Anne de Pontérie. Due to the influence of the Macdonald Rural School Fund, Quebec (which boasted 234 school gardens in 1913) and the Maritimes were well ahead of the West, but continued to lag behind Ontario, the trend-setter.

Even within the provinces, the results differed according to the teacher's ability, the student's dedication, parents' and trustees' attitudes, and school location conditions. One western school inspector sadly noted: "There are too many cases where the little mound of earth serves but to mark the grave of the seed or of the early-departed plant."[44]

Although the act did not generate an immediate boom in school gardens, it did provide the monetary impetus for co-ordinated rural education programs. Provincial programs were varied and broad in the application of the act. Short courses given to farmers and older rural children ranged from livestock care, dairying and farm products marketing to stock and seed judging. Practical demonstrations in weed control, fruit-tree spraying, beekeeping, and vegetable growing were funded.

With school gardening on a much firmer foundation, provincial plant distribution became better organized. Provincial nurseries (at Indian Head, Saskatchewan, for instance) provided tree seedlings; agricultural colleges or departments of education provided seeds, perennials and bulbs. For example, the Manitoba Department of Education distributed the following supplies to 400 school gardens in 1915:

5000	bulbs
8400	vegetable and flower seed packets
1054	parcels of potatoes
27	kilos of alfalfa seed
12 000	tree seedlings for windbreaks
618	perennial roots[45]

Packing seeds for home and school gardens at the Quebec provincial nursery at Deschambault, 1920. This was only one of the many provincial services provided for agricultural education programs.

Circulars were distributed listing varieties, price and date of availability. Town school gardens were usually supplemented by plants supplied by horticultural societies. Children were charged for the plants, because it was believed they looked after their plants better if they had paid for them. Also, in totalling up the expenses and profits (which was a favourite occupation of many school garden promoters), it was handy to have a set price on all supplies.

Money and plant material were now readily available. The next problem was supplying enough qualified teachers to undertake the work. The act provided the means to establish teacher training programs. For example, before 1914 Prince Edward Island had to send its teachers to the Nova Scotia agricultural college at Truro for training. As a result of the federal funds, Prince of Wales College in Prince Edward Island added agricultural teacher training courses and another agricultural professor.

Garden design followed earlier models. However, a new form of garden layout, the municipal school garden, gained in popularity, especially in the west. This was a garden laid out as a rural municipality, each section measuring about .56 square metres with every path representing a road. The garden was managed by an elected municipal council of students: a mayor, aldermen, inspector of weeds, inspector of roads, etc. This design was highly praised and duplicated in many provinces. Children who were involved in such gardens benefited from the experience of civic "duties." This style, which was refined over the next twenty years, remained popular up into the 1930s.

In order to co-ordinate provincial efforts, the act provided funds for the establishment of the *Agricultural Gazette of Canada.* This national publication, published by the Department of Agriculture, recorded provincial advances in rural education, new programs, school garden plans, and school and farm building designs. It was hoped that the *Gazette*, as a forum for discussing problems, theories and current events, would prevent duplication of mistakes and promote the successful aspects of rural education. For now, the weaknesses of the school garden were glossed over by the infusion of federal funds into the movement.

REACTION

In 1916 the *Agricultural Gazette* reprinted a number of its articles on school gardening, distributing them to all teachers of school gardening. This full-scale discussion was the last serious attempt to consolidate a rapidly diversifying movement. Perhaps the school garden did signal the rebirth and revitalization of rural society, but by 1916 fewer spokesmen were as optimistic about the actual date when this would occur. The boisterous enthusiasm of school garden promotions was being slowly replaced by sober reflection and public discussion.

Young trees ready for distribution from the British Columbia provincial nursery in 1917. These trees were for student activities in forestry and school landscaping.

The Christian Brothers novitiate, in Laprairie, Quebec, learning school garden fundamentals in 1915. Teacher training in all phases of agricultural education became more widespread after World War I.

As part of the "new realism" over the school garden, the report dealt at length with the causes of school garden failure: over-enthusiastic projects, gophers, inadequate garden preparation, lack of fencing, the difficulty of obtaining water, rapid teacher turnover, the short school year (140 days in some localities), the lack of summer holiday care and the absence of community support. The most serious problem the provincial school garden directors identified was the great number of ill-trained teachers.

World War I drained off many good teachers, but this in itself did not cause the problem. In spite of agricultural teaching certificate programs (available in every province now), the bulk of a teacher's training was based on urban curricula, given in urban centres. Many teachers continued, whether specially trained or not (and many did not have any formal training), to use the rural school posting as a stepping stone into an urban school where living conditions were better and the salary higher. Leading rural spokesmen repeatedly called for a new class of teacher: one with an intimate knowledge of farm life and who loved the countryside.

Rural teachers (who were mostly young inexperienced girls) were convenient scapegoats for both the opponents and supporters of the school garden movement. L.A. DeWolfe, Director of Rural Science for Nova Scotia, a great supporter of the movement, was particularly direct in laying blame on these teachers. He believed the majority of good teachers had gone west to better opportunities, while the conservative ones remained in Nova Scotia. Too often the teacher started to teach agriculture "without even knowing oats from wheat, cauliflower from shepherd's purse, or sand from clay."[46] It is no wonder the parents would not have it: "Give us good live teachers and we need not worry about the course of study. It will adapt itself to the community."[47] The list of grievances was long and sometimes contradictory: some teachers taught too often from textbooks, others did not use the masses of supporting literature enough.

Other more sympathetic evaluations recognized that there were forces outside the isolated rural teachers' control which magnified the problem:

> Surrounded often by influences that retard, seeing her inspector only twice a year, cut off from her fellow workers, left without any direct means of communication with the educational authorities, and ignorant of the progress of education in the world at large, it is hard to expect any widespread effect from a few girls scattered here and there throughout the schools of the Province.[48]

When rural parents or trustees criticized the movement, however, the criticism usually was characterized as "public apathy" by supporters of school gardening. If the rural folk only knew what they were missing, if they but knew they had the salvation of country life and the answer to rural prosperity right under their noses, the farming community would not hesitate to embrace scientific agricultural teaching: "The farmer of the future, for the benefit of the state, must have a better education."[49] "A wearing down process seems to be necessary."[50] Mounting rural intransigence, however, changed the school garden leaders' exuberance into the strained heartiness of slightly desperate social organizers facing a hostile crowd.

Many rural parents resisted implementation of purely "country" curricula because they felt their children were being discriminated against because of their birthplace. In Ontario, for example, parents opposed this course of study because it was not part of the "educational ladder" (an inter-locking system of courses and examinations) which led from the rural school to the high school, to university and finally to a city career.[51] In eastern Canada, where mechanization had created a surplus work force, the only way parents could see to keep their children from migrating to the prairies was to educate them in non-rural occupations.[52] They saw wealth accumulating in the cities and felt their children had a right to pursue urban goals if they wished. The children who stayed on the farm would pick up what they needed to know from their parents — agricultural courses were not essential to their lives. Farmers may have accepted rural utopian ideas which conferred special status on them, but they certainly did not want to be confined on an agricultural "reserve."

In the midst of this mounting controversy, education departments might have been expected to take a stand, but many did not. For example, the Ontario Department of Education's policy was rather ambivalent. The officials continually referred to the school garden program in very favourable terms, supported it with grants and included the course on curricula lists. But for many years elementary agriculture and school gardening was not included as a compulsory subject on the core curricula, nor as a part of the system of courses and exams on the "educational ladder."[53] Usually the course was tacked onto an already crowded schedule, and never really regarded as important enough to replace any other course. While the two sides continually fired off volleys at one another, education departments in many provinces carefully maintained diplomatic relations with each group.

RELATED MOVEMENTS:

Paralleling the rise of critical discussion over the school garden was the growth of three spin-off movements which later had a profound effect on the school garden.

The first was the school fair — the climax of the school gardening year. The *Agricultural Gazette* helped popularize this movement Canada-wide. In the past, examples of student pen-

The diploma was awarded to members of Boys' and Girls' Clubs by the Manitoba Department of Agriculture, 1918.

manship and drawing had been exhibited at local agricultural fairs. But in 1912, originating in Ontario, fairs dedicated only to student exhibits were being held in schools. As the popularity of the school fair increased, so did the number of types of products and school work exhibited. In time, provincial departments of agriculture supplied eggs and seeds to be raised by students and then judged in the annual fair.

The school fair was soon adopted as another solution to the rural problem. It outgrew its original service role to the school garden, and evolved into a popular community, as well as educational, event. Inspectors' reports from British Columbia, for example, noted that until a school fair was held, little interest in agricultural teaching was voiced by the parents.

The benefits of participating in a school fair were widely publicized: development of a sense of industry and thrift, of an early love of nature, of a devotion to the soil, of an ambition to serve the community and the spread of new agricultural idea. Fairs were usually organized by an elected committee of older students in order to instil a sense of leadership and responsibility.

Another benefit of the school fair was "Canadianizing the foreign born," especially in the west. The fair was seen as a prime place to "mingle the races," providing "the means of learning about other races in a most pleasant manner."[54] Analysis of current labour unrest and the rural problem began to focus on the problem of the unassimilated foreigner. By 1916, articles began to appear linking the solution to the problems of educating non-English-speaking students with the school garden movement. Examples of the capacity of the school garden, and later, the school fair, to produce good Canadian citizens were widely publicized.

Quebec, 1915. The school fair exhibit was only one of many activities of the annual school fair. Some school districts sponsored parades and sports events in addition to the fair competitions.

Ontario, 1917. Although girls were often encouraged to participate in the more domestic competitions of the school fair (baking, canning and so on), they also entered into agricultural competitions such as calf raising.

Speeches were given to audiences of proud parents on the benefits of learning English at an early age, the value of being a Canadian and the worth of the school gardening movement.

While most trustees, teachers and parents were generally in favour of the fair, not all believed it answered every rural problem. In a lively exchange of letters to the editor in the farm journal *Canadian Countryman* in 1915, some parents voiced criticisms of the idealistic aims. All was not the picture of dedication and honest rivalry that many educators described when extolling the merits of the fairs. One farmer noted that it was "only a step to keeping young people on the farm." Other parents felt the fair promoted too much rivalry. Criticism also surfaced over uninformed judging. Some parents were accused of doing the work on projects submitted by their children. Other criticisms centred around money prizes, as children were accused of not competing for the educational benefit, but only to win money, which was said to severely weaken the goals of participation in the fair. More radical parents even accused educators of using the school fair as "part of a conspiracy to compel boys to stay on the farm."[55]

In spite of its shortcomings, the school fair thrived, gaining in popularity up into the 1920s. The school in St. Casimir de Portneuf in Quebec provides an example of the enthusiasm felt. The students ended their program by singing the national anthem and then shouting, "Long live agriculture!"[56] What finally dampened the buoyant spirit of the movement was financial restraint. As provincial support was withdrawn in the 1930s, the movement slowly died.[57]

The home school garden (also referred to as the home garden or home project garden) was described by J.W. Gibson, Director of Elementary Education in British Columbia, as a school garden correspondence course.[58] In British Columbia, for example, a home garden project could only be carried on when conditions did not permit a school garden. Two-thirds of the students had to agree to participate and submit a plot plan drawn to scale. The teacher was to visit each plot twice — late summer and early fall — and then submit a report to the Director of Elementary Agricultural Education. Each student had to keep a dated, written record and report to the teacher weekly.[59]

The home garden was not regarded as the best manner of conducting school gardening, but rather as "better than nothing." Some school districts had no other option. Many rural schools were built on donated land, land that was too rocky or too poor to be farmed. Some school boards were not receptive to school gardening, but were supportive of home plots: a father might give his child manure for a home garden, but would not donate a load to the school.

Every province published guidelines for home project work. In 1917, Quebec instituted a new policy as a result of a questionnaire sent to all rural teachers, when three-quarters of the respondents favoured the home garden. Jean-Charles Magnan, head of Quebec's program, felt the school garden should be the laboratory where experiments were tried, and the home garden the practical plot where field work was actually performed.

Children in their home school garden, St. Casimir, Quebec, 1916. Home school gardens quickly assumed greater popularity than the school gardens in some localities.

In Nova Scotia, the home garden had been the most popular form of school gardening since before the Agricultural Instruction Act. From 1914 to 1915 the number of home plots increased from 700 to 1900. In Saskatchewan, however, the directors of school gardening deplored the growth of home over school gardens, and while Ontario consistently downplayed the home garden, statistics show that the number of home gardens usually outnumbered school gardens.

Boys' and girls' clubs were instantly popular, especially in the prairie provinces. In Manitoba, the growth rate was astounding: in 1913 there were 750 members of various clubs, by 1916 the membership had increased to 10 000. The aim of the clubs (which met outside school hours) was to encourage children (from ten to sixteen years of age) to study and practise any phase of agriculture: calf-raising, poultry-raising, grain-growing, canning, and so on.

The rhetoric used to describe club goals was strongly idealistic, allying the goals with the school garden movement's educational concerns. But, in actual practice, the clubs focused more on occupational values, and aimed at creating junior farmers who produced the finest cucumbers rather than well-educated rural children.

IDEALISM IN CONFLICT WITH VOCATIONAL GOALS

During the time when these smaller movements were developing and gaining strength, a debate was forming over the re-orientation of school garden objectives. Educators for nearly ten years promoted school gardening as an educational, intellectual ideal, hopefully leading to the reconstruction of a viable, contented rural society through upgraded, relevant rural school programs. Yet, by 1915, the vocational motive, which had covertly existed within many school garden programs, had become overt: a garden's success or failure was frequently expressed in bushels harvested and produce sold. But for the "new educationalists," vocationalism was just too narrow and confining a goal. They wanted to create an idyllic rural society, peopled by those who intellectually and emotionally chose to stay in the country. To confine rural re-education to fruit tree pruning or seed grain selection was the antithesis of all they were promoting. Even in the heady early years of the Agricultural Instruction Act, this ideological split had already created small fissures, silently signalling trouble ahead.

World War I was one of the factors nurturing the growing split, and nudged the school garden movement closer to vocational goals. As early as 1916, students sold school garden produce in order to donate money to a patriotic fund or to help purchase a hospital bed or ambulance. The federal program for greater production spurred on greater provincial efforts. Through circulars,

To encourage and reward children who worked in school war gardens, the New Brunswick government distributed a special button in 1917.

teachers' institutes, summer courses and educational journals, officials urged all school teachers to turn their school gardens into war gardens: "Boys and girls cannot be expected to fight, but by assisting in increasing the supply of foodstuffs, they also can be of service."[60] Ornamentals were to be sacrificed for vegetables. Ideals were to be sacrificed for realities — the Allies needed food. Official apologies were given to school teachers and the public for this abrupt reversal of school garden objectives. The emphasis on growing good vegetables rather than good students was termed a "temporary" re-direction of the movement.

As some provincial educators noted, the public was more in sympathy with school gardens used for the war effort rather than as an "outdoor laboratory," "nature's blackboard," or a basis for a new rural society. Some inspectors urged their teachers to take advantage of the situation, promoting school gardens under the protection of production campaigns: "Public opinion is ripe for a forward movement."[61] Gone were vague instructions and philosophical pronouncements, as production and harvesting guided gardening activities.

By 1917, depending on which provincial department (education or agriculture) was given authority in implementing the school garden movement under the Agricultural Instruction Act, either vocational or educational goals would be emphasized. Therefore, in Quebec, where elementary agricultural instruction was supervised by the Department of Agriculture, the emphasis was heavily vocational: "we consider that, at present, it is more important to establish an organization which will foster the inclination for adopting agriculture as a profession."[62] British Columbia's program, on the other hand, was administered by the Department of Education. The Director of Elementary Agricultural Instruction, J.W. Gibson, consistently advocated idealistic, educational goals.

The *Agricultural Gazette* reflected the split in a marked decrease of articles on school gardening. School fairs, boys' and

Two Ruthenian boys with their chickens and produce on their way to the Boys' and Girls' Club fair in Sifton, Manitoba in 1917.

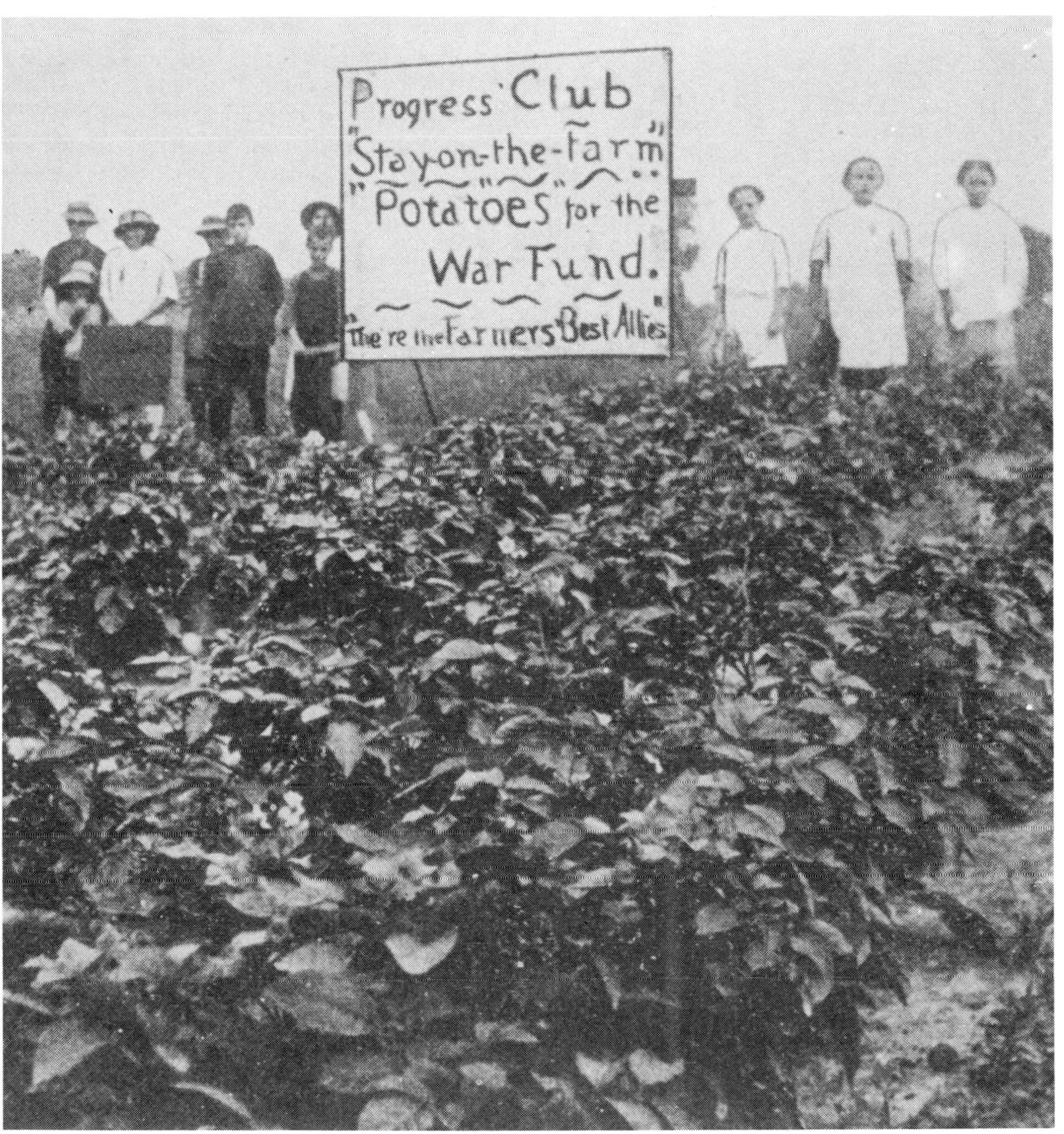

Southwold, Ontario, 1917. School war gardens in many areas were more acceptable than ordinary school gardens.

girls' clubs, teacher training and elementary agricultural programs were occupying much more space. The school garden was frequently referred to as an educational tool which formed the foundation of beginning agricultural education. The "School Gardening" department in the *Gazette* was changed to "Junior Agriculture: Demonstration, Competitions, and Class Room Studies in Rural Life for Boys and Girls."

In the 1920s, the watchword became "rural science," and it was upon this new term that the "orientation" debate now centred. J.B. Dandeno, Director of Elementary Agricultural Education for Ontario, reacted strongly to the term rural science, saying there was no such thing as rural science any more than there was urban science. He felt if this emphasis continued it would defeat the educational goal they all had aimed for. He further stated, in a strange twist of logic and history, that Ontario had never intended to introduce vocational agriculture into the schools since it would only lead to a position of hired hand because the average student could not afford to start up a farm from scratch.[63]

The debate raged on and on, no real conclusions were reached, and no clarification of mounting confusions appeared.

AFTERMATH

Ironically, while the Agricultural Instruction Act was pumping thousands of dollars into agricultural education, temporarily increasing school gardening, the demise of the school garden was being hastened. Teachers may have received the brunt of vocal criticism, but they certainly were not the only reason the movement was gradually weakening. The home garden, school fair and boys' and girls' club movements coupled with the growing dissension within the school garden movement itself were much more at fault.

With hindsight, we see that these ancillary movements were not created to destroy the school garden movement; their eventual destructiveness was more a side effect of their popularity, rather than their intention. Their emphasis on vocational, commercial goals repeatedly detracted from the intellectual, educational goals. Because school garden leaders were constantly fighting on two fronts (one against public opposition and the other against the opposing camp), the leadership was not strong enough to prevent the erosion of their original goals — a wearing away which continued until little remained.

Rural conditions during the twenties were changing, blunting many of the original causes and motives of the school garden movement. Increased communication between city and country, through the media of car, train, radio and telephone, was rapidly urbanizing rural Canada in life-style and values. Rural spokesmen continued to fight valiantly to "countrify" rural curricula, but the reasons had become hollow and codified. Whether anyone seriously listened to yet another listing of the causes and cures of the rural problem is doubtful. In one sense, the problem was disappearing in many urban minds. Commentators pointed out that Canada's true wealth was increasingly stemming from industrial and commercial ventures. After the war, for a while, food prices declined, lessening urban interest in the plight of the farm producer. The farmer had become commercial and political and had lost much of the romanticized "tiller of the soil" image. For many reasons, a growing animosity between city and country was replacing former feelings of concern.[64]

When the funds from the Agricultural Instruction Act stopped in 1924*, the progressive spirit declined even further. An additional blow occured when the movement's main forum for discussion and publicity, the *Agricultural Gazette*, ceased publication when the act's support stopped. Increasingly, junior agriculture clubs replaced nature study and school gardens, perpetuating vocational ideals. Those who were interested in farming maintained their interest through clubs that were not school oriented — clubs that live on today.

The Agricultural Instruction Act had attempted too much, weakening the movement through too great a diversity of ventures. The divisiveness within the school garden movement, fostered by the debate over vocational vs. intellectual and educational goals, greatly undermined the movement's effectiveness. Coinciding with the slow disintegration of the school garden movement during the 1920s was a general lessening of reforming zeal throughout Canadian society.[65] Whether caused by a general disillusionment after World War I over the inability to effect change, or the increasing emphasis on professional, agency and government control over social programs, the middle-class urge to "improve" society sharply waned.

Perhaps the greatest impediment, however, to universal acceptance of the school garden philosophy was its unpopularity with many rural parents and teachers. In spite of the mass of publicity, support and materials to modernize rural schooling, it retained much of its nineteenth-century character up into the 1930s.[67] The school garden's survival in the face of such a negative combination of social, economic and political forces was not promising. When the Depression swept over Canada, most remnants of the school garden movement were finally erased from provincial curricula.

*"owing to the heavy demands upon our Federal revenues, it is only one of the many retrenchments imposed on us by the public demand."[66]

4 Flower Boxes On Main Street:

The City Beautiful

THE OVERVIEW

> . . .the creation of a city beautiful is not only gratifying to our civic pride and satisfying to our artistic senses, but it is also a social necessity, a civic duty, and a profitable investment.[1]

This statement of purpose voiced in 1915 epitomized how the City Beautiful movement had evolved during its twenty years of activity. A vocal portion of North American society was, at first, possessed by an impelling desire to improve their surroundings aesthetically. Later, swept along in the reforming spirit and the growing materialism of the time, the promoters transformed the movement's purpose into a combination of artistic achievement, duty and reward.

In the beginning, the philosophy of the City Beautiful had its roots in the growing appreciation and utilization of the expertise of "new" professionals such as landscape architects, town planners, architects and engineers. Chicago's World Columbian Exposition of 1893 was the premier example of what a co-ordinated group of professional "beautifiers" could create. A carefully chosen committee, collaborating with selected painters and sculptors, produced a uniform, aesthetically-pleasing site: the exposition buildings, designed in a neo-classical style, were painted white, sited on landscaped grounds and integrated into an equally well-designed park and parkway system. For the first time, many North Americans realized the possibilities of planned, visual harmony in civic design.[2]

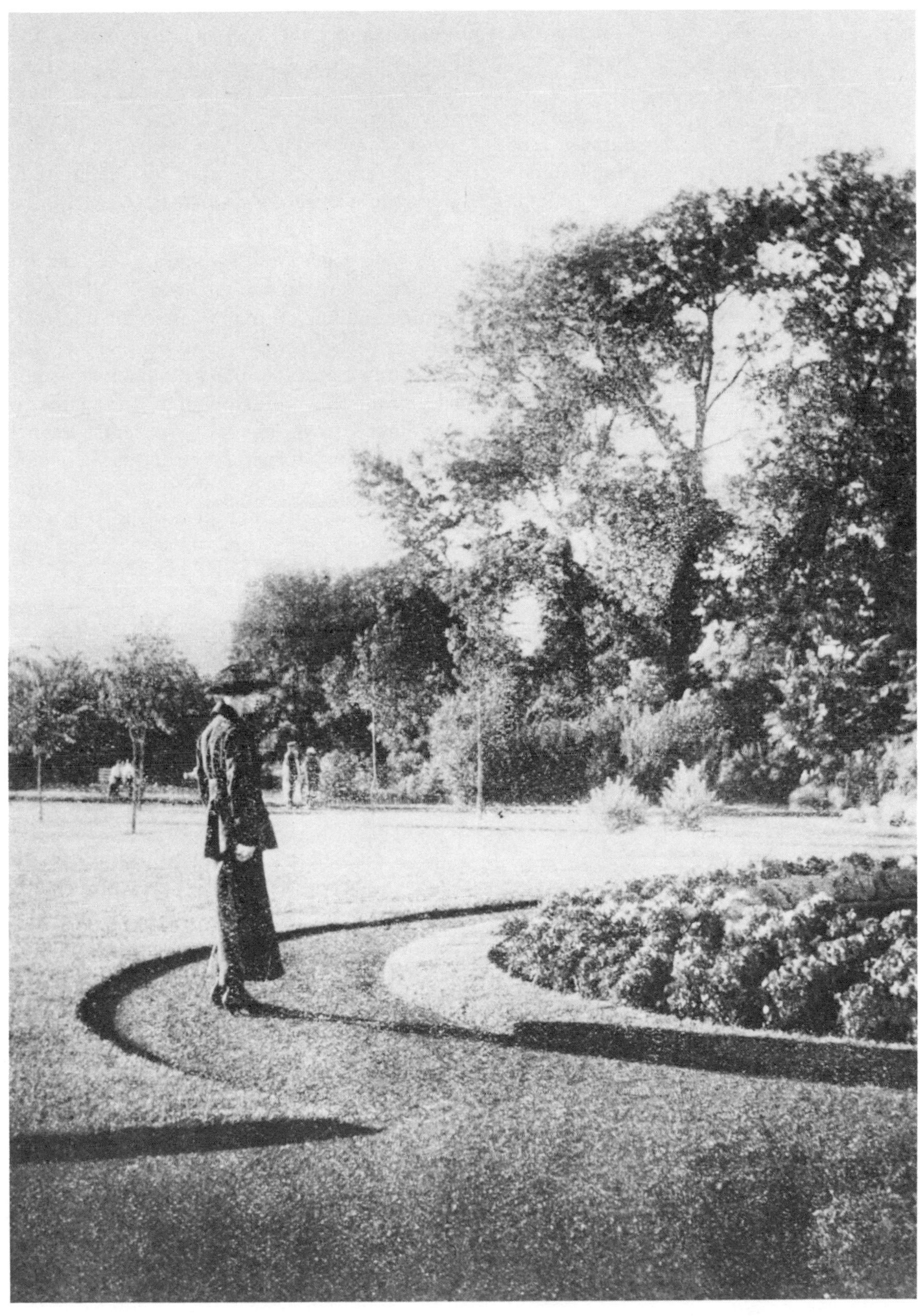

Another influence on City Beautiful thought was the example of magnificent buildings and vistas of many European cities. More North Americans were travelling to Europe to see these marvels first hand, and returning with glowing reports of all they had seen.[3] By 1904, a few years after Charles Robinson's pioneering book, *The Improvement of Towns and Cities, or the Practical Basis of Civic Aesthetics*, appeared in the United States, many professionals, civic spokesmen, and members of the lay public were engaging in the "world-wide civic battle between Ugliness and Beauty."[4]

In Canada, the Chicago exposition, foreign travel, and international writings on the new movement stimulated reassessments of our urban surroundings. In many cases, the contrast in the late 1800s between the beautifier's goals and actual conditions was jolting. Downtown areas in many of our major centres suffered aesthetically from the profusion of utility poles, tall buildings, billboards, over-crowding and a general drabness. Many residential areas were unadorned by either parks or home landscaping.[5] According to current psychological thought, an ugly environment damaged the viewer's mental health. This theory was soon used to bolster the improvers' sense of purpose and

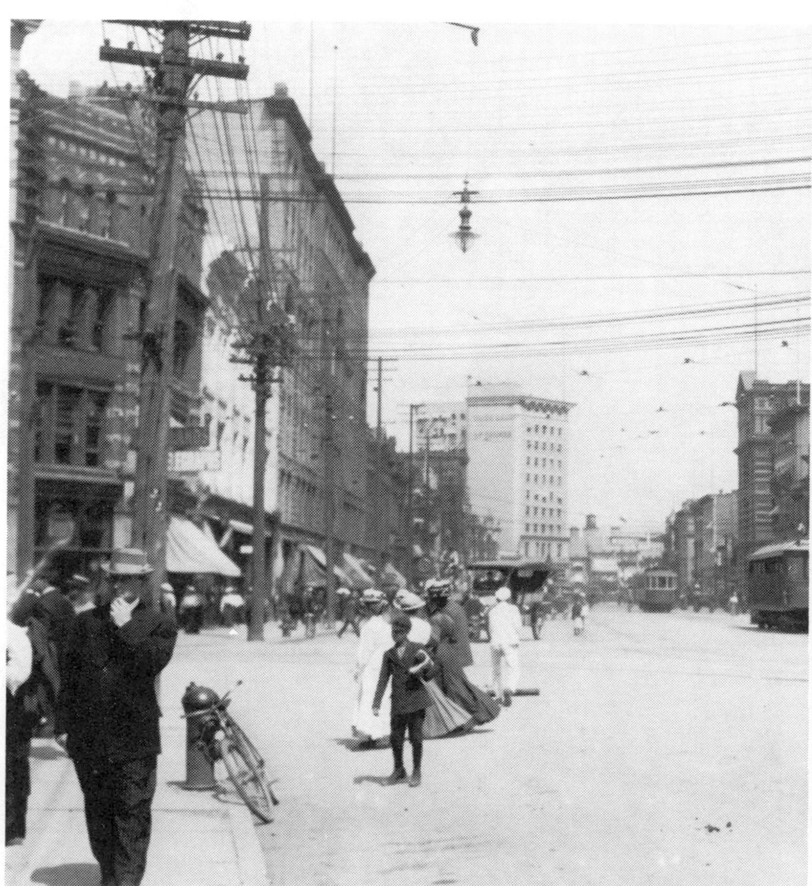

Winnipeg, about 1909. Urban beautifiers were challenged by the many obstacles blocking their vision of a perfectly planned, aesthetically pleasing city.

A Toronto factory in 1906 was improved with vines and lawn, as part of a civic campaign to beautify eyesores: ". . . to give an air of brightness . . . to cheer and brighten the sometimes monotonous character of the labor of the employees . . ."

duty. If the streetscape were cleaned up and beautified, a "social duty" would be performed. On the prairies, performing this social duty often meant starting from "scratch":

> [Saskatoon in 1901 was] a sprinkling of rude shacks dotted upon a raw prairie and housing merely 113 sanguine souls . . .One tiny single-room school; no streets, no sidewalks; neither sewers nor waterworks; no light, no newspaper, no telephones, — in fact, nothing that bore the faintest semblance of simplest comfort.[6]

Yet, it was in the older, eastern Canadian cities where civic beautification first took hold. The turn of the century witnessed a flurry of activity as professionals began drawing up plans to achieve the ideal city — one of parks, trees, boulevards and stately buildings.[7] Coherence of design, with elements of visual variety (landscaped streets, inspiring vistas and parkways) would enhance the civic grandeur of a planned design.[8] Attaining this ideal involved not only tremendous amounts of money, but also a great degree of regulation over the city dweller's life. Regulating bodies of architects and engineers were to have the power to approve or disallow municipal building plans, supposedly eliminating the "haphazard mixture along a street of architectural style and building size."[9] Professional beautifiers were convinced that society as a whole loved beauty, wanted to be surrounded by it, and did not differ in aesthetic judgement from their own ideals.

City Beautiful thought slowly trickled down from the professionals to the rest of the populace, stimulating smaller, less grandiose beautifying efforts. Unfortunately, the Canadian City Beautiful movement lacked both an integrated philosophy and an articulate national spokesperson. Further, worsening economic conditions before World War I severely curtailed implementation of larger projects. Coupled with this, beautification projects

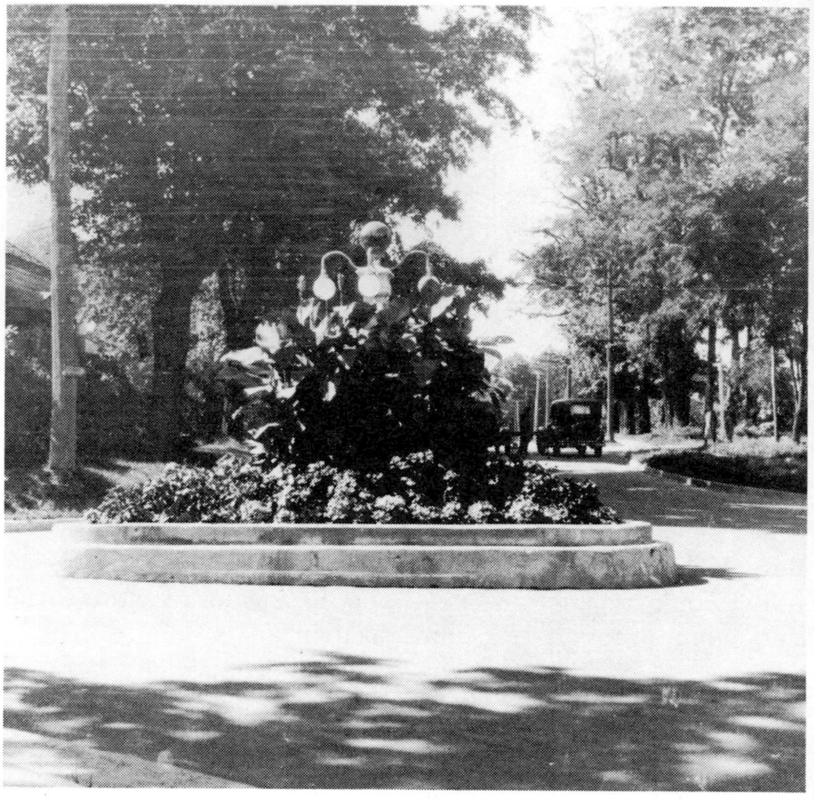

Street planters in Grimsby, Ontario, 1925. These became increasingly popular. One Ontario town turned the centre of its business district into beds and planters full of cannas and caladiums, maintained by the merchants themselves.

began to be criticized in the face of housing shortages, public health problems, and the need for legislation to control our growing cities. Beauty was gradually phased out of the urban planner's criteria for social change and was not re-admitted until the 1920s. City councils planned great architectural innovations and park commissions designed large acreages, but few of these plans were executed. However, smaller, amateur groups (horticultural societies, improvement associations and sometimes Boards of Trade) went about "planting up" the city. These smaller groups carried on the fight against ugliness when official City Beautiful programs failed.[10]

HORTICULTURAL SOCIETIES

Horticultural societies were slowly becoming a part of Canadian life by 1900. The first horticultural society in Ontario was formed in 1834 and in the prairies in 1893 in Brandon, Manitoba. Originally outgrowths of local agricultural societies, horticultural societies were organized by men interested in amateur and commercial growing of fruits, vegetables and ornamentals. (There were women members, but the official positions were nearly always held by men up into the 1920s.) By the early 1900s, many eastern Canadian societies were catching the "beautifying fever," and breaking out in a rash of City Beautiful rhetoric:

> If we are to provoke a revulsion against untidy streets, hideous alleys, tumble down houses, repulsive garbage heaps, offensive advertisements of black and yellow on dead walls and mountain sides, we must become teachers of beauty . . . Missionaries of beauty are wanted to enlist in this crusade against ugliness.[11]

Horticultural duty to society, when performed well, not only would insure beautiful surroundings, but also, as a side benefit, would "purify home life. . .promote a greater love of home. . .and thereby lay the foundation of a patriotism worthy of the land we possess."[12] Professor William Hutt of the Ontario Agricultural College in 1909 further outlined various ways a horticultural society could "reach out" to improve the environment. Horticultural societies should lead educational campaigns for civic beautification, leading the public to an "appreciation of the value of neatness, order and beautiful surroundings."[13] Societies should support children's flower competitions to instil a life-long love of flowers.[14] The society should not work alone, but co-opt other civic organizations: school boards, town councils, and boards of trade.[15] The local press should never be ignored, but used to the best advantage in publicizing civic beautification.[16] By 1903, the *Canadian Horticulturist* had instituted a monthly department called "Civic Improvement," devoted "to the interests of the Horticultural Societies of Ontario, and of all other bodies interested in the improvement of the surroundings of our Canadian town and country homes."

IMPROVEMENT ASSOCIATIONS

Improvement associations were also being formed by groups of concerned citizens. The composition of improvement societies was similar to horticultural societies (that is, ministers, doctors, lawyers, municipal officials, businessmen), the town's élite forming the core membership. Often an improvement association would join forces with a local horticultural society, or enthusiastic promoters would be prominent members in each group.

The City Improvement League of Montreal, founded in 1909, grew out of the success of an anti-tuberculosis crusade. The League initiated improvement activities, and acted as a central clearing house of information for other societies and individuals working toward civic betterment. Among their many activities (ranging from "child life problems," to Montreal's water supply, to a city plan for Montreal), the League also sponsored children's gardens — some made on unused land at home or in nearby vacant lots: a child's garden "makes for physical and not a little for moral cleanliness."[17]

Hamilton, Ontario, however, claimed to have the first civic improvement society in Canada in 1899, an organization which

The Empress Hotel, Victoria. These grounds were part of the CPR garden system, but were also influenced by Civic Beautification programs.

raised "the moral tone of the community."[18] Improvement societies generally espoused the same ideals as horticultural societies, but sometimes with an added element:

> So we have found that what we have done with very little inconvenience to ourselves has proved a good advertizement for the place and its people, and the present prospect is that we shall get back many times the value of the labor and money expended in improvement, for several sales of property have been made at much better figures than prevailed before we began our work.[19]

Parliament Buildings, Edmonton, Alberta. Landscaping around government buildings was designed to enhance civic grandeur.

BOARDS OF TRADE

Boards of Trade, certainly not known for their civic reticence, sometimes instigated beautification programs, believing beautiful surroundings were "a potent factor in attracting citizens and increasing trade."[20] This certainly was true for Saskatoon. The Commissioner of the Saskatoon Board of Trade was responsible for attracting settlement to a region characterized by "variable" weather and a short growing season. The Commissioner from 1908 to 1919, F. Maclure Sclanders, cultivated a garden plot full of fast-ripening varieties of vegetables, flowers and grains in front of the Board of Trade office. One year he optimistically grew banana plants in the garden.[21] However, this touch of whimsy was unusual. Most improvers were serious, dedicated people with a mission.

The spirit of civic rivalry helped fuel the growing improvement movement. Floral boosterism added its voice to the already strident clamour of the boosterism of the times: real estate promotions, rivalries over factory locations, and general civic advertising of a city's attractions.

By 1910, many Canadians had heeded the improvers' message; a variety of public plantings had been successfully initiated. Among these smaller scale efforts were schemes such as street tree planting; public grounds beautification, including churches, civic buildings and schools; clean-up campaigns; and the beginnings of urban and rural home beautification. The two larger movements of public park building and vacant lot gardening were also emerging at this time.* Many of the same people were involved in the various activities and sometimes the various schemes were combined in one local campaign. However, for a clearer picture of what was done, the activities will be treated separately.

Street tree planting, Lorne Avenue, Brandon, Manitoba. "There is nothing which tends more to beautify the general appearance of a city, to impress its visitors, to add to its healthfulness, and to inspire its residents with a desire to improve and beautify their homes . . ."

STREET TREE PLANTING

One of the earliest civic beautification projects was street tree planting which was also allied with the growing popularity of boulevarding — creating strips of lawn and trees and sometimes flower beds alongside or down the centre of city streets. In Winnipeg this practice was begun in a limited way in 1896, supervised

*Details of Canadian town planning are largely irrelevant to this horticultural story. Town planning focused more on zoning, legislation, town layout, housing and public health, rather than on landscaping or gardening.

by the City Council's Board of Works. By 1900 it had become so popular with residents that the Parks Board took it over and extended tree planting throughout the entire city.[22] The Board quickly and efficiently bureaucratized the plantings. A special assessment was enacted and maintenance was streamlined by dividing the city into districts. A few disasters convinced the Board that the best trees to plant were the ones dug out of the bush* by farmers, for which they were paid thirty-five cents per tree.[23] By 1908 the Board proudly announced they had 138 kilometres of boulevard, planted with 20 000 trees.[24]

Elsewhere, tree planting was less officially pursued. In 1901 readers of the *Canadian Horticulturist* were told it was their civic duty to plant shade trees.[25] In 1907, Professor D.P. Penhallow, professor of botany at McGill University, lent scientific backing to tree planting. In addition to their aesthetic appeal, he stated, trees also provided an atmosphere of "greater purity and more bracing quality."[26] Educationally, shade trees were also beneficial:

> . . .to bring up children habituated to association with those forms of vegetation which typify great beauty and grace of form, which represent the embodiment of plastic strength and great virility, is to insensibly shape their moral natures in such ways as to develop character and self-reliance, as well as an appreciation of those more gentle graces which contribute so largely to the characteristic qualities of the cultured and refined.[27]

The planting campaign was further embellished by claims that street trees attracted visitors and encouraged settlement. The contrast between an unimproved street (a mud road, bordered by deep ditches, ornamented by weed patches between ditch and sidewalk) and an improved one (a paved street, bordered by ribbons of lawn and rows of trees) was a powerful incentive in many cities for increased tree plantings.[28]

However, by the 1920s, problems had emerged from over-enthusiastic tree planting. In Ottawa, street tree vendors had not only sold unsuitable trees but recommended planting them too close together. In 1923, Ottawa passed a tree by-law prohibiting the planting of certain trees† and appointed a street tree inspector to oversee planting and spacing.[29] The Ottawa Horticultural Society led the campaign for better street tree regulations: little gardening was occuring in older sections of the city because of over-shading and over-drainage of front lawns and gardens.[30]

---

*American elm, white ash, basswood, Russian poplar and box elder.

---

†Butternut, cherry, chestnut, Manitoba maple, sassafrass, walnut, cone-bearing evergreens, poplars and willows.

Other cities were having similar problems of maintenance and care. Calgary had planted 29 000 trees by 1921, but the attempt to involve its citizens in tree care had failed. Asked to water the trees directly outside their homes during dry spells, many home owners refused.[31] Because of citizen neglect, other cities as well were forced to hire arborists to maintain the plantings and to remedy untutored tree pruning, much of which amounted to "butchery": "Preach against the destruction and mutilation. Preach tree planting. Raise your voices until our municipalities enact laws for the preservation of the trees and grant a bonus or award prizes for trees well planted."[32]

But by 1929, in spite of a great deal of voluntary and municipal participation, large centres, such as Toronto, were still beset by street beautification problems:

> There are streets without boulevards, where boulevards ought to be; there are streets with boulevards in the wrong place; there are streets with badly cared for boulevards; streets without trees on them, streets with the wrong kind of trees; streets with too many trees on it [sic], all kinds of disfiguring things.[33]

Dr. Frank E. Bennett, president of the St. Thomas, Ontario, Horticultural Society, was a force behind many horticultural initiatives in Ontario.

BEAUTIFICATION OF PUBLIC PROPERTY

The continuing battle to eliminate "disfiguring things" was not limited solely to tree plantings — the attack was manifold. Typical examples of common beautification programs pursued before 1925 are illustrated by the activities of the St. Thomas, Ontario Horticultural Society.

The Society, from 1912 up into the twenties, was run by an energetic president, Dr. Frank E. Bennett, a man who fervently practised floral boosterism. Bennett only accepted the presidency on the condition that $100 was granted by the city council to plant fifteen flower beds by the city railway lines.[34] In 1913, the Society planted fifty-five flower beds (on average six metres by one metre) along the streetcar route, in parks, and in front of public buildings such as the City Hall, public library and post office. Nearly sixteen thousand tulip bulbs were used in these public plantings.[35] Where land was not available for flower beds, the Society in 1915 bought and filled twenty-five one metre high cement urns.[36]

The St. Thomas Board of Trade (at the instigation of the Horticultural Society) offered a silver cup for the best kept factory grounds — which provoked a great deal of wholesome rivalry.[37] Many factories without extensive grounds competed by planting vines around the buildings and installing plant-filled window boxes. Window boxes graced other public buildings as well, especially post offices — the focal point of most small towns.

By 1921 the St. Thomas Horticultural Society had been so successful with its public plantings that it was given sole responsibility for beautifying all public buildings, major stores, factories and railway property. Dr. Bennett was very pleased, saying the Society now could co-ordinate colour schemes throughout the city.[38]

Factories were also drawn into the beautifying spirit. The *Farmers' Advocate*, a farm journal, for one year sponsored competitions for the beautification of cheese factories in Ontario and western Quebec.[39]

Churches and hospitals were other public buildings said to need "floral beautifying." The Hamilton City Improvement Society complained in 1902 that far from the support and activity they expected from churches, there was practically no improvement shown.[40] The reverse was sometimes shown in other cities. In Winnipeg, an outstanding and rather astonishing example was the grounds of St Luke's Anglican Church. Landscaped and maintained by J.E. Smith (former gardener for the Grand Trunk Pacific Railway and then head gardener for the CPR), the grounds were a mixture of natural and geometric styles. Scattered around the ivy-covered grey stone church were wide perennial borders and lawn. Dotting the lawn were various flower beds. Near the rectory was

Virden, Manitoba. Horticultural reformers were often disappointed that landscaping around churches was not more elaborate. The reformers felt that churches should set an example in their communities.

an oval bed filled with gladiolus. A circular bed on the main lawn and one around a large elm were filled with flowering shrubs and perennials. Nearby a shamrock-shaped bed sported snapdragons, while a crucifix-shaped one was filled with petunias. In front of the church there were three flower beds — one of which was shaped like a fleur-de-lys. All were filled with assorted annuals.[41] Churches and hospitals benefited from the beautifying spirit in other ways. In St. Thomas, as in many other small towns, the horticultural society donated cut flowers for church decoration and for hospital patients' bouquets.

SCHOOL BEAUTIFICATION

Children's participation in beautification was also stimulated. Horticultural and improvement societies capitalized on the growing interest in school gardening by advocating school grounds improvement. They further enticed school children into the "love of the beautiful" by seed distributions and special exhibitions of their floral harvests.

In the early 1900s horticultural societies were beautifying many schools. From descriptions of unimproved schools, this must have been a challenge:

> How barren, how uninviting are the average school grounds — not a tree to offer a hand's breath of shade, or a shrub or vine to break the painful monotony or hide the unsightly outbuildings. Does it not seem, then, a poor, insignificant thing, this plain little building in its patch of hard ground?[42]

Beautified school grounds would assure "better and more contented attendance of pupils, will inspire [pupils] with higher ideals of living and of citizenship and will implant in their minds loving and imperishable memories of the happy days spent at the old school."[43]

Arbor Days were held to encourage community participation. Usually a May Friday was designated for cleaning grounds, planting trees and sometimes constructing flower beds. The response was not always enthusiastic: the editor of the *Canadian Horticulturist* in 1904 surveyed fifty Ontario schools on their Arbor Day observances and discovered only three schools active.[44] The New Brunswick education journal, *Rural Education Monthly*, recorded a variety of responses to provincial Arbor Day promotions, ranging from: "What's the use," to "As we are is good enough," "No use fixing up the school, the children would only spoil it," to the conventional "I haven't time."[45] One Saskatchewan teacher, undaunted by community opposition to Arbor Day, gathered the willing children together and with one dull spade and an axe, managed to plant thirty maple trees they had dug from the bush.[46]

As official school garden programs increased in influence, departments of education took over school grounds improve-

Ontario, 1902. School grounds beautification was promoted as an uplifting element in the community's cultural life and as a psychological boost to the child's appreciation of nature, beauty and country life.

J. C. Magnan, Official Agriculturist of Quebec, plants a tree during Arbor Day at the St. Casimir school in 1925.

ment, diminishing the participation of horticultural societies, Women's Institutes, and improvement associations. Provincial departments offered grants to teachers, supplied ornamentals, and, in general, included school beautification in official school garden policies.

With increased official recognition and support, the landscaped rural school was championed as a worthy community centre, reflecting the area's spirit and intelligence.[47] Children's mental health would improve because of the positive psychological effect beautiful surroundings would have on them.

Competitions, the most popular form of horticultural encouragement, were held, sometimes sponsored by local horticultural societies, or funded by provincial ministeries. For example, the Quebec Department of Agriculture in the late 1920s awarded silver cups to schools making the greatest improvement.[48] A nation-wide competition was sponsored by the Horticultural Council of Canada, which awarded silver cups to each provincial winner.[49]

The ideal, which a few schools achieved, was a properly landscaped site with perennial beds, shrub borders, and a lawn and circular drive at the entrance. The Horticultural Departments of Macdonald College, Quebec, and of the Ontario Agricultural College, free of charge, would draw up landscape plans for any school which sent in a proper sketch of their grounds showing placement of buildings, existing trees and playgrounds.

As with school gardens, where the school grounds movement was accepted improvement was quite successful and resulted in many aesthetically pleasing school sites. Most rural schools remained unadorned, victims of a district's unreceptiveness or poverty, while city schools fared better because of the additional support of horticultural and civic improvement societies.

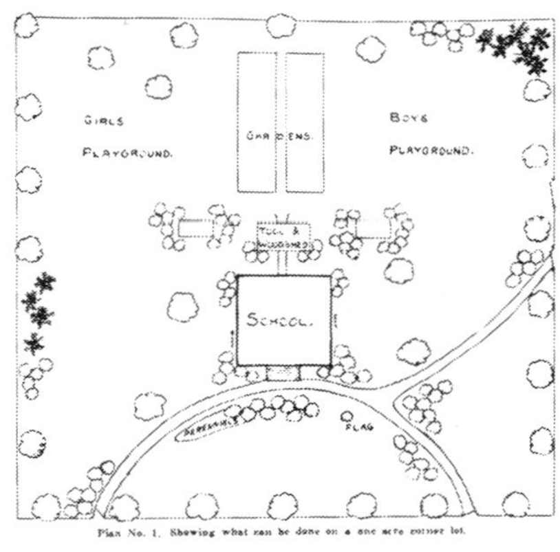

A school grounds landscaping plan suggested in 1916.

HOME BEAUTIFICATION

As ambitiously as they had tackled public and institutional beautifying, civic improvers directed their energies into home beautification, to further a "greater intolerance of ugliness."[50] In eastern Canada a priority project was tearing down the high board fences surrounding home properties. In Charlottetown, these eyesores were said to give residences "the appearance of aslyums for the insane or of prisons for the criminal classes."[51] Professor William Hutt saw the removal of street fences as the initial step which would initiate a series of improvements: proper cement sidewalks, proper grading of lawns and boulevards, neater lawns, and more tree planting.[52]

Clean-up weeks were another popular horticultural attack on civic eyesores. Often, in large centres, the clean-up campaigns concentrated on one or two neighbourhoods, while in smaller towns, the entire community would be involved. Usually campaigns focused on back-yard clean-ups. Back-yards in many urban centres were generally neglected, littered with debris — places where dish water and garbage were thrown. Home owners were further encouraged to plant a few flowers and shrubs for aesthetic, hygienic and emotional values:[53] "An ugly environment too often means a soul distorted, dwarfed and destroyed by the absence of sympathetic and subtle influence — a soul untouched by the influence of a home scented and adorned with things fair to look upon."[54]

In the larger cities, some clean-up campaigns were linked with slum improvement projects. A minor theme in the overall movement, slum improvement provoked outbursts of action and idealistic rhetoric:

> It had been very encouraging to see the transformation of ugly little backyards littered with broken furniture, boxes and cans, without plants or flowers, and cheered only by an occasional bright-hued garment on washing days, into little green and flowering places, where the family can refresh their minds and bodies, rest and think, and perhaps dream a little.[55]

But the magnitude of slum conditions overpowered any lasting horticultural remedy.

More lasting was the clean-up work directed to vacant lots, grounds of public buildings, and private front lawns. The St. Thomas Horticultural Society, with its green fingers in every gardening pie, pursued these campaigns so energetically that by 1920, they boasted:

> The effect of the work has been remarkable. Hardly a waste area exists in the city. Unsightly spots have been transformed into beauty places, unsightly fences have been removed, nearly every home, however humble, is a bower of flowers. Law and order are more respected and fires are practically eli-

Before and after pictures of back-yard improvement projects were often printed in periodicals as encouragement and proof that the transformation of an ugly site could be effected in a short time.

> minated. An air of cleanliness exists, and the whole town has transformed in a few years at a very small cost.[56]

Beautification efforts were also encouraged by home garden competitions. The earliest were in Hamilton, Ontario in 1902, sponsored jointly by the Hamilton Horticultural Society and the Improvement Society: gardens, children's bouquets, window boxes, and rockeries for corner lots were among the competitive categories. Corner rockeries, usually laid along a line from a corner of the house to the angle formed by the two front sidewalks, were highly praised. They were not only ornamental, but also useful, preventing people from cutting corners, destroying the lawn.[57] In 1905, the rockery competition had become so popular that $300 in prize money and five gold medals were awarded.[58]

Ottawa's garden competitions were organized and patronized by the wives of two Governors-General. Lady Minto in 1902 inaugurated garden competitions for the

> . . . encouragement of neatness and order in the keeping of grass plots and flower beds in the private homes . . . the encouragement of flower growing, and their tasteful arrangement in beds or borders; and to awaken increased interest in horticulture in general, so that the gardens and lawns entered in the competitions might be object lessons to the rest of the citizens.[59]

Following the usual custom, Ottawa was divided into judging districts, and the gardens into two classes — those maintained by amateurs and those cultivated by professional gardeners. In the first year gold, silver and bronze medals were awarded, while in the second, money prizes were given. After Lady Minto left Canada, Lady Grey sponsored the competitions for a few years more.

The amount of participation in clean-up days, back-yard beautification, garden competitions and flower shows varied across Canada. Depending on the energy of local improvement groups, a town's eyesores might be eliminated. Gardeners seemingly were never satisfied — there was always room for one more planter, one more boulevard. One famous Ontario gardener, R.B. Whyte, bewailed the horticultural ignorance of many Canadians who (he felt) retarded the movement.[60] Others worried that our gardens and horticultural improvements would not compare favourably with the beautiful gardens our soldiers had seen in England and France: "We as horticulturists must live up to these visions of our soldier boys." In some quarters, improvement societies were being criticized for *over*-enthusiastic improving. Frederick Todd stated that the Ottawa Improvement Society had improved much of the individuality of several scenic drives "out of existence until a sameness exists . . . which destroys the interest."[61]

(Top)
The Calgary Public Library. Window boxes and flower beds were favoured "weapons" in the beautifiers' war against ugliness.

(Bottom)
A winner in the Hamilton Rockery Contest in 1905. Garden competitions were promoted as part of clean-up campaigns held in towns and cities.

PUBLIC PARKS

Another phase of civic beautification was the emerging movement to create public parks. The enthusiasm which prompted neighbourhood clean-ups or municipal flower beds soon was directed into this new cause. Open areas for public use were not a recent innovation — the town square probably is as old as settlement itself.[62] What was innovative in the nineteenth century was the idea of an urban tract of land devoted to public recreation. Prior to this parks were part of a gentleman's private property, and not open to the public.

The industrial revolution brought the plight of working people, crowded into dirty, congested, polluted urban areas, before British social activists. The Romantics had bequeathed to the Victorians the notion of nature as a restorer of moral and physical health, and the idea of parks as "breathing spaces," where the worker could revive himself with the healing properties of nature, began to gain in popularity.[63] An aesthetically designed park would lend the extra support of the Beautiful on the worker's trek into the bourgeois ideal of rightful living. Some park enthusiasts advocated parks purely for recreation or sports, while others called for parks designed for aesthetic enjoyment for everyone — not just for the workers.

The landscaped public park entered North America in the 1830s through the "rural cemetery" movement. Burial grounds were landscaped, serving as ". . . a quiet place in which to escape the bustle and clangor of the city — for strolling, for solitude, and even for family picnics."[64] But it was not until the 1860s that the first American park, landscaped for recreational and aesthetic enjoyment, was created. New York City's Central Park was the first park to be made on public land, developed with public funds and open to all.[65]

Both park development and the profession of landscape architecture owe a great deal to Frederick Law Olmsted, who designed New York's Central Park in the 1860s. A self-taught landscape gardener, Olmsted was always drawn to parks during his early, extensive trips around Europe. In subsequent years he also had a profound impact on Canadian park creation. He may have emphasized the practical basis of nature, but the real foundation of his belief was metaphysical, that nature had the power to lift the mind and spirit into the realm of the poetic.[66]

In 1874, he was invited by the city of Montreal to design a park out of various parcels of land collected together on the urban fringe. By this time Olmsted was the pre-eminent landscape architect in North America, with more than a decade of experience in designing parks, college campuses, private estates and residential subdivisions behind him.[67] In designing Mount Royal, Olmsted was guided by three major design themes: his continu-

The bandstand in the Halifax Public Gardens. Sunday concerts in the park were commonplace in the larger cities.

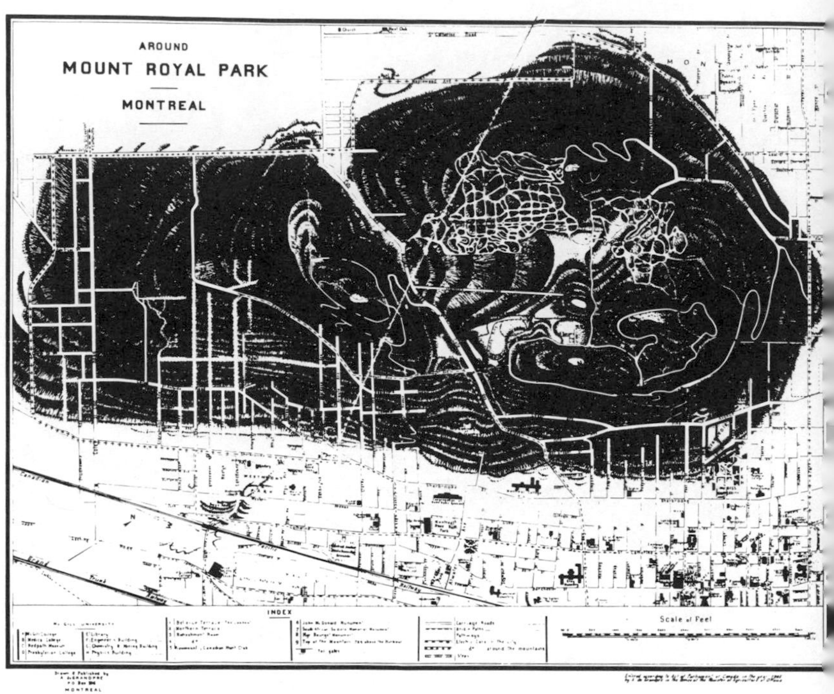

Topographical map of Mount Royal Park, 1905, designed by F. L. Olmstead. He feverently believed that "Charming natural scenery acts in a more directly remedial way to enable men to better resist the harmful influences of ordinary town life and recover what they lose from them."

ing belief in the mystical and healing effects of natural landscapes on city dwellers; his belief that the site was best developed if its special qualities were respected and incorporated into the design; and the precept that the landscape design must be unified, not fragmented.[68] Since the site was composed of eight distinct topographical areas, a unified design was a challenge. But Olmsted, despite political, economic and geographical obstacles, persevered and created a magnificent park, basically true to its natural features. Until the 1870s, Canadian park development had been minimal. The impact of Olmsted's Mount Royal on Canadian park design was immeasurable.

Canada had also been affected by the cemetery-as-park phenomenon in the mid-1800s. British immigrants were active in certain urban areas in agitating for landscaped cemeteries as well as parks. They had imported the ideals of the English landscape style, which had also influenced Olmsted: rolling hills and long stretches of lawn created vistas of shrub and tree groupings, based on an informal, naturalistic design. Another imported style influencing our early park and cemetery design were the geometrical, formal arrangements recently popularized in Victorian England.[69] We have already seen examples of this style in our discussion of railway gardening.

An early example of a formally designed park is the Halifax Public Gardens. Originally this small park was a botanic garden founded by the Halifax Horticultural Society in 1836. It featured flower beds, fountains, an archery court, and a grotto with a spring. The park was open only to those buying a membership.

In 1875 the city of Halifax purchased the Gardens from the Horticultural Society which could no longer support them. Under the supervision of Richard Power, who we are told had trained under a famous British landscape gardener, the public gardens were combined with a small park created on the Halifax Common. The resulting park was essentially Victorian in character: "Rich floral displays in geometrically situated carpet gardens, memorial statues, urns, fountains, artificial ponds and streams, and a gingerbread bandstand are linked by endless winding paths."[70]

Another early attempt in park-garden creation was Queen Square in Charlottetown, Prince Edward Island. In 1884, when concerned citizens could no longer bear the ugliness of the square, a group formed to improve its appearance:

> Its absolute hideousness could not be described. Brick bats were the most ornamental things to be seen, next came wisps of grass, looking forlorn, and growing in a spasmodic fashion . . . Cows and horses frequently found their way into the

One of the scenic drives through Mount Royal Park winding around the reservoir.

Court House Square, Winnipeg. Landscaped city squares were more numerous than larger parks. After World War I, such squares were popular sites for war memorials.

> square, proofs of whose presence could always be seen by the admiring tourist. The summer dust, to be appreciated, had to be seen and felt. A post and rail fence, of portentous ugliness, had been erected around the square.[71]

These public-spirited citizens instituted Arbor Days to plant trees in the square as well as other deserving sections of the city. Arthur Newbery, secretary of the Queen Square Committee, was the main promoter of a planned garden in the square, a garden to equal in beauty the Halifax Public Gardens.[72]

Public awareness of the need for parks was slowly emerging. In late 1876, British Columbia passed an Act for the Management of Public Parks,[73] and Manitoba in 1892 passed a Public Parks Board Act.[74] However, the creation of large, planned and designed parks, on the scale of Mount Royal, was not a high priority of city planning in these early years. Rather the main emphasis was on establishing small urban parks, ornamental squares, or small "breathing spaces" throughout the city, as in Winnipeg, and in many other urban centres at the turn of the century.[75] Eight parks were created in Winnipeg between 1893 and 1897 — in spite of the feeling at the Parks Board that the city had the great handicap of not having many natural sites "to catch the eye."[76]

Greater interest in park building was also reflected in the media. The *Canadian Horticulturist* by 1902 was printing articles detailing notable Canadian and European parks — even to the extent of publishing a plan of a park in Mainz, Germany. Nor had the promotion of park-like cemetries languished after the turn of the century in Canadian periodicals. The *Canadian Horticulturist* was also in the forefront of this enthusiasm, as seen in an 1903 article extolling the virtues of a well-designed cemetery. If the cemetery was nicely landscaped and well-maintained, "patronage would so increase that the sale of lots would soon make the cemetery a paying investment and the pride of the countryside."[77] A beautified cemetery would be a place where "mourners will not mind to lay aside a loved one."[78] Too many cemeteries, according to various commentators, were sadly neglected: uncut grass, broken fences, and desecrated gravestones "shame the living, and speak loudly of their lack of reverence for their ancestry."[79]

The City Beautiful movement had by 1900 embraced the cause of cemetery improvement and park creation. As with other improvement projects, park and cemetery work had a professional as well as an amateur side. While landscape architects (some imported from England and the United States) and parks boards landscaped large tracts of urban and suburban land, horticultural and improvement societies oversaw the beautifying of smaller pieces of land. The merits of recreational versus aesthetically-oriented parks were debated with each group.

The years before World War I were a period of intense park creation. For example, Ottawa in 1898 had only one park, but by

1908, mainly through the efforts of the Ottawa Improvement Commission, the city was ornamented by six more. By the 1930s many Canadian cities and towns boasted at least one new park (usually named Victoria) and beautified cemetery.

Reasons for park promotion in these pre-war years ranged at times far beyond Olmsted's spiritual bond-with-nature philosophy and breathing-spaces-for-the-worker justifications. Not that these viewpoints lacked promoters, but the booster mentality of the era had begun influencing park creation: the economic benefit of parks began to be noted as the value of land adjacent to parks rose. Thus in many cities parks were created near the "better" residential areas, sometimes due to the vested interests of members of parks boards and improvement societies.[80] Parks were touted as visible proof of a prosperous community, a community concerned about the welfare of its residents. For this reason, parks would attract a better class of residents to the town, while also acting as tourist attractions.[81] Certainly the few large public parks the CPR created were mainly for this purpose.

Parks were also said to be economically beneficial for the horticultural industry. Parks kept a community conscious of floral beauty, creating a need for flowers for indoor and outdoor use. To maintain the growing horticultural industry, parks must be continually created. A dismal picture was painted of a town which did not "mould public sentiment towards a love of horticulture and parks."

Certainly the professional landscape architect received a boost from the increased interest in public parks. But while there was much activity, travelling to and fro, drawing up plans and presenting them to civic committees, larger projects either never left the drawing board or just continued at a slow pace. For example, in 1903 Frederick Todd submitted a detailed report to the Ottawa Improvement Commission illustrated by numerous photographs, outlining an integrated park and parkway system, but lack of

(Left)
Old Burying Ground, Saint John, New Brunswick, 1890. Cemetery grounds were often nicely landscaped, affording an aesthetically pleasing location for a Sunday stroll.

(Right)
Mount View Cemetery, Galt, Ontario, 1911. Formal bedding designs were popular in cemetery parks in the twentieth century.

Winnipeg in the 1920s. The long view across Assiniboine Park to the pavilion.

money and political obstacles seriously curtailed the implementation of the entire scheme at that time. However, most of Todd's recommendations for the Queen Elizabeth Driveway were completed by the end of 1903.

Thomas Mawson, one of the most famous British landscape architects and city planners, toured Canada for three months in 1912, lecturing and accepting commissions from Halifax to Vancouver. His best-known contributions to Canadian park development were the public grounds and park surrounding the Regina Houses of Parliament and Coal Harbour Park in Vancouver.[82] Other large projects included the landscape plan of the University of Saskatchewan campus, and a town plan for Banff, Alberta. But even some of his large proposals met with uneven success.

At this time there were also a few large Canadian-designed projects under construction. George Champion, Superintendent of Winnipeg Parks, designed the 121 hectare Assissiboine Park in the English landscape style — à la Olmsted — with large open meadows and lawns defined by borders of native plant materials. The park was officially opened in 1909 although work had been in progress since 1904, when the 114 hectares were bought. By 1914, 9261 trees, 18 257 shrubs, 2970 perennials and 2000 annuals had been planted. Formal areas, wild areas, and recreational areas were all contained in the plan. A concentrated effort was made to grow native flowers, trees and shrubs, labelled for educational purposes.[83]

Park expansion was more intense in our smaller cities and villages, where concerned citizens devoted cheerful weekends of

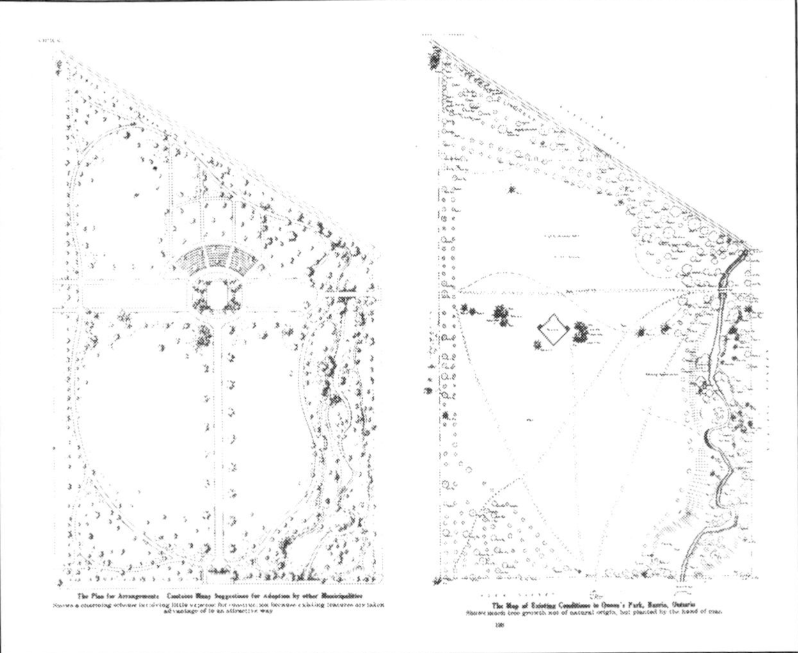

Before and after plans for improvements to Queen's Park, Barrie, Ontario, 1909. The influence of the English landscape style as interpreted by F. L. Olmstead is evident in the improved park version.

planning and planting. Galt, Ontario was often cited for its progressive, energetic parks policy — out of 567 hectares of city land, fifty hectares were devoted to parks and playgrounds. By 1908, it had "three good sized parks and seven or eight small plots and squares about the town."[84] Its Victoria Park of fifteen hectares was considered one of the "most beautiful natural parks in Ontario."[85]

As park building intensified, professional advice on plant material and design increased, supporting amateur efforts. The advice ranged from the succinct "for solid, bold effect, nothing equals geraniums and cannas,"[86] to the detailed. While most spokesmen stressed supervision by an elected parks board, the more thorough articles offered guidelines for any enthusiastic park builder. Plant lists of desirable park material stressed the use of native plant material, both for its educational value and its reliable hardiness. Design advice was rudimentary: "Decide what purpose the park will serve," "Do not put formal flower beds in natural settings," "Strive for simplicity" and so on.[87] The idea of linking a town's park system with connecting "parkways" was another popular idea in the advice columns. Parkways, according to City Beautiful theorists, provided visual variety and aesthetic pleasure. They were treated somewhat like boulevards in that wide grassy strips alongside the road were planted with ornamental trees and shrubs, becoming long extensions of the parks they linked. Unfortunately for many cities and towns, parkways were often too expensive, and had to be omitted from final plans.

The collapse of the real estate boom coupled with the onset of

World War I left many cities unable to finance civic beautification schemes. Park building was halted until war memorials rekindled interest and released civic money. While most war memorials were of concrete or marble, some horticultural societies planted memorial trees commemorating the town's fallen soldiers. Cemetery beautification also increased at this time. Children's parks — "peace memorials" — were also advocated by a number of horticultural societies after the war.[88]

Up into the 1920s, this great variety of park projects, both professional and amateur, continued to be implemented. A notable amateur park project was developed at this time in Davidson, Saskatchewan. A city councillor, a Mr. Arnold, decided that a rubbish-filled plot in the centre of town was a disgrace, and began to clean it out. He attracted help in ploughing the land and fencing it. The next spring he set out paths, flower beds, trees and shrubs. To finance this civic venture, Mr. Arnold instituted annual park concerts followed by a lunch and dance. The proceeds provided for the purchase of plants and the hiring of a caretaker. As the shelter belt of caragana grew higher, he added perennials, garden seats and bird houses. It became a popular place for school nature study. The townspeople in his honour named the park Arnold Park.[89]

Many parks created in the 1920s, however, were products of bureaucratic supervision. Most large urban centres by now had a well-entrenched parks board and a consulting, if not on-staff, landscape architect. Horticultural societies seemed to be losing their former community influence, as red tape replaced enthusiastic "green thumbs." In a sense the power of creating parks had been taken from the people, but coinciding with the bureaucratic take-over was the realization of the basic need for parks in growing communities. The Depression may have slowed down major park building projects, but the idea of public space devoted to beauty and recreation never waned.

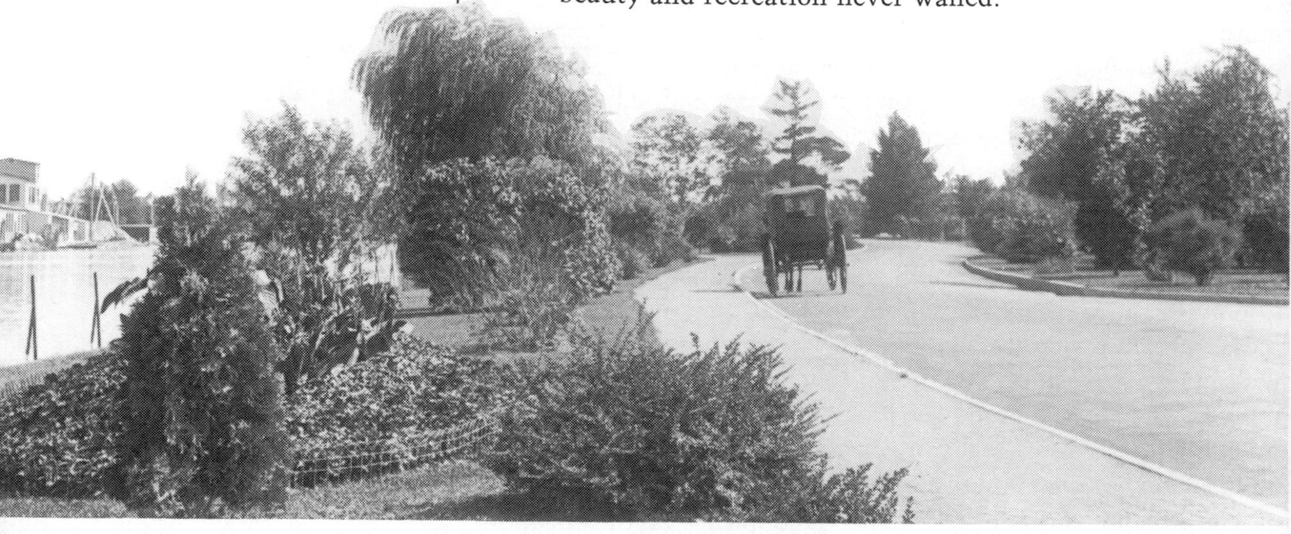

The Ottawa Driveway. Visual variety affording aesthetic pleasure was the main objective of parkway design.

VACANT LOT GARDENING

While organizations and individuals were labouring to beautify their cities with planters, parks, trees and shrubs, others promoted more utilitarian civic embellishments. By 1910 vacant lot gardening, where rubbish heaps were turned into lush vegetable gardens, was rapidly becoming a popular gardening movement.

Historically, vacant lot gardening is related to allotment gardening, originally popularized in Britain. By 1898, the allotment idea had gained a foothold in North America, Philadelphia being the first city to sponsor it.[90] As the City Beautiful movement gained strength, so did the vacant lot garden idea in the early 1900s. Vacant lots were included in the list of civic eyesores needing beautification, but ornamentation also gave way to charitable impulses. By 1910 in Canada many civic groups promoted vacant lot gardens to aid the poor and uplift the working classes: the gardens "would mean so much for the moral and financial improvement of the dwellers in the slums of our rapidly growing cities."[91]

The real estate bust in the western provinces and the general depression gripping Canada in the two years before World War I stimulated the growth of this movement. But not until 1915, when the effects of World War I were becoming more evident, did vacant lot gardening receive serious attention from municipal, provincial and, finally, federal authorities. Federally, vacant lot cultivation became synonymous with the greater production campaigns strongly supported by the Department of Agriculture. Every able Canadian, rural and urban, was to participate in the war effort by raising food on any available piece of ground: "Plant a garden in 1918, and your harvest will include financial gain, a better diet, better health, assistance to our Empire and through it justice and liberty to the world."[92]

Many sponsoring organizations began depicting the gardens as problem solvers. Not only would patriotism and civic beautification be served when these areas were cleaned up, but a city's noxious weed problem and sanitary condition would also be controlled. Unemployment would be mitigated, and vacant lot gardening would teach thrift and industry to the working-class poor. This in fact was the main aim of the Toronto Vacant Lots Cultivation Association, founded in 1914. Self-help charity was seen as the best solution to the financial and moral burden of poor relief: "It would not be a charity tending to pauperize and degrade. . ."[93] The unemployed who worked a garden were publicly praised and contrasted with those who "lazed about."[94]

Other socially-minded citizens proposed vacant lot gardens as the perfect solution for the problem of the unemployed woman. It was easily learned, light work especially when "two or more girls" shared a plot.[95] When a serious scheme to send unemployed

PRODUCTION is PATRIOTISM

Back Yards and Vacant Lots

THE EMPIRE'S CALL TO FEED YOURSELVES

The farmers are responding in their thousands to the call of the Empire for greater production. They have realized that every bushel raised means a bushel more for export to Britain: that this is one way of displaying patriotism. With favorable weather, Canada's crops this year will be the greatest in her history; far greater than any of us thought possible a year ago.

Now, to round out the scheme requires equally patriotic action in the towns and cities. The people of every community, large and small, should make vacant lots and back yards productive by raising their own vegetables and garden stuff. Every pound raised, remember, is another pound furnished toward Britain's needs.

Send for the Government Bulletin

This Department will forward free a special bulletin entitled "The Vegetable Garden." The simple instructions are easy to follow and make success practically certain, even to those without experience. The best methods of cultivation for the following vegetables are fully described: Tomatoes, Onions, Cabbage, Cauliflower, Celery, Melons, Watermelons, Cucumbers, Squash, Pumpkins, Carrots, Parsnips, Beets, Turnips, Salsify (or Oyster Plant), Radish, Peas, Beans, Corn, Egg Plant, Peppers, Spinach, Lettuce, Parsley, Sweet Herbs, Asparagus, Rhubarb.

You will enjoy amateur gardening, and profit in health and pocket as well. Children are immensely benefited, get a liberal education in the most practical manner, have outdoor amusement away from the street, become the possessors of rich red blood, strong lungs, alert minds.

Identify yourself with the national movement. Be a grower. Send for the bulletin and get your neighbors to do the same; everybody will benefit by the friendly rivalry thus started. No stamp is required on your envelope, for your coupon is truly "On His Majesty's Service."

What Local Civic Bodies Can Do

City and town councils, boards of trade, charitable bodies, women's clubs, horticultural societies, civic improvement leagues and other organizations working for the common good can accomplish a great deal locally by identifying themselves with the movement and energetically furthering it by every means at their disposal.

It will mean a thorough and permanent clean-up without cost to the community, a partial solution of the unemployed problem, and the institution of a genuine up-lift work. Vegetables and flowers will make better citizens.

This Department has formulated a plan telling how the various civic organizations may be brought together to further this worthy aim, and giving suggestions how to launch and carry on the work to a successful issue. Write at once for the form of organization and get your community properly started in performing its share of "Greater Production."

Canadian Department of Agriculture, Ottawa, Can.

No Postage Required.
Publications Branch, Canadian Department of Agriculture, Ottawa, Canada.
Please send me Bulletin entitled "The Vegetable Garden."
Name . .
Address
Town or City Prov 17

The call for greater production was advertised in various types of publications. This ad appeared in a 1915 issue of the Agricultural Gazette of Canada.

At work in a vacant lot garden, 1917. Most members were charged a small membership fee covering rental costs and sometimes including ploughing, fertilizing and perhaps a few supplies.

males to farms as farm labourers gained support during the early years of the war, an Ontario agricultural official, C.C. James, campaigned instead for vacant lot gardens. Here a man could grow labour-intensive crops such as potatoes without any farming expertise whatever.[96]

The poor and the unemployed were not the only beneficiaries of this new movement. Montreal and Ottawa florist associations reported that since vacant lot cultivation had begun in their cities, their business increased significantly. These merchants stocked an unusually large number of vegetable plants in 1917, which sold out early in the season.

By 1916, the vacant lot gardening movement was well represented in most urban centres in Canada. Many cities now supported vacant lot associations in addition to the usual horticultural or improvement society. (Some horticultural societies totally changed into vacant lot associations for the duration of the war.) Vacant lot association officials involved entire groups in cultivating large plots, as the emphasis changed from self-help to greater community involvement due to the war.[97] By 1917, groups such as Boy Scouts, Girl Guides, policemen, firemen, Women's Institutes, church organizations, ratepayers associations, and factory workers' groups were being encouraged to raise vegetables.

Generally, vacant lot gardening was not controlled by legislation. Associations and community participation were purely voluntary. Initially, concerned citizens formed a vacant lot association, then surveyed existing vacant lots in their city — which in many towns could be quite extensive. When suitable lots were identified, the owners (sometimes located by using assessment records or by newspaper advertisements) were contacted. Most organizations reported that many lot owners were delighted with the free clean-up of their property and usually volunteered the use of the lots for a small fee.[98] Lot size varied and lots were awarded on a "first-come" basis.

Returning soldiers, their wives and dependents were preferentially granted lots free of charge. One commentator in Ontario remarked that cultivation of vacant lots by returning soldiers was an excellent means of bringing them back into civilization.[99] In Toronto, seventy-five soldier gardens were cultivated in 1917, increasing to 181 in 1918.[100] A past president of the Toronto Horticultural Society even promoted war gardens at the Belgian "front" — men of his unit were given flowers and vegetable seeds, competitions were held and medals awarded.[101]

Although vacant lot gardening was not legislated, rules governing the use of a lot evolved over the years into a tight set of regulations. Most members were charged a small membership fee which covered rental costs, and sometimes ploughing and fertilizing, as well as some supplies. Many city councils voted grants to cover these expenses. In 1918, the Toronto Vacant Lot Association was awarded $3000 by the city to continue their work.[102] When an individual accepted a plot he was to have it

First prize vegetables in a vacant lots competition, 1917. Often the entries would be judged not only on the final results, but also on observations made during several visits by the judges in the course of the summer.

cleaned up and cultivated by a set date, or the lot would be forfeited back to the association. At the end of the season, the association usually wanted a list of crops grown and their estimated value.

While ploughing and fertilizing were either supplied free or charged to participants, the buying of seed varied. Some cities such as Halifax, Edmonton and Victoria made arrangements with merchants to sell seed at cost to association members. Other cities, such as Stratford (Ontario), Winnipeg and Regina, allowed lot owners to purchase seed at their own option. Some associations bought in bulk at wholesale prices and re-sold seeds and seed potatoes at cost to their members.[103]

The most popular crop was potatoes. Medicine Hat, Alberta for the first time in many years actually exported potatoes in 1915.[104] Guelph, Ontario officials stated that their vacant lot association raised fifty per cent of the city's potatoes in 1917. In addition to this staple, the usual vegetables were grown: cabbages, onions, beans, tomatoes, turnips, parsnips, carrots, corn, lettuce, peas, pumpkins, radishes, squash, Brussels sprouts, and a number of smaller fruits, such as strawberries and blackberries.

Some associations such as the one in Fort William, Ontario required lot holders to plant at least one row of flowers in addition to vegetables. The flower borders were usually composed of bright annuals such as marigolds, asters and nasturtiums.[105] A.J. Cowling, in his description of how he won first prize in the Calgary Vacant Lot competition, went even further in beautifying his fifteen by thirty metre lot: next to the sidewalk, he planted a perennial border nearly two metres wide, the foreground filled with annuals. Winning first prize two years running he felt "makes up for a little back-aching."[106]

One enthusiast noted that while many commented on how soothing vacant lot gardening was, he was of a different opinion:

> When I came in from my Vacant Lot and in my own garden passed budded lilacs running to a forest of suckers, precious paeonies lost in a jungle of delphiniums and beautiful spreads of climbing roses ablaze with flowers even then against a background of brown, thrip-riddled leaves, the joys of the Vacant Lot Garden did not soothe my mind.[107]

Despite the occasional grumbler, vacant lot gardening was an expanding, popular movement. Out of 1600 lots in Guelph, Ontario, only two were given up in 1917. Montreal officials noted that their 5000 lots were so popular that three times that many would have been taken if they had been available.[108]

The methods of publicizing the movement varied. Many towns relied on newspaper ads, notices and editorial support. Windsor, Ontario officials distributed circulars with government ads on one side explaining the production campaign, and on the other, details on how to lay out and plant a vegetable garden.

School children delivered the circulars to every door. In Sherbrooke, Quebec, the association sent out explanatory leaflets along with the electricity and water bills. Street cars and telephone poles were also placarded. Lectures and demonstrations were given by provincial and federal agricultural officials, and park board members. Horticultural society members also lectured in the hopes of generating support. The horticultural media contributed with masses of how-to articles.

To sustain the enthusiasm, garden competitions were sponsored, prizes awarded and grand totals of produce and market values were published. Some associations combined garden judging with the fall fairs of horticultural or agricultural societies. One of the most publicized exhibitions was the Toronto War Gardens Show held in September, 1918. Billed as the largest vegetable show ever held in Canada, the show featured produce from an estimated seventy-five per cent of the 2060 vacant lot gardens in the city. Toronto was divided into five districts with top prizes given in each section and a grand championship prize over all.

A satisfied Calgarian vacant lot gardener, 1920. As the winner of a poetry contest put it: "Behold my Vacant Lot, vacant no more,/Here grow my cabbages, dew-pearled at dawn./There stand my corn, beplumed like knights of old . . ."

There were problems and some disgruntlement among the public outpourings of enthusiasm. Some lot holders were dissatisfied with poor soil, a shady location, or lot owners revoking rental agreements. While most cities reported little trouble with theft, a few cities, like Ottawa, found it necessary to establish night patrols.[109] One Toronto gardener decided to plant potatoes around the boundaries so not "to tempt the public or attract their attention."[110]

When crops were harvested, another problem surfaced: storage and marketing. The city of Guelph operated an amateur market garden shop to sell off the surplus. In Saskatoon, the City Parks Board erected a root house and invited gardeners to store their products for three cents a bushel. In 1917, between four thousand and six thousand bushels of potatoes were stored. The Calgary Vacant Lots Club maintained a warehouse with a capacity of 54 650 metric tons.[111]

In 1917, the *Agricultural Gazette of Canada* wrote to mayors in every city with a population over 10 000 to amass statistics on the movement: Guelph led in membership and number of gardens, Calgary led in number of acres cultivated, and Ottawa and Calgary were tied for amounts produced.

The high-point of the movement came in 1918: everything was well co-ordinated and public participation at its peak. A minister even used his vacant lot gardening experiences as the subject for a Sunday sermon — "When God Speaks in Your War Garden": "The war garden underscores His name . . . (and He says) 'If I can hang emeralds and topazes on the bean bushes, rubies on the tomato vines, and amethysts on the eggplant, I can take care of you.' "[112]

When the war ended, the movement's energy began to dwindle. By 1920, most vacant lot organizations had ceased, or their memberships were severely diminished. The Calgary Vacant Lots Garden Club was an exception; the members maintained an enthusiastic participation up into the mid-1920s.[113]

Why most vacant lot associations died out was explained by a Calgarian vacant lot gardener: people were more affluent and did not need to supplement their incomes with foodstuffs. Potatoes, the chief crop on these lots for a number of years, had finally exhausted the soil. Gardeners sometimes lived too far from their plots to grow vegetables that needed more intensive care, and soon lost enthusiasm. Some members begrudged the membership fee, while many others were lured away from gardening by the increased entertainment opportunities: cars, movies, and other social amusements.[114] While it lasted, the vacant lots movement surpassed in enthusiasm most other civic beautification schemes, with the sole exception of park-building.

Just as other social movements lost their sustaining energy in the 1920s, so did the urban beautification movement. However, while movements such as railway gardening and school gardening had a definite end, beautification did not. Certain ideals stayed in the public mind. Parks, tree-lined streets, well-tended front lawns and public plantings never really lost their champions. Nor did the urge to grow vegetables in the city totally disappear — victory gardens abounded in World War II, re-emerging as allotment plots in the 1970s. Finally, another legacy of the City Beautiful movement endures, an emphasis on home landscaping for all classes.

5 The Righteous Trowel:

The Home Garden

WHY GARDEN?

Predictably, the home garden was also affected by the motives and rhetoric surrounding the major horticultural movements. Elevated from mere "soil and toil," many home owners found trowels in their hands and garden plans in their heads because of the widespread belief in the psychological, spiritual, moral, economic, social, and healthful benefits of gardening.

These benefits were expanded in publications and lectures directed to the impressionable home gardener. Religiously-inclined gardeners promoted the sentiment that ". . .no other agency will lift one to God as much as does the garden."[1] Statistics were generated by others to prove the healthful benefits: in one year, more saloon keepers died than gardeners.[2] The character-enhancing qualities of gardening were quantified: in an informal survey it was discovered that the number of gardeners in penitentiaries were far fewer than any other class — including ministers.[3] A house was not a home until it was beautified: this philosophical premise was transferred into the political area. Those who landscaped their homes were characterized as yet another group constructing the bulwarks against the Bolshevik menace. The home gardener was enlisted, not only in the battle against external enemies, but also against those within: the forces which prevented beautification, forces which could be overcome by home gardeners performing their horticultural duty.

Ottawa, 1918. Foundation plantings were popular in the early 1900s. They covered unsightly foundations and also created a transition from garden to house — a popular technique in landscape theory.

This action was termed "contagious," a beneficial communicable disease: "A well-planted and neatly kept front lawn or back yard affords an incentive to emulation, until in some cases the residents of whole blocks are brought under the spell of gardening."[4]

The home gardener was not only instructed on why to garden, but also on how to do it properly. Horticultural education was to include design as well as technique and plant selection. In the early 1900s, Canadians were actually to be re-educated in garden design. The new horticultural standard was based on the nascent British garden design revolution which influenced a whole new generation of European and North American gardeners.

HOW TO GARDEN: BRITISH ORIGINS

The pervasiveness of British garden influence was not solely tied to our colonial history — it was just as much a reflection of the predominance of British garden styles throughout the Western world. From the early eighteenth century onwards, England ruled the garden world as a style setter, a pioneer in plant collecting, a disseminator of horticultural knowledge, and as the site of magnificent examples of the art of gardening.

Beginning in the late 1700s, the style of the British ornamental garden underwent profound changes. These changes were due not only to alterations in artistic perceptions, but also to the availability of new plant material. Before this time landscaped gardens were composed of lawn, shrubs and trees, with the lawn coming right up to the house. Grand vistas, rolling hills and meadows were the hallmarks of the English Landscape Style. The succeeding style, the Picturesque, was less concerned with pleasant vistas and more with creating natural pictures — landscape painting in three dimensions. Often this meant nature in its wilder and more rugged aspects. Flower gardens were often hidden from view, languishing in the kitchen garden or in a neglected corner away from the house.

However, in the eighteenth century, after centuries of neglect, the flower garden was slowly re-introduced as a garden element of prime importance. Humphrey Repton, a British landscape designer in the late 1700s, was a major catalyst in this slow evolution. He was a proponent of the older English Landscape Style, but with new interpretations. He added a new element: balustraded garden terraces next to the house used as a transitional device between house and garden. Within these terrace divisions, flowers once more appeared.

Coinciding with changes in landscape design, the British Empire was growing. Voyages of exploration brought back horticultural treasures. A preoccupation with botany and horticulture resulted and some plant hunters were nationally renowned. Not surprising in this age of enthusiastic scientific enquiry, the addi-

"Ravenscrag," residence of Sir Hugh Allan in Montreal. Many of the larger estates had extensive greenhouses attached to the main house.

tion of a greenhouse to a house became as "*de rigueur* as a membership in a scientific society."[5]

By the 1840s other horticultural events in Britain altered the landscaped garden even more. The rise of a newly affluent middle class, taking their cue from the upper class, regarded a garden as a social necessity. They created a demand for a wider variety of plant material and garden furnishings. Technological advances also aided the developing horticultural industry to serve this expanding market. Heating of greenhouses using the cheaper, cleaner, more efficient method of steam pipes evolved; new techniques in using iron profoundly affected greenhouse design, making them more open to light and fire resistant. When the glass tax was lifted in 1845, the middle-class gardener could afford a greenhouse — formerly only available to the wealthy. The lawn mower was invented, and cast iron garden furniture and horticultural appliances such as fruit trainers, arches and trellises entered the commercial market. Regular horticultural journalism emerged, disseminating gardening knowledge to a wide audience. All these factors greatly influenced the next phase of garden design.

John Claudius Loudon in the early 1800s popularized a style (called Gardenesque) reflecting the influx of new plant material, and the new emphasis on the flower garden. Loudon, a horticultural writer, designer and practitioner, designed gardens which were meant to be walked around, gardens designed to display the skill of the gardener and the individual beauty of plants, shrubs and trees.

By the mid-1800s the flower garden dominated landscape designs. Hedges, trees, and shrub groupings, traditional focal

A Victorian-style garden in 1909. Dorothy Perkins, a Canadian garden writer, denounced this style: "We do not want gardens, whose only charm lies in wonderfully accurate geometrical designs. They are dead! They lack soul!"

points in a landscape, became backdrops for flowers. The Gardenesque style with its emphasis on botanical collections and winding paths gave way to the bedding-out style. This Victorian garden style was based on the practice of growing tender annuals under glass until blossom time. The plants were then massed in geometrically-shaped flower beds — usually circles and rectangles, but also stars and crescents — artistically arranged around the lawn.

The object was to create broad colour effects (sometimes quite glaring) in regular patterns, a style characterized by one British garden historian as "trumpets and massed brass bands. . ."[6] Bedding plants meeting the special requirements (identical bloom time, neatness, and prolonged blooming) were found in semitropical plants — annuals such as lobelia, geranium, calceolaria, alyssum, canna and salvia, all requiring greenhouse protection until frost-free weather.

Victorian gardens, in addition to their blinding colour combinations, were also stiff, formal and fussy. The garden did not escape the Victorian's penchant for collecting. Shrubberies, conifer collections, willow collections, ferneries, and other specialist collections were common components of more ambitious gardens. Ironwork garden furniture, gazebos, urns, statuary, arches and pergolas might also ornament the lawn.

Some home landscapes sported carpet-bedding, a direct offshoot of bedding-out. Long, thin "ribbon" beds, floral clocks, messages and curious pictures were created by planting brightly-coloured foliage plants in patterns: alternantheras, iresines and sedums were the most popular.

Acceptance of the bedding-out system and all its ornamentations was not universal. By the 1870s, dissenting voices were becoming more audible, as opponents denounced the bedding-out system for causing a serious deterioration in the practice of horticulture, by limiting the number of plants grown and by consequently reducing horticultural knowledge. The acknowledged leader of what was to become a crusade against bedding-out and carpet-bedding was an abrasive Scot, William Robinson. In strongly-worded lectures and articles he advocated an acceptance of a more natural, informal style of gardening, emphatically stating that bedding-out and all its relations were affronts against nature. He was strongly influenced by the living tradition of the cottage garden — harmonious mixtures of perennials, climbing plants, shrubs and trees planted naturally around the cottage — humble creations of rural people, and sometimes idealized by romantically-inclined painters. In Robinson's view, old perennial favourites should be rescued from oblivion, and placed in a harmonious mixed border, along with selected annuals (to extend the flowering season) and the interesting floral introductions entering the horticultural trade.

Another major horticultural figure soon joined in the battle. Gertrude Jekyll, an artistic gentlewoman, through her refined attacks and her detailed alternatives, greatly aided Robinson's crusade. She became the most famous designer and proponent of the informally designed herbaceous border: an artfully filled border of perennials, annuals and shrubs, carefully graded by colour and natural effect. Miss Jekyll's artistic eye "painted" the

Toronto, early 1900s. Victorian conventions persisted into the 1900s. The castor bean plant, for example, continued to be a favourite focal point in circular flower beds.

flower border, creating a garden mirroring the variety of nature.

Robinson, Jekyll and their followers popularized a horticultural revolution which affected the whole Western garden world. By the 1890s as the bedding-out system began "dying of repetition,"[7] it was no longer *au courant* in certain horticultural circles to display star-shaped flower beds filled with the glaring juxtaposition of scarlet salvia and purple lobelia. Informal, tasteful arrangements of hardy plants were now becoming the acceptable mode of gardening.

CANADIAN DEVELOPMENTS

Canadian gardeners had not been untouched by British trends and styles.* As seen in Chapter One, Canadian examples of the major British garden styles — from the Picturesque to the bedding-out style — existed before 1900 in Canada. But although these styles were present, highly-stylized gardening efforts were not very widespread.

In the early 1900s the general lack of professional design was decried, especially by the small group of professional landscape architects in Canada. Frederick Todd, a Montreal landscape architect, stated in 1901 that it was still the "rule rather than the exception to see costly private residences and public buildings standing bleak and lonely without a tree or shrub to relieve the hard outline of architecture. . ."[8] And where designed plantings did exist, he felt they were usually untutored, injuring rather than helping the general appearance.[9] Another landscape architect, H.B. Dunington-Grubb of Toronto, complained of the same early lack of enthusiasm:

> I was once informed by a prominent Canadian architect that there is no garden so beautiful as plain trees and grass. A well known patron of the arts told me that love of wild nature and the primeval forest were so deeply instilled into the Canadian consciousness that garden design was likely to make little progress in this country.[10]

Conversely, there was praise for the advances we did make. "Landscape art" was perceived to be on the rise, as the value of proper home landscaping was better understood. One early twentieth-century gardener noted that "much appreciation of the aesthetic has been kindled."[11]

Whether or not professional landscape architects and gardeners were satisfied with our horticultural activities, they did agree that Canadian gardening should be guided into proper aesthetic modes of gardening:

---

*Québécois gardens (which have not been adequately studied and are unfortunately outside the scope of this work) were mainly influenced by styles from France.

> How can the unskilled or semi-skilled gardener be convinced that his garden is not as distinctive as it should be? It is necessary that the knowledge be imported to enable them to improve their standard, for only as the work of the individual improves will our gardening standards be elevated, and it is time that our thoughts were turned in that direction.[12]

The new style, the natural style, had an impact in Canada. Enlightened gardeners would no longer be receptive to pamphlets such as *Semi-Tropical Bedding and Carpet Bedding* — a manual written by a Montreal horticulturist, George Moore, in 1888. Nor would his enthusiastic promotion of this system, which he called "the best method to derive pleasure from the cultivation of the Flower Garden during the summer months, thus adding to the beauty and value of the homestead"[13] find as sympathetic an audience as it might have in 1888.

Canadians were now urged to plan their gardens as if they were painting a picture. The gardener was to combine lawn, trees, shrubs and flowers into an artistic whole, with nature as teacher and example. But the garden designer was to create nature idealized rather than nature real. The new, natural school acknowledged their debt to nature, but reminded their followers that any garden created by man was by definition artificial. One was to follow nature by rejecting formalism, not emulating rustic scenes.

Toronto, 1924. A classic example of the Jekyll style in North America.

The focal point of the design revolution was (as noted before) the flower border. In these wide, long beds, bordering fences, hedges or tree and shrub backdrops, the gardener was judiciously to group bulbs, perennials and annuals. Gardeners were urged to mass their plants, arrange them by size, blooming time and colour, rather than display them individually. In 1905 one eastern Canadian commentator noted the favourable increase in the variety of available perennials.[14] Articles with descriptive lists and detailed cultivation tips extolled "old fashioned" flowers — grandmother's perennial garden. Gardeners were urged to expand their horticultural horizons beyond red salvias and cannas to embrace old-time favourites, so disfavoured during the bedding-out era.

Writers contrasted the natural informal garden with the bedded-out, formal style. Garden beds filled with annuals flowered for only four months, and the rest of the year the beds looked bare and unattractive, conveying "a depressing feeling." Bedding-out was transitory, perennials were permanent. Bedded-out gardens were "monotonous in ever recurring uniformity, and monotonous in never varying colours for the few short months . . . that our short free-from-frost season will permit."[15] Perennials were hardy and needed less maintenance than annuals. The lower cost of perennials in the long run was compared with the yearly expense of annual bedding plants. One noted Manitoba gardener, Dr. H.M. Speechly, could not understand why more Manitobans did not garden with perennials, for they included the earliest-blooming plants for that climate.[16] While it was quite ingenious to cut beds in the shape of a Maltese cross, Dr. Speechly felt it certainly was not *real* gardening, nor gardening in good taste.[17] It was suggested that more would be gained artistically and tastefully by increasing the size of flower and shrub borders, rather than by haphazardly planting trees, shrubs and flowers all over the lawn: "A little reserve in gardens is as necessary as in people."[18]

The natural style of planting was not without its problems and drawbacks, but this knowledge did not deter the promotion of the perennial border. Horticulturists soon realized that inexperienced growers needed help.[19] Note was made of the frequent garden failures or haphazard designs created by those who knew little of the growth habits of trees, shrubs and flowers. It was recognized that not everyone was blessed with an artistic sense of form and colour, so necessary for "painting" a garden picture. Other writers appreciated the difficulties of the perennial border, especially in summer. Many gardeners did not have an adequate, nor easily tapped, water supply. Therefore, when summer drought occurred, gardens could not be watered properly and the display mirrored this neglect. Perennial borders did require work, a fact seldom discussed until much later in the 1900s. Staking, pruning, weeding and thinning were coupled with the difficulties of design and massing the right plants for continuous bloom.

Enthusiastic gardeners may have had the best intentions and the proper knowledge, but they might not have had the means of obtaining the varieties they wanted. As late as 1920, Irene Parlby noted that westerners faced difficulties and great expense procuring high quality varieties. She laid the blame on government import restrictions, and the unwillingness of local nurseries to cultivate a wider range of plants.[20]

The horticultural societies definitely felt it their duty to educate the tastes of the gardening public. To this end their members spoke and wrote on a great variety of gardening topics, always hoping to educate and to convert. Dorothy Perkins, a garden writer in the 1920s, noted:

> The last few years have seen great advances in garden craft. People are tired of pokey, patchy gardens in which a practical gardener — usually a furnace man — thrusts into the soil a few dozen red geraniums; tired of having a few packets of seed thrown ruthlessly on top of poor soil . . . Thanks to the horticultural societies in our cities and towns, the gospel of gardening has been and is being preached, and we are being educated to indulge in real constructive gardening.[21]

Also in this period of intensifying gardening activity, an increasingly large spectrum of garden types became visible. The home garden could now be classified into broad categories. The commonest form of gardening occurred in the small, urban residential lot. The next category consisted of rural gardens — some commentators felt that this garden type lagged behind in style and numbers. These two categories generated a lot of garden writings ranging from landscape plans to tool descriptions to lists of easily-grown plants. Enthusiasts' gardens (devoted to a particular plant family or plant collecting and testing) comprised another group. A division existed between the amateur and the professionally designed garden. The professional ones were further divided by size: the smaller, urban grounds and the larger suburban and country estates, some of which became gardens of note — our few garden showplaces.

A sophisticated town garden was designed by L. A. Dunington-Grubb in 1916. She was an active Ontario landscape architect and promoter of City Beautiful programs.

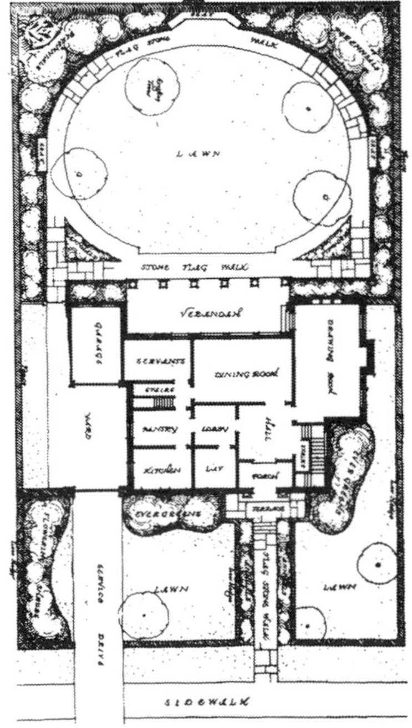

COMPONENTS OF THE TYPICAL HOME GARDEN

Home owners were urged to design their domestic landscapes in the new natural style. In the early 1900s, accelerated house building was occurring in the developing suburbs, on homesteads, and somewhat in the cities. The scope for garden creation was immense, Canada's "raw" edge was to be softened by the civilizing presence of landscaped homes. However, creating beautiful gardens was not only a "civilizing" activity, it was also a socially enhancing activity. If one gardened in the latest mode, using the proper furnishings, fencing and plant material, the garden would be judged favourably. The garden as a social yardstick was not a new concept, but was more blatantly voiced in the 1900s than before: "To the majority of people, however, the garden stands for what the owner is."[22] If one wanted to be judged as "wide-awake," progressive and prosperous, one must garden. Properly relating the various landscape components became more important than ever.

For the uneasy amateur gardener, there were definite rules to guide him or her to fill in the blank landscape. The owner's first consideration was to lay out the lawn: "It is the canvas, and on it you paint with flower and shrub the picture that your fancy desires or your purse can gratify."[23] It was to be kept open, unscarred by flower beds or solitary shrubs and trees. The invention of the lawn-mower had made maintenance much easier and allowed the introduction of finer mixtures of grass seed. Before a practiced man with a scythe would crop the lawn into a stubble of weed stalks and coarse wild grasses. Now it could be maintained by the owner who easily could create a lawn of even height and velvety texture.

The next important component was foundation planting. This newly popular concept of grouping trees, shrubs and climbers around the house united home and garden by smoothing the transition from the natural to the man-made, and hid the ugly features of the newer style house foundation. Some gardeners favoured evergreens and conifers, others flowering shrubs — the most popular was the spirea. Together, lawn and foundation plantings were said to "set the scene" for the home garden.

Walks and drives were also a part of the garden framework. Proponents of the natural style minimized the number of passages, because all too often the tendency was to "cut up" the lawn with paths: to outbuildings, around flower beds, or to garden seats. Expensive upkeep and the change in aesthetics stopped these excesses. If the property was large, the drive up to the house was ideally composed of graceful curves — curves which should appear necessary, either by the placement of trees or other objects (which could be located after the drive was plotted).[24] Smaller properties were much more utilitarian, with walks and drives going from point A to point B with little deviation.

Another element in the home landscape was the hedge. It served as a backdrop for the perennial border, a privacy barrier, or a boundary marker. On the prairies, hedging was indispensable as part of a shelter belt system. Hedges were also an alternate answer to the problem of fencing. Beginning in the late 1890s, fencing was increasingly seen as an aesthetic problem, but in some urban areas, the elimination of fencing caused a few unforeseen problems. Trespassing, plant theft, and cutting across corners were the main complaints.[25] Wire fencing (invisible and cheap) was soon advocated as an alternative. (The best fence was

Ontario, 1902. Over-ornamentation was frowned upon; judicious placing of planters was now the rule.

Red Deer, Alberta. Walks and drives were to be laid out in graceful curves according to the new garden theorists.

Ottawa, 1911. Pergolas were popular garden structures which were often used to exhibit prize roses and clematis.

the least seen and the best seen through.)[26] Low stone or brick walls were also permitted if the property was extensive.

Annual and perennial climbing vines were widely promoted as perfect solutions for hiding permanent eyesores. Objectionable views, ugly outbuildings, "tasteless" fencing, all could be hidden under the luxuriant growth of climbing vines.

Once the basic landscape framework of lawn, foundation planting, walks, drives and fencing were in place, the amateur landscaper was encouraged to fill in the garden "canvas."

Perennial borders and flower beds were preferably to be sited near the house. Irregular massings were stressed, along with proper choice of plant material. Some of the most popular perennials were Rudbeckia or "Golden Glow," peonies, iris, delphinium, lilies, poppies, phlox, and asters. Annuals such as marigolds, nasturtiums, petunias, vincas, geraniums and salvia maintained their popularity from the earlier style, but their use was less static.

While vases and other garden decorations continued as focal points in flower beds, their extensive use was increasingly frowned upon:

> . . . well intentioned but unsightly assortment of odds and ends placed on the lawn such as the flower box made of an old boiler, tripods of birch poles holding a tin can suspended filled with flowers and the grotesque edging of beds and paths with whitewashed stones and even inverted bottles or auto tires. We are all familiar with these cheap and puerile attempts at gardening which are crude and should be carefully avoided.[27]

Verandahs were not only to be ornamented by planters and baskets, but also by various vines. Dutchman's pipe, clematis, climbing roses, honeysuckle, and a variety of climbing annuals not only provided colour, but shade as well. Verandahs were often used as outdoor rooms for family entertaining and the occasional meal.

The home owner had a wide choice of garden structures. Depending on the landscape design, size of property and prevailing taste, the gardener might choose to construct a summer house (also called a gazebo, belvedere, gabrietta, teahouse, kiosk or pavilion)[28] and plant vines around it. The arch, another popular structure, might be placed at the house entrance or at the front of the garden. Usually the arch (covered in vines) was a transitional device from the drive into the back-yard, forming a living doorway into the garden. The arch could be freestanding as well. While the summer house and the arch have definite associations with Victorian gardens and declined in popularity during the 1920s, the pergola persisted up into the 1930s. Essentially constructed of a series of connected arches, pergolas varied in design and plantings. They were favoured for creating a shady spot in the garden and for tastefully displaying climbers, especially roses.[29]

The home owner might also want to place a few chairs, benches and tables in suitable places. At the turn of the century, garden furniture was usually in the "rustic" style. These pieces would be constructed from unrefined twigs, branches and stumps or iron which imitated knotholes, bark and other wooden imperfections. Later on, wickerwork and canvas furniture were more favoured.

While not as common as the preceding categories of garden structures, conservatories and greenhouses were popular among those who could afford them, and as such had a certain social value. These structures were essential on the larger estates to provide the large supply of bedding plants required to fill in formal designs. Conservatories, usually attached to the "better" houses, extended the growing season and served as fashionable sitting rooms. The *Canadian Horticulturist*, as early as the 1890s, published greenhouse plans. By the turn of the century, greenhouse parts were available in Canada — imported from the American firm of Lord and Burnham.[30] But Glass Garden Builders of Toronto, which called itself the first all-Canadian greenhouse company, was not formed until 1914.[31] Greenhouses of all sizes were used by affluent gardeners for growing exotic varieties and starting seeds.

Canadians had definitely advanced out of our so-called untutored gardening into a greater awareness of garden design and an increased horticultural sophistication. One group, however, did not share in this upsurge to the same extent.

RURAL GARDENING: BASIC BEAUTIFICATION

Rural gardeners were not as embroiled in fashionable modes of gardening as were their city cousins. In fact, farm journals, from the late 1800s on, periodically bemoaned the state of rural home landscaping. A quote from the *Canadian Horticulturist* in 1900 is typical of a rural observer's concern: "Our Canadian farmers and fruit-growers give too little attention to the decoration of their home surroundings."[32]

After the homesteading phase, the farmer and his wife were encouraged to turn their thoughts to beautification, for a home could not be considered a home unless it was surrounded by natural beauty. There were some rural gardeners of note who designed and maintained contemporary-styled gardens, but they did not seem to be in the majority. Irene Parlby was a noted rural gardener who enthusiastically promoted ornamental farm gardens. She strongly urged farm women to simplify their work and meal preparation to better enjoy this satisfying hobby, a hobby which gave "a real interest in life," refreshing minds and spirits.[33] When she immigrated to Alberta from England, she

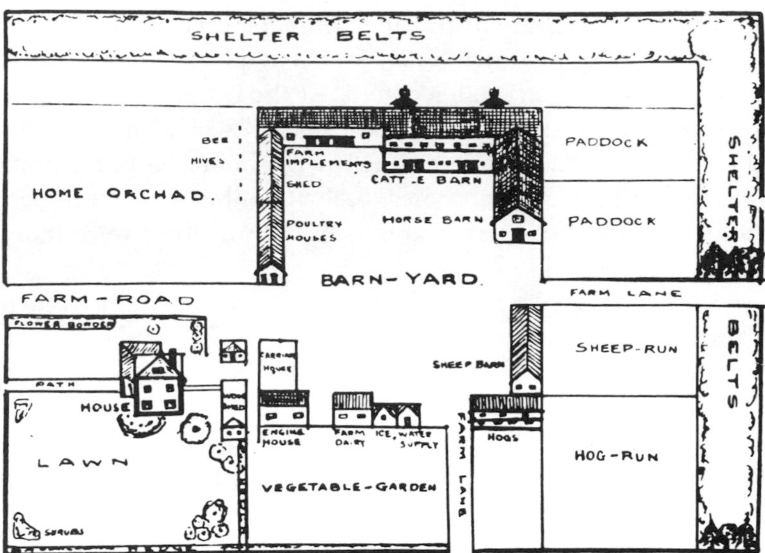

Plan for a well laid out farmyard, 1916. Farm flower gardens were promoted as a solace for the busy wife and an uplifting sight for the rest of the family.

planted two small beds of annuals by the front door. Within a few years, this modest garden had expanded into extensive perennial borders and shrubberies.

Gardening in Alberta was a continual challenge and experiment for Mrs. Parlby. The wind was so strong around her garden that a high board fence was built around the grounds. When visitors opened the gate, it was like entering another world:

> Border beds flaming with brillance and over-hanging shrubs, creepers, vines, trees shedding an underlying coolness and peace. There is, too, a small flag garden wherein the gardener has placed all manner of specially sweet scented plants, — stocks, nicotiana, mignonette, — in addition to all the little unobtrusive plants creeping shyly between the flat stones . . .[34]

She mixed her garden advice in various agricultural journals with philosophy, observations on rural life and practical hints on what to plant. Other rural writers contributed advice on how to recycle tins and other containers as planters, how to assemble window boxes, the best wild flowers to use as ornamentals, and how to landscape the farm property. However, the most practical, necessary and popular gardening advice given as the west was being settled centred on shelter belts, how to construct them and what plant varieties to use.

A typical prairie shelter belt consisted of Russian poplar, cottonwood, Manitoba maple, golden willow, or caragana. Traditionally, trees were first planted on the north and west sides of the immediate farm yard and house, in three rows: the outside one of willows, then four feet away a row of poplar, cottonwood or maple, and then the inside row of caragana or a smaller willow.[35]

Once shelter belts were in place, the farmer could garden with more hope of success. According to one writer in 1915, there was now no reason why farm grounds could not be properly landscaped. While farmers were urged to landscape in the natural style, using trees and shrubs and perennials rather than high-maintenance formal plantings, such formal gardens persisted:

> "Here is his plan for a real old-fashioned flower garden. See the stars and circles and borders and walks." "Oh well," apologetically the husband answered, "You know my wife will have a flower garden, so she might as well have it right. . ."[36]

However, no matter how the landscape was designed, the desired outcome was a well set-up homestead. By 1930, farm landscape design had become so sophisticated that one commentator spoke of designing the grounds as a three-roomed area. The first room was public, extending from the front of the house out to the gate. The most suitable landscaping here was to be executed in a plain and dignified manner. The second room was the private area designed for family use. Hammocks, summer houses, specialty gardens (although these were never promoted as intensively for the farm garden as they were for the urban garden) were to be placed here. The third area was the service area: drying yard, ash pile, pump-house and driveway.[37]

Sometimes as farmers prospered, more attention was given to the farm grounds, but generally the design and contents were less sophisticated and less varied than urban gardens.

Duffield, Alberta, 1920. Windbreaks were effective in checking the force of strong prairie winds and in preventing massive snow drifts among farm buildings.

FADS AND FANCIES

Specialty gardens, devoted to one plant family, theme, or construction, were often found in urban and estate gardens. They contrast sharply with the basic beautification practised by so many rural gardeners. Like the major garden styles, specialty gardens were direct imports from Britain, and subject to the whim of horticultural fashions. Whatever the current fad, the fashionable gardener would follow, and some Canadian gardeners were no exception. Many specialties survived an initial enthusiasm to become permanent features in the modern garden, while others were doomed to the short life of a fad. Canadian gardeners built ferneries (a late nineteenth-century madness), Japanese gardens, rose gardens, water-lily ponds, rock gardens, Italianate terraces, and woodland gardens. The choice of specialty was seemingly determined not only by a gardener's talents, ambitions, natural resources, and money, but also by the current craze. Understandably, many of the grander ones appeared in more affluent gardens, but this did not always guarantee quality.

Southern Ontario, 1919. Rose gardens have always been popular in garden plans, but in the 1920s they were characterized as a necessary component of the fashionable garden.

For example, some commentators decried the many unfortunate interpretations of the Japanese garden where either taste or money was lacking to do the job properly.

Lady Eaton's Japanese garden, located at her summer home, Villa Fiora, sixty kilometres north of Toronto, was an example of a highly-praised North American interpretation. One garden writer termed it "one of the finest Japanese gardens east of the Rockies."[38] The garden contained Japanese structural elements ("stepping stones, tinkling water-falls, pagodas, lanterns and tiny high-arched bridges leading to fairy-like islands"),[39] but the plantings were more Western than Eastern. There were lots of dwarf evergreens and the usual Japanese maple, but in among these traditional plantings were distinctly Western touches: spirea instead of wisteria, compact lilacs, Iceland poppies, veronicas, violas, and lupines.[40] Perhaps Villa Fiora would have merited the diplomatic remark made by a Japanese diplomat when viewing a Japanese garden in Britain: "Magnificent. We have nothing like it in Japan."[41]

One of the most popular of the twentieth-century horticultural fads taken up by Canadian gardeners was the rock garden. In Britain the rock garden began as "the rockery" — often just a pile of rocks, bricks, cement "rocks," and occasionally tree roots.[42] By 1910 the rockery had progressed from an insignificant ornament into a popular garden fad — the rock garden. Its popularity was strongly influenced by the mountaineering vogue which in turn spurred on a study of high altitude flora.[43] The herbaceous border was soon found lacking as an adequate display area for these often tiny plants. When influential gardeners began

Water lilies and other aquatic plants received a great deal of attention in the horticultural press in the 1920s.

The layout with rock gardens, lily pond, and rose garden is an example of the ideal promoted in international garden publications.

collecting alpines and constructing imitations of the alpines' home environment (taking a "lesson from nature"), other gardeners began to follow suit.

By World War I in Britain the rock garden was considered an integral part of any garden with pretensions. But its great popularity was largely due to the influx of so many new high altitude plants and to the promotional writings of the plant explorer and gardener, Reginald Farrer. His greatest work, *The English Rock Garden*, did more than any other book to popularize this style of garden.

The Canadian rock garden followed the progression of the British rock garden with a bit of a time lag. The pre-World War I rock garden was often a rockery and occasionally was harangued in print: "The man who builds a rockery in his garden in Winnipeg is a lost man."[44] After World War I, there were more enthusiasts building naturalistic rock gardens and stocking them with alpines. The specialty did prosper within the more affluent gardens, and periodically articles appeared stating that rock gardening was "sweeping" the nation now that middle-class gardeners realized they could afford them. However, the middle-class rock garden was usually a small construction, and not always filled with rare speciments. The showplace rock gardens remained on larger estates where property, money and labour (rock gardens involve high maintenance) were plentiful:

> At the Angela Hotel . . . Victoria, Mr. Rant has a garden which is different to any other on the island. It is not large, probably three city lots in size, but in that small space there is a collection which has few equals in Canada . . . the big rock wall which bounds the property on the west is a sight which when once seen is never forgotten.[45]

Until the 1920s, Canadian alpine enthusiasts imported their seeds and plants, because there were no Canadian firms specializing in alpines. Around 1922, John Hutchinson and Norman Rant began Rockholme Gardens in Victoria — one of the first such firms.[46]

Plan of F. Cleveland Morgan's estate garden outside Montreal in 1923.

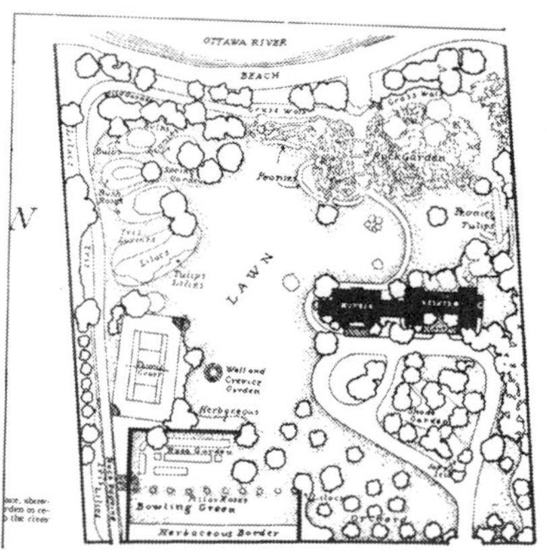

F. Cleveland Morgan, the wealthy Montreal art collector, designed and executed a world-class rock garden on his estate outside Montreal. The garden was highlighted in *Country Life in America* in 1923, and in 1936 Mr. Morgan gave a paper detailing its design and plant content at the prestigious London conference on rock gardens and plants. While large enough for a bowling green, tennis court, rose garden, house, garage, shrubberies, flower borders and beds, extensive lawn, and a large rock garden, Morgan demurely stated that his garden was "no vast estate but a Lilliputian affair calling, therefore, for imagination and also for intensive cultivation so that no spare foot shall be overlooked."[47]

Morgan stated that since 1916 he had been working on the garden without the aid of a landscape architect. The rock garden

Scene in the Morgan rock garden. Alpines are notoriously difficult and time-consuming plants to cultivate, and the rewards are often limited to a spring display.

was built on a natural site on either side of a gully leading down a steep bank to the lakeshore. He had local stone brought in and placed and also had places dug out to expose the existing rock. A pool was created at the foot of a portion of the rock garden, and special alpine conditions were duplicated to provide conducive environments for the more finicky plants. His garden was characterized as a continuing experiment: "it must be difficult for a Britisher with his wealth of Public Gardens, Nurserymen, and eager specialists to realize the comparative isolation of a venturesome gardener in so huge a country as Canada."[48] He did to this end maintain contact with the major gardeners in Canada and Europe, exchanging plants and cultivation tips. Morgan reputedly helped Lady Byng, an enthusiastic gardener, design a rock garden at Government House. She was said to have supervised the building of it so enthusiastically that five years' work was accomplished in three:

> Her Excellency's recipe for the making of a rock garden was sufficiently simple that it might be imitated by most garden lovers. She gathered her stones from the closest neighborhood, which happened to be Rockliffe Park. She planned her planting so that she would have bloom from May until Autumn frosts. She planted all kinds of flowering plants from all corners of the globe, many of which she had collected for her gardens in England and in Canada. Then she added a plentiful selection of Canadian plants. In every individual case she had studied the native soil and surroundings of her plants, and then she sought to reproduce the home as closely as possible.[49]

All too soon, the fad of the rock garden was, like last year's

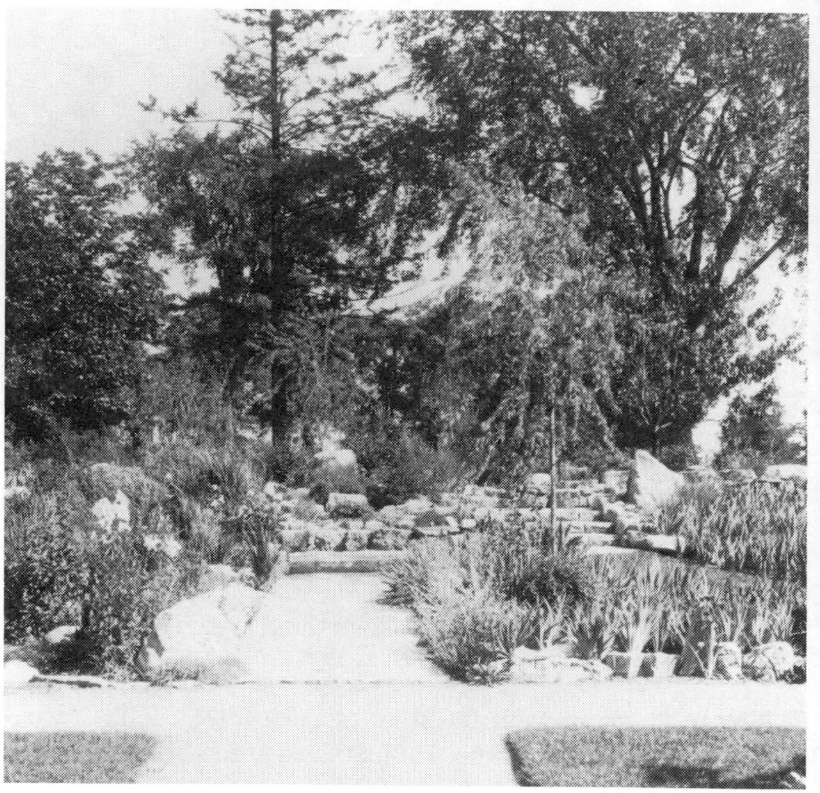

The rock garden at Rideau Hall, Ottawa was a pet project of Lady Byng. After she returned to England, she sent some prize plants to the Department of Agriculture for testing in Canada.

hemline, out-moded, and ridiculed by some garden commentators. The depression ended the large scale garden make-overs and proliferation of garden specialties.

ENTHUSIASTS' GARDENS

Enthusiasts' gardens (another group in the classification of garden types) usually mirrored interests in hybridization, plant introduction or collecting. R.B. Whyte cultivated one such garden in Ottawa — a garden that was not only famous in Canada but was also written up in *Country Life in America*. His property enclosed house, outbuildings, lawn, a tennis court, a small vegetable garden and a half-acre flower and fruit garden. Whyte continually juggled the intricacies of insuring continuous bloom with his overwhelming desire to grow as many varieties of flowers as possible. The garden was admired for its mixed borders as well as its more utilitarian aspects:

> The garden has supplied a family of nine the year round with all the fruit desired, including thirty-five varieties of grapes, and two hundred and ninety-nine quarts of preserves. It produces a fair quantity of fresh vegetables in season.[50]

To maintain this challenging, crowded garden, Whyte gardened for two hours every morning before going to work — evenings were reserved for rest: "I like to keep that time to look around and enjoy it."[51] Design was subordinate to experimentation, as Whyte liked to "take-up" one genus at a time, growing every species and variety he could locate. Inferior varieties were ruthlessly discarded, while the better ones were kept and distributed later to gardening friends.

His gardening altruism coupled with his view of gardening as a force for improvement made Whyte a model twentieth-century gardener and citizen. He was a founding member of the Ottawa Horticultural Society and the Ontario Horticultural Association. He sponsored children's gardening contests ranging from potato growing to flower cultivation to school gardens. He wrote numerous articles in support of children's gardening and co-authored a pamphlet on Ottawa gardens and their care as a contribution to civic beautification.

R. B. Whyte of Ottawa was an extremely influential member of the gardening community of Ontario, and was also greatly admired for his civic betterment programs.

Part of R. B. Whyte's garden in Ottawa, which he cultivated for over forty years. The perennials alone numbered over a hundred varieties.

URBAN, PROFESSIONALLY LANDSCAPED GARDENS

Professionally designed urban gardens differed from the enthusiasts' category in their very designed look. In the 1920s many of these gardens were designed in a mixture of formal and informal treatments. This style, which generated some very sophisticated gardens, became quite fashionable. While not totally popular with advocates of the Jekyll-style garden, some, such as Dr. Speechly of Pilot Mound, Manitoba, gave grudging praise when visiting one such garden: "This is called a formal garden because it is laid out in rectangular beds, but it looks so lovely that you can forgive any formality."[52]

Generally, these gardens designed by landscape architects also contained a variety of specialty gardens. Miss Bessie Baldwin's garden, which prompted Dr. Speechly's praise, also boasted a fountain, a lily pond, and a terrace ornamented by perennial and shrub borders.

ESTATE GARDENS

The larger estates contained spacious landscaped grounds as well as a number of specialty gardens. They were usually designed by a landscape architect and maintained by a garden staff. In the 1920s, when many of these gardens flourished around our major urban centres, the accepted style was also the formal-informal mixture favoured in the smaller, designed urban gardens. Interested gardeners could derive direct inspiration from these larger gardens. Some of them had established "open days" or permitted garden tours (usually led by the head gardener) by appointment.[53]

GARDENS OF NOTE

Nearly every region in the country by the 1920s boasted at least one grand estate garden. The Gaspé Peninsula, for example, was the site of Métis Park. Mrs. Elsie Reford was given the property of Métis Park by an uncle in 1919, and by 1927 she had transformed eighteen hectares of wilderness into an internationally acclaimed garden. A self-taught gardener, she devoured books on gardening and botany, and corresponded with the leading horticulturists of the day. Her aim was not only to exchange information, but also to exchange plant material world-wide.[54] Her husband owned a busy transatlantic shipping company so her exchange program was easily arranged. Her garden reflected her maturing horticultural knowledge and enthusiasm, as well as the ample amounts of leisure time, money and help available. She herself often put in eight-hour days watering, weeding and supervising. Her husband installed clocks throughout the enormous garden which would chime at one o'clock, reminding Mrs. Reford it was time for lunch.[55]

The garden is located in a very protected site on the St. Lawrence River. The estate is bordered on all sides by effective cedar windbreaks. The resulting shelter enabled Mrs. Reford to grow a much wider variety of plants in this mild micro-climate than could be grown a few kilometres further inland.[56] In addition to the many other rare perennials she grew, Tibetan blue poppies (*Meconopsis betonicifolia*) grew two metres tall and self-seeded — a horticultural feat. She also cultivated Asiatic rhododendrons and azaleas — plants most Canadian gardeners cannot grow.[57] The garden was (and is) a series of specialty gardens (alpines were featured), other plant collections, perennial borders, winding walks and forest.

Another enthusiastic gardener who designed and planted his own extensive grounds was Sir William Van Horne. In the late 1880s he purchased a major portion of Minister's Island — an island lying just off the coast of St. Andrews, New Brunswick. Van Horne landscaped the grounds with drives, walks, hedges, flower beds (filled with imported, choice varieties), orchards and bathing pools. This summer estate, Covenhoven, provided a grand scope for his horticultural abilities to the end of his life.[58]

Van Horne was not a neophyte gardener at the time he landscaped Covenhoven; his gardening experience dated back to earlier days in the United States. He was as determined and competitive in his horticultural pursuits as in his other ventures. In Lacrosse, Wisconsin he grew roses, producing finer, larger blooms than his neighbours. The height and vigour of his very showy castor-oil bean plants amazed his friends. He also dabbled in hybridization, producing a triple trumpet-flowered datura. He even produced magnificent forced hyacinths in his basement.[59]

His horticultural competitive urge never abated as the following anecdote shows. One day Van Horne returned to Covenhoven, roaring for his head gardener. The gardener, Mr. Clark, came running and found a furious Van Horne. "Rip them out," he shouted, "rip out the front beds, and replant them — now!" His rival, Thomas Shaughnessy, had planted his front beds with the same flowers as Van Horne. Van Horne shouted that he would not be matched by Shaughnessy, even in gardening.[60]

View from the house out into the garden at Covenhoven, 1928, the summer home of William Van Horne.

Not all gardeners were as aggressively competitive as Van Horne, nor all estate grounds as extensive. In Lower Fort Garry, Manitoba, an exclusive settlement called "Old England" had developed:

> Slowly but surely something of the quaint rural peacefulness that permeates little Surrey towns a few miles out of London is being developed as the pathways leading to the houses are half-hidded in green mantles of creepers. Gardens that suggest an English atmosphere surround the buildings. . .[61]

The gardens were characterized by hedges, roses, perennial borders and fruit and vegetable gardens.

Southlands, Fraser River, B.C., 1927. Gardens in British Columbia usually exhibited a lushness and variety not possible in other sections of the country.

Further west in British Columbia, large gardens were even more prevalent, due no doubt to the salubrious climate. Especially around Vancouver and Victoria, beautifully landscaped gardens, with a wide variety of plant material, were the norm. The estate garden, Shannon, located on the Fraser River was not unique to the area, but still evoked the fulsome praise of one garden writer:

> The garden . . . is an example of stately pleasure grounds planned to lead one on a pilgrimage by straight stone-flagged walks between formal rose beds to a summer house half hidden under masses of American pillar bloom, down winding paths past parrot-green tennis lawns, lily-gemmed ponds, and lavender plots to a balustraded terrace, from which the outlook to the Fraser River across acres blazoned with the scarlet insignia of the vine maple (*Acer circinatum*) is enchanting. Vast plantings of flowering shrubs and foreign trees flank wide parterres of colour. . .; herb gardens. . .flourish; in short all kinds of cultivation marks the site where in 1885 an impenetrable forest was overlord.[62]

Within a radius of ten kilometres of Vancouver, gardens devoted to a single plant family, rock gardens, water gardens, wall gardens, or topiary could be found.

Another often-cited western garden, notable not only for its plantings, but even more for its location, was Ben-My-Chree. The creation of Mrs. Otto Partridge, the garden was located on the Taku Arm River in a nearly inaccesible part of the Yukon:

> The flowers were sweet-peas, delphiniums, asters, columbines, paeonies, pansies . . . and many others besides — a pool of colour under the sheer precipices . . . we passed on, a little quiet, spellbound, for we had expected nothing like this, wilder wilderness, perhaps, but not a garden in it. And finding it, the contrast with the scene round us made it all the stronger. Having walked through that oasis of colour we came to a house beside which was a small conservatory.[63]

Residence of J. Pendry, Victoria, B.C., about 1909. Topiary was a British horticultural fancy imported into Canada which never became a widespread garden feature.

Mrs. Partridge, even when elderly and widowed, carried on the garden and ongoing northern hospitality with the aid of a Japanese servant and a gardener.

Butchart Gardens, one of our most famous gardens, was the creation of another woman of means, Mrs. Jenny Butchart who directed the gardens for over forty years. The estate near Victoria, British Columbia comprised 52 hectares, surrounding the house, her husband's quarry and cement factory. She began gardening in a small way in 1904, at first with a gift of sweet peas and roses from a gardening friend. Jenny Butchart reputedly knew little at first about gardening, but from this humble beginning, she became more absorbed in the study and practice of horticulture, until it became a passion.[64] Within a relatively short time, she and the garden had become internationally renowned.

Five years after quarrying began, the quarry site near the house was exhausted. A two hectare area, twenty-three metres deep, was left, filled with rubble and discarded rock. The old quarry was an ugly offensive thing to Jenny, an unaesthetic sight for her husband to pass daily on his way to work.

Hatley Park, Victoria, was one of the most impressive estate gardens in British Columbia. The estate is now the home of the Royal Roads Military College.

The quarry in Butchart Gardens, Victoria was once a rubble-littered hole. Due to the enthusiasm and organization of Jenny Butchart, thousands of visitors a year enjoy this superb garden.

As the story goes, Jenny decided to make it into a garden, saying to her husband: "We've made it ugly. Now let's make it beautiful again. Let's put some flowers in there."[65] It was a formidable task — loose rock had to be gathered together, top soil brought in by horse cart, and plant material had to be chosen and planted. Congratulating her when the garden was well settled, her husband then wondered what could be done about the bare walls. Soon the enthusiastic Jenny was seen swinging from a bosun's chair, dangling over the sides of the quarry, merrily planting bits of ivy into every crevice. The bare walls soon also flowered with choice alpine plants. Asked how she accomplished this horticultural wonder, Mrs. Butchart replied: "It is easy, quite easy and simple. I got the seeds from Europe, and just took a watering can and filtered them down with the earth amongst the rocks and crevices — like nature would do it with her rains."[66]

This section alone gave her an international reputation. On one occasion as she was showing her garden to a prominent British adventurer, Frederick Marshman Bailey, he remarked that he knew one flower she probably did not have — a Himalayan blue poppy named after himself. Jenny merely smiled and led him to a bed devoted entirely to this poppy (*Meconopsis betonicifolia Baileyi*):

> 'Impossible!' exclaimed the dumbfounded Captain Bailey. 'I only just discovered it myself in Tibet!' But Jenny's contacts had been so good that the Edinburgh Botanical Garden — to whom Bailey had sent some seed — had shared the prize with the distant, but renowned, Mrs. Butchart.[67]

The garden was full of rarities as well as an exhaustive selection of native British Columbia flora. By 1915, the fame of Butchart Gardens had spread so widely that 18 000 people visited it that year.

When asked why she opened her gates to the general public, Jenny said:

> When I first came out here . . . I used to feel so badly because I never could get a glimpse of the really beautiful gardens of this place . . . And at first I had no garden of my own to speak of. But everybody here had high-walled gardens — very English and seclusive . . . Do you know I thought such a garden policy was very selfish. Anyway, I vowed that if ever I had a garden, less fortunate people than myself should have the privilege of enjoying it.[68]

Jenny evidently enjoyed people as much as she did flowers. She was often to be found helping the staff to conduct tours through the garden or to serve tea, although thousands of visitors did not know who she was. Once a customer offered her a tip after she had served the lady tea. Jenny demurred with: "Oh, I couldn't take it; Mrs. Butchart would never let me accept a tip."[69]

Water lilies, roses, alpines, and successions of spring flowering bulbs, annuals and perennials graced this spectacular garden. Workmen were requested to "never let the ground be seen,"[70] a policy which insured continual bloom in this garden from spring until late fall. The 1930s saw more innovations, a lake, a conservatory, Italian gardens, and so on, but the original sections and structures remained virtually unaltered. The gardens, one of the few privately-owned horticultural legacies we have from the early 1900s, still hosts thousands of visitors annually.

The Supporters

6 Clothing the Rhetoric:

Canadian Nursery Development

Kensington Park Nurseries, London, Ontario, 1885. Early nurseries concentrated on growing mainly "economic plants" such as fruit trees, and windbreak material such as conifers.

Ornamental gardening in Canada gradually came to rest on three essential supports: the tripod of the nursery industry, horticultural writing and plant breeding. Demand for plant material stimulated nursery development; increased gardening activity stimulated a demand for greater varieties of hardy plants and encouraged publication of gardening instructions. As public knowledge increased, more demands were made, hybridists and nurserymen were motivated, garden writing was stimulated, greater gardening activity resulted, more demands were made, and so on. Our examination of this triple support will begin with a look at nursery development in Canada.

Nineteenth-century British immigrants, who came from a garden tradition that had been developing since the sixteenth century, found the scope of Canadian gardening quite limited. Where were the favoured varieties of roses, or the unique range of polyanthus, for that matter? These were to appear in Canada only after years of experimenting and testing in our rigorous climate. It was not a simple case of importing material from Europe and the United States. It was a major challenge to produce hardy, beautiful, disease and pest resistant plants to ornament the new nation. The basic test for any new plant — whether introduced or hybridized — was, of course, hardiness: would it survive our winters?

Obviously, the pressing concerns of early settlement — clear-

Eng. For FARMERS ADV.

ing land, building shelter, planting crops — diminished purely aesthetic activities. Nurseries were consequently quite basic and confined to larger population centres. Before 1900, nurseries and seedsmen mainly sold fruit trees, bush fruit, vegetable seeds and some ornamentals. Nova Scotia distributors were selling flower seeds as early as the 1770s.[1] There are records of Montreal firms existing in 1810[2] and lists of nursery stock in New Brunswick were advertised in the 1820s.[3]

There was a range of responses to these early establishments. Some affluent home owners patronized them, while others only ordered supplies from British and American seed houses. The general trading of plants and seeds between friends, and the cheaper alternative of digging wild flowers and shrubs from the bush also continued.

Expansion and prosperity of the nursery trade were not equally distributed across Canada for many years. One of the earliest nursery catalogues published in southern Ontario was described in 1827 by William Custead of New York; it advertised ornamental as well as fruit trees.[4] For some time, the national nursery business was dominated by nurseries in the Niagara Peninsula region of southern Ontario. As Upper Canada prospered, other nurseries were established.

An example of a successful nineteenth-century Niagara Peninsula business was the St. Catharines Nurseries. Reputedly established in 1830 by Chauncey Beadle, an American immigrant

Belleville Nurseries, Ontario. Some nurseries landscaped their grounds as a living advertisement of their stock and also to demonstrate the appeal of home beautification.

doctor, it mainly featured fruit trees — many were grown from scions imported from an Albany, New York nursery.[5] By 1845, the nursery was so successful that Beadle gave up his medical practice and devoted himself fully to his horticultural interests. This was also the first year he offered ornamental trees: horse chestnut and yellow locust.[6] The business continued to thrive into the next generation. Chauncey's son Delos White Beadle returned from a New York law practice in 1854 and began a thirty-three-year career as a nurseryman.[7] Delos Beadle's influence was quite far reaching, extending into ornamental plant introductions and the formation of the nationally recognized Fruit Growers' Association of Upper Canada (later of Ontario). He was the first editor of the *Canadian Horticulturist*. The St. Catharines Nurseries survived until 1895.[8]

These early nurseries were characterized by individualistic management, and moderate commercialism. Sources of supply were varied, with significant importations from Europe and the United States (the survival rate was equally varied). The number and size of eastern Canadian nurseries expanded and prospered as settlement increased, towns grew and transportation links multiplied. Well before 1900, many Niagara Peninsula nurseries had begun to switch from fruit trees to ornamental stock — hedging, evergreens, shade trees and shrubs.[9] And when the early beautification programs such as city tree planting and park formation began in earnest, the nursery industry was further enriched.

One of the larger concerns was Morris and Wellington Nurseries near Fonthill, Ontario, founded between 1837 and 1842, and passing through a succession of owners.[10] By 1904, business was measured in the "hundreds of thousands," had penetrated into every leading town and city in Canada, and boasted a European clientele.[11] Fruit trees were the largest stock (hundreds of thousands of apple trees were planted annually), but a significant number of ornamentals was also handled: 75 000 rose bushes, 15 000 elm trees, and hundreds of varieties of other trees, shrubs and flowers. Mr. Morris noted:

> The demand for new and rare plants is increasing rapidly. Most of it has sprung up within the last ten years, more particularly the last few years, until now it has become one of the most important branches of our business. I can remember when we only planted 500 elms. This increased to 1000, a few years later to 3000, and last year [1903] I planted 15 000.[12]

The operation became so extensive that the owners had difficulty keeping in touch with the foremen on their nine farms. To solve this problem Mr. Morris installed a private telephone system connecting all the branches — an exciting innovation at that time.

Morris and Wellington Nurseries employed seventy-five men full time, and two hundred part time — a figure which did not in-

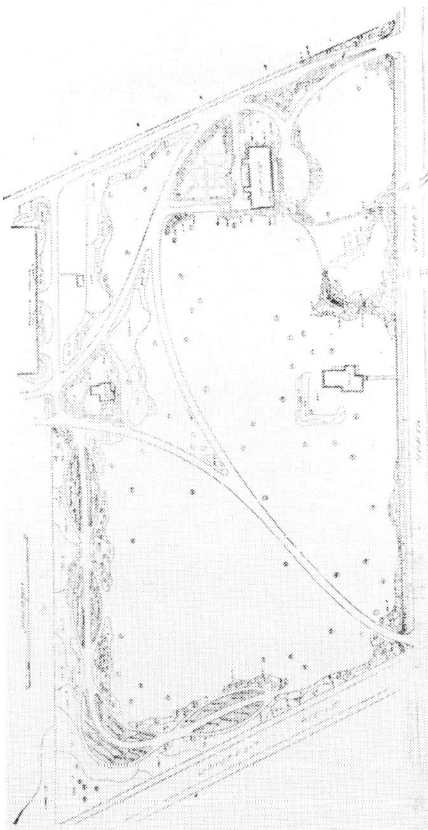

Landscape plan of Belleville Nurseries, Belleville, Ontario.

clude office staff or nursery agents. Brown Brothers Nursery, another leading Ontario nursery, in the same year was said to employ between 1200 and 1500 agents.[13] Morris and Wellington did its packing outside under the protection of pine trees. Brown Brothers, on the other hand, had a storage cellar built which could house 500 000 trees prior to packing and all packing was done under cover.[14] This firm also provided two boarding houses — one for office help, the other for the nursery "hands."[15]

Prairie nurseries were not as numerous nor as affluent as eastern establishments. Plantings were not as extensive, varieties were limited and the market smaller. However when the tidal waves of immigrants, many of whom came from horticulturally sophisticated backgrounds, engulfed the west, more interest was shown in garden material. Some early western horticulturists were embued with a sense of horticultural mission, but progress was slow unless they were willing to experiment.

One of the pioneer western nurserymen who conducted experimental work was A.P. (Sandy) Stevenson. This Scottish immigrant settled with his wife near Dunston, Manitoba in 1874, where he established Pine Grove Nurseries in about 1882, in a sheltered position in the Red River Valley. Stevenson, an early promoter of shelterbelts, increased the natural protection with plantings of Scotch pine, Manitoba maple, and white spruce.

Although Stevenson was renowned for his pioneering work in apple orcharding, he also grew and distributed various ornamentals: bush honeysuckle, lilacs from Bulgaria, caragana from Siberia, roses, and various perennials.[16] He also read papers before the Manitoba Horticultural Society's annual meetings on the varieties of ornamental trees, shrubs and flowers. In time, Stevenson, an amiable man with a quiet sense of humour, became one of the leading Manitoban horticulturists, whose opinions were constantly sought by officials and settlers alike. He was referred to as "one of the fathers of the principles and practice of Forestry and Horticulture" in Manitoba.[17]

While Stevenson was more of an experimental nurseryman and hybridist, H.L. Patmore laid claim to being the first commercial nurseryman in Manitoba. Born in England, he immigrated to Canada in 1880 at the age of nineteen. By 1888 Patmore was a partner in a Brandon nursery specializing in strawberries and Manitoba maple. Later in that year he took it over and named it Patmore Nursery Company.[18] The years before 1900 were lean ones, when settlers, in the words of Patmore:

> . . .have grown to look upon nursery stock as a luxury, while many others have formed the opposite idea that nursery stock growing was much of the nature of the cultivation of weeds, and that it should be so cheap as not to be considered of any value.[19]

A. P. Stevenson in his apple orchard near Dunston, Manitoba, in the 1920s. His reputation spanned the testing of economic as well as ornamental plants.

Packing nursery stock at Morris and Wellington Nurseries, Fonthill, Ontario in 1904. Nursery stock had to survive many rigours before arriving at its destination.

Birdseye view of Patmore Nursery, Brandon, Manitoba, about 1921. Patmore declared that ". . . another requirement of a nursery is the continuous preaching . . . of the necessary conditions for successful tree growing."

Patmore was an articulate spokesman and writer who often analyzed the fortunes of the prairie nursery industry. He found a great contradiction in the west's need for nurseries and their poor survival rate:

> Western Canada should be the home of many nurseries, and with its need for trees, the vast extent of land, and the number of homes requiring tree culture, the nursery business should be one to afford good returns for the growers of nursery stock; but, for some reason, up to the present [1915], nurseries have not been successful in the west, and we are of the belief that this has been to the disadvantage of the prairie country.[20]

Patmore felt that the lack of horticultural knowledge among both customers and some plant sellers may have been partly responsible for the slow growth of the industry. Often customers would not plant trees properly — that is, where the soil could be continually cultivated to retain moisture — and the trees would die.

Other commentators highlighted the problems of distance — both for spreading horticultural knowledge and for delivery of nursery stock. Most nursery business was conducted through the mail, with the stock sent by train. Nurserymen constantly complained about mishandling of their material by railway officials: "the railway people will delay packages ten days or a fortnight on the road, and in consequence the plants do not live."[21]

The continuing reliance on out-of-province sources of supply was another factor which hindered the growth of western nurseries. Western growers understandably felt some animosity towards eastern nurseries: "one Ontario nursery alone received $14 000 from this province [Manitoba]; had none of these orders been sent, it would have been better for the country, as not one percent of that stock will grow."[22]

Allied with this dissatisfaction, was western anger with federal restrictions on plant importation in the late 1890s, due to the danger of importing destructive insects. In 1900 the Western Horticultural Society (centred in Winnipeg) addressed itself to one such irritation: the federal San Jose Scale Bill. The San Jose scale (a destructive insect particularly injurious to fruit trees and some ornamental trees and shrubs)[23] flourished in epidemic proportions at the turn of the century. The bill severely restricted the importation of plant material from the United States where the insect thrived. From the late 1800s, many westerners had been ordering predictably hardy trees and shrubs from northern American nurseries, but when this source of supply was halted, they were limited to eastern Canadian nurseries and less hardy stock. The western growers, in a formal protest, stated that the resulting restriction forced them to rely on the Niagara district in particular — a district they noted was full of this insect. There were even allegations that Ontario nurserymen lobbied energetically (and successfully) to keep the bill in force only to protect their financial interests. A positive result was the realization by westerners that prairie-grown stock was the most reliable.

Two other factors were generally recognized in discussions on the progress of the nursery industry and horticulture in general. The first was the founding and programs of the federal Experimental Farms System, and the second, the activities of tree pedlars and nursery agents.

EXPERIMENTAL FARMS SYSTEM

The emergence of the Experimental Farms System as a force in Canadian horticulture had an agricultural origin and purpose. In the early 1880s, Canada, as well as much of the Western world, was experiencing a severe depression which badly affected the farmer's fortunes. Investigations conducted by the Department of Agriculture, attempting to discover causes and remedies, noted that in the west new agricultural methods needed to be developed, while in the older sections of the country:

> primitive agricultural methods no longer sufficed and their consequences were becoming only too apparent . . . . Canada's possible future as a great nation depended on a contented and prosperous people; that such contentment and prosperity were impossible unless agriculture were put upon a permanent and profitable footing. . .[24]

In 1884, a select committee, headed by the Quebec Member of Parliament G.A. Gigault, was appointed by the House of Commons to investigate the need for agricultural improvement. In its final report, the committee recommended that an experimental farm system be established.[25] On May 12, 1886 "An Act Respecting Experimental Farm Stations" passed in the House of Commons.

The system's organization corresponded quite closely to a report written by William Saunders who had been engaged by the Minister of Agriculture, Sir John Carling, to collect detailed infor-

William Saunders (1836-1914), first director of the Experimental Farms System. Even before his federal appointment, Saunders was a leading figure in Canadian agricultural and horticultural circles.

mation on the organization and scope of similar institutions in Europe and the United States. Saunders included all that he had learned on his various trips, as well as recommendations for the organization and personnel of the future Canadian system. When the act passed as law, Sir John Carling named Saunders as the first director of the system.[26]

William Saunders was a logical choice for such a role. By 1880 he was regarded as a leading horticultural and agricultural authority in Canada.[27] He had begun his career as a druggist in London, Ontario, but soon branched into serious amateur study of fruit growing, entomology, and medicinal plants. Before long he had a mini-experimental farm of his own in London, and was a frequent speaker at scientific and agricultural society meetings.

When he assumed directorship of the Experimental Farms System, Saunders oversaw the establishment of five agricultural stations:* the central farm in Ottawa, serving Ontario and Quebec, a substation in Nappan, Nova Scotia, serving the Maritime provinces, a station at Brandon; serving Manitoba, one at Indian Head, Saskatchewan for the (then) Northwest Territories, and one at Agassiz for British Columbia.[28] Saunders also appointed an entomologist, a superintendent of horticulture, a superintendent of forestry, a botanist, a veterinary surgeon, and substation superintendents.[29]

The initial programs centred on economically oriented agricultural and horticultural projects. When the prairie stations were established, one of their main objectives was to promote windbreak plantings. By 1891, Brandon Station had planted 111 316 shrubs and trees of all kinds and distributed 70 000 trees to prairie farmers.[30] The next year the demand far exceeded the supply. In some areas, federal authorities had difficulty persuading farmers to plant shelter belts — especially Ontario immigrants. Many Ontarians were less than enthusiastic about tree-planting, remembering stories or having personally experienced the tremendous task of tree clearing that had to be done on Ontario land before one could farm.

However, the idea must have been promoted properly and have become popular, for in 1901 the federal government decided "to commence free distribution of seedlings, cuttings and tree seeds in sufficiently large numbers to help a settler grow a really practical shelterbelt."[31] In 1904, when the Indian Head Station took over tree distribution, an estimated one and a half million trees were distributed, and by 1917, seven million trees.

*By 1924, the five stations had multiplied to twenty-six farms, stations, and substations, with a corresponding expansion of departments and interests pursued by the system.

The superintendant's residence at the Dominion Experimental Station, Kentville, Nova Scotia. Often the superintendant's house was landscaped as an "object lesson" in an ornamental garden layout using varieties hardy in the region.

Not just any farmer could receive such largesse — federal regulations and inspections were instituted:

> To qualify for free trees, the recipient had to be an open prairie man; had to agree to follow specified planting directions including summer-fallow, and to fence in his trees; plantings to be at least thirty yards from permanent buildings; and do reasonable cultivating between the rows. To see that tree planters understood and made reasonable attempts at what was required of them, qualified inspectors were employed and assigned both to check on the plantings, and to instruct, advise and encourage them.[32]

A.P. Stevenson was one of the best known inspectors. While he was away working for the federal government, Mrs. Stevenson ran the household of six children, the farm, and the nursery business — much to the amazement and praise of outsiders.[33]

NURSERY AGENTS

Before the federal program was established, prairie settlers relied on the few local nurseries supplying tree seedlings. Or the farmer could purchase trees and other ornamentals from "tree pedlars."[34]

An illustration from the nursery agent's catalogue used by Belleville Nurseries, Belleville, Ontario. Often the pictures in these catalogues were idealized versions of plant material which was not always hardy in the regions where it was sold.

The tree pedlar was known in Canada from the mid-1800s. Initially, they came from the States, sometimes attached to little-known American nurseries. Unfortunately many tree pedlars acquired unsavoury reputations — stories abounded about their dishonest dealings, selling worthless stock and tender plant material. The Ontario-based *Canadian Agriculturist* noted in 1855: "Yankee pedlars have made frequent inroads into this province with 'cheap' and worthless trees." Some pedlars were supplied with leather-bound books full of coloured plates depicting idealistic representations of their wares. These forerunners of the nursery catalogue gave the pedlars a scornful nickname: "the picture book gentry."[35]

As the west was settled, it became a new area for the tree pedlar to conquer. Soon there were warnings issued in horticultural society reports against these dealers who were now coming from eastern Canada, as well as the United States:

> The tree agent with his 'fancy pictures of impossible fruits,' his cuts of magnolias, horse chestnuts and flowering plums will soon be intruding his presence on you for spring orders for plants at magnificent prices. My advice is to buy only from nurserymen and florists of good reputation, buy through catalogues and correspondence and let the smooth-talking agent severely alone.[36]

Understandably, struggling prairie nurserymen were quite unhappy in the early days over the destructive encroachment of these outsiders. The selling of worthless plant material (often at inflated prices) severely damaged the nurserymen's "missionary work."[37] Gardeners who had bought and lost such material were often reluctant to purchase more material, even when it was perfectly hardy.

However, in this age before mass advertising, many nurseries discovered that the employment of an agent (the next level up from tree pedlar) was very profitable, and their use multiplied in the west as it had in eastern Canada. To offset the frequent criticism arising from the average agent's ignorance of what he was selling and his treatment of the job as just a temporary, seasonal way to earn money, some nurseries issued "certificates of agency" to their agents and a few nurseries elevated the agent's role to an educational level.[38] It was noted that wherever knowledgeable, interested nursery agents had travelled, they usually left behind a feeling of good will, an understanding of how to plant the stock, and profits for their nursery.[39] By the 1920s, some nurseries, such as the Prairie Nursery in Estevan, Saskatchewan, were holding "sales schools" to give their salesmen "instruction in Landscape Gardening, Planting and Care of Nursery Stock, etc."[40] Agents had become such an integral part of the larger nurseries that they were spread out all over the Dominion and into the United States.

Rose garden in the B.C. Nurseries, Sardis, British Columbia. Many such nurseries found it difficult to compete with foreign imports.

PROGRESS AFTER WORLD WAR I

The early 1900s were characterized by the continuing expansion of eastern nurseries, the struggle for survival of the western nurseries, and the emergence of the Experimental Farms System's widening sphere of influence. But World War I slowed down the nursery trade, European sources of supply were cut off, and many nurserymen were called into action. The Experimental Farms System became heavily involved in the greater production campaigns, and had to cut back the few early experiments and programs in ornamental gardening.

The years after the war were marked by accelerated expansion of the nursery business Canada-wide. Western nurseries were becoming better organized; they hired their own agents and supplied mail order catalogues to customers. In the post-war boom, both west and east benefited from the increasing amount of hardy material available, and the increased patronage of nurseries generally. Not only was there more money to spend on luxuries, but an increased urban population and settled communities also contributed to the growing interest in ornamental gardening. (Some nurseries landscaped their grounds as living advertisements and concrete examples of the art of home landscaping.) Expanded transportation routes and improved methods of packing and shipping also aided the nursery boom.

With expansion came diversification. Prior to the 1920s, many Canadian nurseries supplied a wide selection of ornamentals and fruit stock. But the boom enabled some firms to specialize. For example, Patmore Nursery in Brandon had outlived the years of struggle to emerge as the "largest growers of Caragana in the world." In 1926 they sold 2 421 500 caraganas to customers on the prairies, British Columbia, the Yukon, northern Ontario and the northern United States.[41] Scarboro Gardens Company near Toronto specialized in dahlias (a hundred varieties in 1928) and peonies (two hundred varieties).[42] Others specialized in bedding plants, roses, or perennials. In 1930, the results of a questionnaire sent to large-scale growers across Canada were published: in the previous year, 364 661 rose bushes, 620 613 ornamental trees, 800 037 shrubs, 591 445 perennials, and 1 683 868 bedding annuals had been sold.[43]

By the 1930s the nursery industry was solidly established in Canada — in fact, it was big business. The transition of nurseries from innovative, pioneering institutions involved in a mission to beautify the nation to money-making ventures did have an effect

Spruce tree nursery, Winona, Manitoba, about 1911. Spruce trees were not only viewed as ornamentals, but also as integral parts of shelterbelt systems.

on the type and range of material Canadians could purchase. Many firms specialized in a few types of ornamentals. Others went with the fads — geraniums, pansies, petunias and spireas on a grand scale — and this, in the long run, had beneficial effects, making more reliable material available at low cost. It also resulted, however, in the standardized appearance of many gardens. Advertising by agents and mail-order catalogues became more sophisticated, informative and wide-spread. Improved transportation lines insured that people in remote locations would receive plant material in a healthy condition. The nursery industry, with its supply of varied plant material, had evolved into one of the three firm supports of the home garden and public beautification programs.

But besides buying lilacs and cedars and all sorts of plants, gardeners were also reading about the whys and hows of planting and caring for their plants. The next chapter will examine the role of our horticultural press — the second leg of the horticultural tripod.

7 Gardens in Print: Horticultural Writing in Canada

Horticultural writings appearing in Canada before 1870 were not particularly Canadian. Adaptations of British works, reprints of British and American books and articles, and settlers' accounts comprised our early horticultural press. By 1900 this situation had begun to change, and by 1930, the Canadian horticultural media had begun to have an impact on our lives. Gardeners, depending on their means, could buy gardening books, magazines or newspapers with daily or weekly garden columns. Free copies of federal or provincial horticultural bulletins, circulars, and pamphlets were available. Free publications were also available from provincial agricultural colleges. Some early nursery catalogues included information on choice of site and layout, and cultural advice, in addition to their price lists.[1] Gardeners who were members of large horticultural organizations, such as the Ontario Horticultural Association, received informative annual reports. Libraries also provided an extended range of garden writings.

BOOKS

Before 1870, gardening books were mainly found in private libraries and were usually the works of British and American authors.[2] For example, the innovative Andrew Jackson Downing's works (recognized as the first major American landscape architectual books) were available in Canada in the 1860s.[3]

THE BEAUTIES OF NATURE COMBINED WITH ART BY H. A. ENGELHARDT

MONTREAL, PUBLISHED BY JOHN LOVELL. 1872.

FOR SALE AT ALL BOOK AND SEED STORES AND BY LESLIE & SONS, TORONTO NURSERIES.

Title page from H. A. Engelhardt's book, distributed by Leslie and Sons Nurseries in Toronto.

In 1868, an adaptation of a British book was published in Toronto: *The Cottage Florist: Being a Compendious and Practical Guide to the Cultivation of Flowering Plants, Adapted to the Late Province of Upper Canada*. As well as in private collections, horticultural works could also be consulted in the libraries of scientific or natural history societies such as the library of the Montreal Horticultural Society.[4]

Yet it was not until 1872 that eastern Canadian gardeners could consult an extensive all-Canadian garden book. Delos W. Beadle in that year wrote the *Canadian Fruit, Flower and Kitchen Garden*. At this point in his career, Beadle had been involved in

Delos W. Beadle in 1904. He was the first editor of the Canadian Horticulturist.

his father's nursery business in St. Catharines, Ontario for nearly eighteen years. This self-taught horticulturist was soon one of the most influential men in Ontario horticultural circles.

The 390-page book was a compendium of horticultural knowledge and the distillation of Beadle's experience, and included cultivation advice, descriptions of available plant varieties, special techniques (such as fruit tree grafting), and information about insect pests and their control. The climatic range of his advice encompassed Ontario, Quebec, Nova Scotia and New Brunswick. The book was written in very matter-of-fact prose, but Beadle occasionally gave way to personal exhortations:

> Take courage, then; the Canadian's motto is 'to make a path where he cannot find one,' and if the floral treasures of the tropics do not grow naturally in our northern land, we will set about our homes those things which harmonize better with the natural features of our country. . .[5]

Nineteenth-century readers of Beadle's book could learn how to prune dwarf pear trees, but unfortunately they could not gain any information on how to landscape their property. Beadle was quite aware of this inadequacy:

> The time, we trust, is near at hand when the desire for home embellishment in the planting of trees shall attain such a position among us, that Canadians will require and receive, from abler hands, a work that shall treat specially of the planting of ornamental trees, and give hints concerning their arrangement and disposition. . .[6]

But the gap was filled by a book written in the same year by a German immigrant, H.A. Engelhardt — *The Beauties of Nature Combined with Art*, published by John Lovell in Montreal. Engelhardt became known chiefly for his design and superintendency of Mount Pleasant Cemetery in Toronto. In 1872, he was well in the vanguard of civic beautification thought. His slim volume contained chapters on prison beautification, school house landscaping, street tree planting, cemetery beautification, public building landscaping, and railway beautification.

In addition to the theoretical and philosophical content were sections on practical landscaping. Engelhardt presented succinct instructions on laying out drives and placing statuary, as well as plant lists of desirable North American trees, shrubs and roses. The landscape style he worked within was the Reptonian style, with overtones of the Picturesque — grottoes, ruins and hermitages.

Neither this book nor Beadle's book went into a second printing. After the appearance of these two volumes, there was an interval of thirty-one years before another significant Canadian book on ornamental gardening was published. In 1884, Robert McNeil of the Little Saskatchewan Nurseries wrote the booklet:

Practical Tests on Gardening for Manitoba and North-West Territories. Here, flower cultivation advice was sandwiched between vegetables and livestock, and the booklet contained only the rudiments of flower gardening for the new settler: "In the push and hurry of the first years of a settler's life these ornaments of our homes are apt to be neglected; but it will not be found wasted time to give a little attention to these old friends."[7]

In 1903, George Moore* published a book, *The Farmer's Vegetable, Fruit and Flower Garden* — a revision of Alec Santerre's 1902 book, *Le potager, jardin du cultivateur*. The revision contained a section on "Fruits and Flowers in the Vegetable Garden." The floral information was not extensive, nor uniform, but Moore did attempt to cover a representative sample of annuals, perennials and bulbs. Other than these composite garden manuals, Canadians had to rely on the increasingly available American and British publications.

This reliance was quite evident in a 1904 book list published in the *Canadian Horticulturist*. Eighteen of the general horticultural books were devoted to ornamental gardening — only one of the eighteen was Canadian. Five of the eighteen were written by the phenomenal American, L.H. Bailey, whose works were extremely popular in Canada. (He was not only a prolific writer, but he devoted considerable energy to rural betterment, founded the Nature Study Movement, and promoted a wide variety of beautification schemes.) The remaining twelve books were divided between American and British authors.

1885. Mrs. Annie L. Jack.

Annie Jack (1839-1912) was a Canadian gardener and writer who influenced gardeners all over eastern Canada through her book and journal writings.

The sole Canadian book on the list was written by Annie Jack and published in 1903. She was born in England and immigrated to the United States when she was thirteen.[8] In the 1860s she married Robert Jack, "a Scotch fruitgrower of intelligence and position," and moved into his home on the Chateauguay River southwest of Montreal.[9] Here Mrs. Jack for the next fifty years designed and cultivated her garden, a garden which L.H. Bailey praised in 1905 as "one of the most original gardens I know."[10] She not only experimented with new plants, but she also wrote numerous articles and books ranging from horticulture to social issues to short stories and poems. She regularly contributed to the *Canadian Horticulturist*, the *Canadian Horticultural Magazine* (published by the Montreal Horticultural Society) and the *Montreal Daily Witness*.

The Canadian Garden: A Pocket Help for Amateurs, written in her sixty-fourth year, was a distillation of a lifetime's gardening

*Moore, at this time, was assistant editor of the Quebec government's *Journal of Agriculture and Horticulture*. Formerly he was a nursery owner and the author of a pamphlet on carpet bedding mentioned in Chapter Five.

experience. It went into a second edition in 1910, and as late as 1914 readers of the *Canadian Horticulturist* could order a copy for one dollar postpaid or receive it free as a subscription premium.[11]

The book was full of concise, nicely worded advice on the usual spectrum of gardening topics. She could also be quite technical. For example, in the chapter on "The Kitchen Garden," Mrs. Jack listed common vegetable seeds and how long they could be stored without losing their germinating ability. The book's appeal lay in its calm, wise assessments of garden problems, especially how to start a garden from "scratch." There was a strong sense of a "real" gardener behind the printed word: "The picture framed on the lawn is always unfinished; a new flower, a newer fruit, lures on at planting time, while constant changes must be made with plants that are condemned or misplaced, and though perfection is aimed at, it is never reached."[12] Throughout the book, underlying this practical content, was a recurring belief in the higher purpose of gardening: "New gardens, too, contain a prospect that one may almost envy, for there is no pleasure can surpass that of anticipation, when it is for the betterment of humanity, working hand in hand with nature."[13]

Eight years later the next all-Canadian ornamental gardening book was published. In 1918 Dorothy Perkins published the *Canadian Garden Book* (sometimes titled *The Dorothy Perkins Canadian Garden Book*). In comparison to Annie Jack's warm, gentle prose, Dorothy Perkins' writing was sharper, occasionally shrill. Miss Perkins wrote with great verve and many exclamation points, intermingled with frequent sentimental observations: "The little woodsy flower faces have a message all their own — they are pure and innocent, for they have not been hybridized and crossed by ardent horticulturists who seek to outstrip nature."[14]

Dorothy Perkins was the *nom de plume* of Adele Austin,* daughter of a wealthy Toronto banker. Since little has yet been discovered about Miss Austin's life, we can make few assumptions. Certainly we can assume she came from a horticultural background — her father ran a large fruit farm at Port Dalhousie, Ontario for many years as a hobby.[15] We also assume from evidence in her book that she actually gardened, rather than just supervised a garden staff. There are extensive family records of the garden development of her family home, "Spadina," in Toronto. Her choice of pseudonym was also horticulturally apt — "Dorothy Perkins" was the name of one of the most popular early

---

*Pleasance Crawford kindly passed on an "Author's Note" from the May 1927 issue of *Canadian Homes and Gardens* which revealed the true identity of Miss Perkins.

twentieth-century North American hybrid climbing roses.

While Miss Perkins did dwell on practical items such as lists of perennials, grouped by colour, or where to locate shrubs and creepers, her main emphasis was on gardens that the more affluent might create. She featured specialty gardens — that post-World War I pre-occupation. For example, two chapters out of seven were devoted to rock gardens and rose gardens. In her typical style, Miss Perkins praised the rose garden: "It is in a rose garden that one learns. . .that pleasure is always mixed with pain. There's always a thorn in life, put there that we may be better able to appreciate the joys."[16]

Her high-spirited prose brooked no argument with her plant selection advice, her aesthetics, nor her love of English gardens. She certainly adopted, if only for purposes of the book, quite a dashing (and sometimes humorous) persona to further her gardening philosophy: "Take courage, those of you who have city lots, for a little well done is better than a lot half done."[17]

The next gardening book to appear was not a "how-to" manual, but rather a garden autobiography.* The garden autobiography was (and still is) a staple of British horticultural publishing. This genre first appeared in the Victorian era, probably influenced by the rise of the smaller, more intimate home garden. Generally, a garden autobiography is

> . . .a book in which the writer tells the life-story of his garden rather than of himself. Study of these books shows that they vary from works in which the garden itself has a definitely starring role, often serving as a sort of manual for the gardens of others, to works in which the garden is mainly an extension of the owner's personality.[18]

Canadian garden writers did not seem to favour, nor did the book publishing industry seem to support, this type of writing, even though the public seemed to enjoy British and American examples. *My Garden Dreams* by Ernest P. Fewster (a Vancouver writer and poet), published in 1926, was the only *bona fide* Canadian garden autobiography of the time. Fewster's style was rather coy, sometimes whimsical, often sentimental. He used his garden and all its occupants (the plants were very real to him) as the basis for horticultural information, plant lore, his personal opinions on a wide variety of subjects, and as a vehicle for his ornate prose. Fewster was at his best on nasturtiums:

> What have you seen, O golden strangers from the mysterious

*The useful term "garden autobiography" was coined by Beverley Seaton, British garden writer and historian, in "The Garden Autobiography," *Garden History*, Vol. VII, No. 1, Spring 1979.

> Southland, strangers indeed to my body's eyes, who yet have such friendly communion with my soul, who seem so intangibly, yet so surely related to a yesterday of mine that perchance was a thousand centuries ago: I am not wise enough to answer you as yet, little flower, nor as yet is my memory awakened sufficiently to know.[19]

MAGAZINES

The rise of the garden magazine also dates from the Victorian era when gardening and gardening interest became more widespread. In Britain, the influence of these informative periodicals was credited with "the encouragement of interest in gardening, the propagation of new plants and the development of new techniques."[20]

A similar case can be made for our own small horticultural press, especially its encouragement of an interest in gardening. In fact, magazines of all types, ranging from the cultural to the agricultural, rather than books, were the main forum for a great variety of horticultural writing in Canada. Nevertheless, our publications industry was somewhat curtailed by intense American competition; the United States had witnessed an explosive multiplication of magazines in the 1880s, many of which were sold in Canada.[21] For example, an early twentieth-century American periodical, *Garden Magazine*, was received by many Canadian gardeners and was offered as a subscription premium by a few Canadian magazines and horticultural societies. The Ontario Department of Education distributed it free to all primary teachers involved in school gardening. British magazines were also read even though the advice was not often pertinent to our climate. The only serious competition Canada offered for many years was the *Canadian Horticulturist*, founded in 1878.

Our first horticultural publication was established by the Ontario Fruit Growers' Association (founded in 1859) which had long wanted a publication to regularly communicate items of interest to its members. The first editor was Delos W. Beadle who held the post for nearly ten years. Under his direction this monthly magazine increased its circulation from a few hundred to 2000. By 1904, the journal had tripled its number of pages and more than doubled its circulation.[22]

From the beginning the journal concentrated on the individual grower and gardener. In fact, up into the 1880s a major portion of the magazine consisted of informative letters from readers, on subjects ranging from fruit cultivation to houseplant care, along with the inevitable reprints from foreign journals. Most issues began with a coloured frontispiece of a plant or fruit labelled "especially painted for the Canadian Horticulturist." The lead article would then describe the plant and what was known of its cultivation. Often, at the end of the article, the editor would ask

(Opposite)
Cover of the April 1895 Canadian Horticulturist, *one of the most influential Canadian horticultural publications of the period.*

APRIL, 1895.

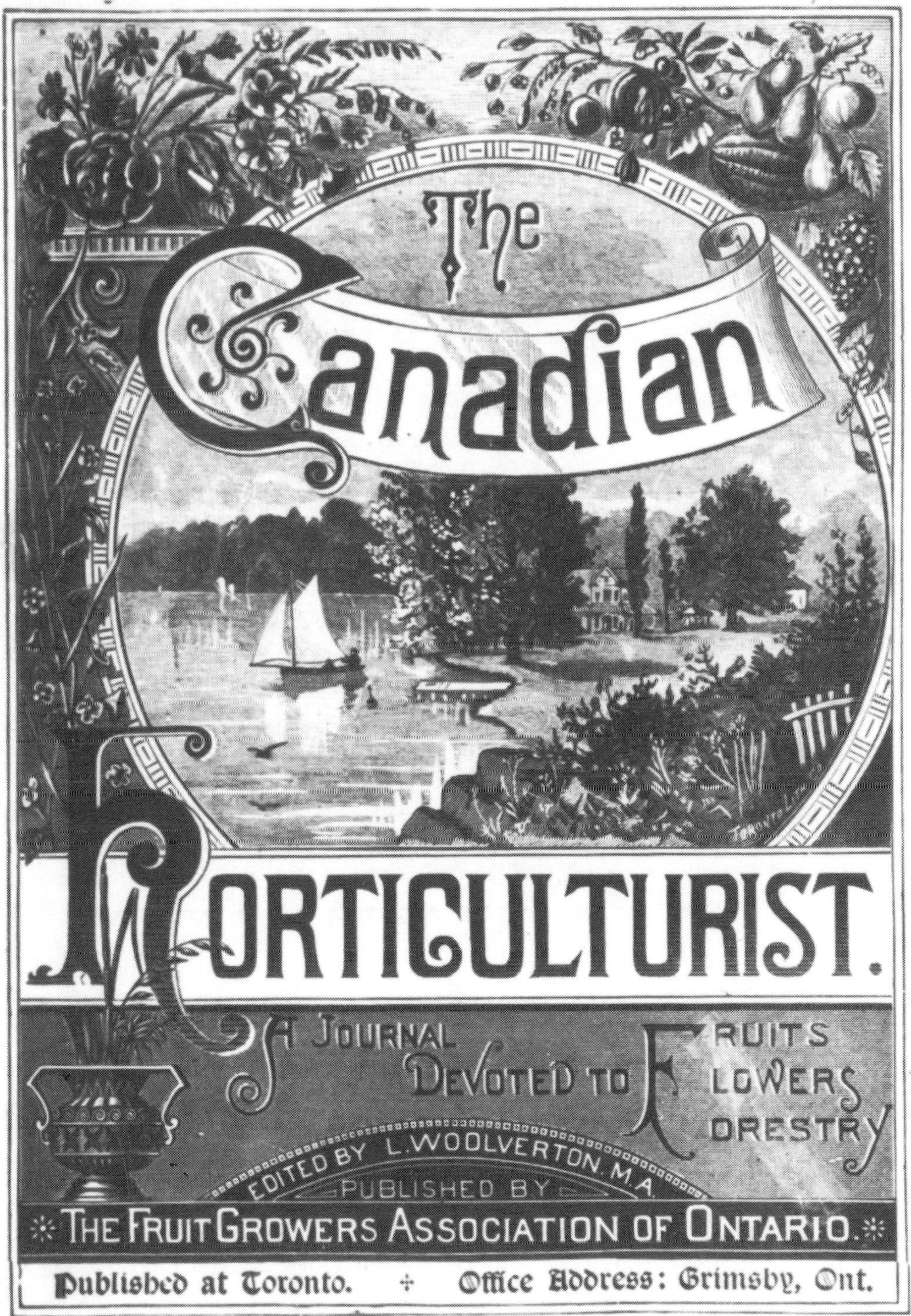

The Canadian Horticulturist.

A Journal Devoted to Fruits Flowers Forestry

Edited by L. Woolverton, M.A.

Published by

The Fruit Growers Association of Ontario.

Published at Toronto. ÷ Office Address: Grimsby, Ont.

$1.00 per ann. (including Membership, Annual Report and Share in Plant Distribution). **Single Copy, 10c**

Price, posted to Europe (with Annual Report), 5s., payable to J. Nugent Johnston, 21 Victoria St., Liverpool, Eng.

Linus Woolverton (in 1904), second editor of the Canadian Horticulturist, *was from a well-known fruit-growing family of Grimsby, Ontario.*

for first-hand information from his readers. The plea in the January 1885 issue, highlighting *Bignonia radicans* (Trumpet Flower) was typical of the magazine's early consciousness of its role in Ontario (and later Canadian) horticulture:

> We trust that our readers will enable us to verify this statement [the geographical limits of its hardiness], for if this be so, it will be gratifying to know that a climber as showy and desirable as this, can be confidently planted over the greater part of this Province. [p. 1]

The magazine also sent out yearly premium plants to all subscribers. In 1885, readers had a choice (one of five) of the following:

> a yearling tree of Russian apple; or, a yearling tree of the hardy Catalpa; or a yearling plant of Fay's Prolific Currants; or, a tuber of a choice double Dahlia; or, three papers of Flower seeds, one each of the Diadem Pink, Salpiglossis and Striped Petunia. (January 1885, p. 3.)

The early issues also contained sentimental poetry, a few engravings or line drawings, a few advertisements, and book lists — usually with a promise that the magazine would try to order them for readers if desired.

Under Linus Woolverton, the second editor of the *Horticulturist*, the magazine altered its focus from fruit to a more balanced selection of horticultural topics. The Canadian content was much higher and the practice of reprinting foreign articles had declined. The format was larger, the paper glossy, and the use of black and white photographs extensive. The articles continued to be written by subscribers, no longer in letter-to-the-editor format, but as journalistic pieces.

By this time, the magazine had taken various positions on beautification and other horticultural improvements. Emphasis on the small lot owner's garden increased, and the home garden department ("Flower, Garden and Lawn") became a monthly feature. While reflecting the garden issues of the day, the *Horticulturist* persistently called for reader action to effect horticultural change, especially when the response did not fulfill the editor's expectations. Within the framework of beautification, the magazine published information on the care and cultivation of both new and familiar plants. Plant premiums also continued, but the former call for information was muted.

By 1910, circulation of the *Horticulturist* had reached 9000. The magazine was striving for a national audience by featuring articles on prairie and maritime topics, while still retaining reports from Ontario provincial representatives. Articles continued to be written by prominent amateur horticulturists, but pieces by experts — professional horticulturists, academics, and nurserymen — were increasingly appearing in these issues. How-

NARCISSUS.

ARISE from thy slumber, lovely Narcissus,
The south winds now carol over thy bed;
Old Sol is waiting to greet thee with kisses,
You have nothing to fear now; Winter has fled.

The fearless wee Crocuses—Paradise immigrants!
Have arrived on our borders with God's message of peace,
And you, too, sweet Narcissy, must try to be diligent,
Improving Time's lessons, which never shall cease.

Your Sleepy old Sisters, Rose and Rose Mary
Have promised to visit me early in June,
I never have found the dear beauties contrary,
But timely arrayed in their queenly costume.

So bonnie Narcissus, hasten your toilet,
I weary to see you, don't tarry so long;
Bring with you your incense, sweet odorous Pilot!
And waft my old soul back to childhood and home.

For The Canadian Horticulturist. GRANDMA GOWAN.

A poem written in 1890 by Grandma Gowan for the Canadian Horticulturist. *Sentimental floral poetry was extremely popular in the Victorian era.*

ever, few articles were written by professional journalists and writers. The *Horticulturist* consistently contained the type of information needed by amateur and professional gardeners alike — for fun, profit, or duty.

In the early 1900s, a number of other Canadian gardening publications appeared. *Garden Magazine and Home Journal* was published in British Columbia. It offered gardening information, while focusing on homemaking topics. In 1911, the Ottawa Horticultural Society sponsored a garden journal which unfortunately lasted only one year. The *Ottawa Horticulturist* featured very practical, informative articles on all phases of ornamental gardening, many of which were written by prominent federal horticulturists. The Manitoba Horticultural Society entered magazine publishing with the appearance of the *Manitoba Horticulturist*. From 1914 to 1921 this little magazine published articles from its readers on a wide variety of prairie garden topics, as well as updates on the various horticultural societies' activities. In 1927 *Gardening in British Columbia* began publishing ornamental garden articles, but this too only lasted a year. In 1925 *Canadian Homes and Gardens* began a successful thirty-seven year run. This publication seemed to cater to upper middle-class readers who appeared to reside only in British Columbia, southern Ontario, and along the St. Lawrence. It was a professionally written publication, slick, glossy and well-illustrated. There was a wealth of information on gardens of prominent people, and practical articles on horticultural topics, written by well-known amateur gardeners as well as professional horticulturists.

This then was the extent of our horticultural press before 1930, in spite of periodic calls for more popular horticultural journals.

In addition to the horticultural magazines, many readers obtained gardening information from articles published in other types of periodicals. Rural magazines, such as the *Grain Growers' Guide*, *Farmer's Advocate* and *Country Life in British Columbia*, were popular sources of horticultural information. The editor of the *Grain Growers' Guide*, George F. Chipman, was an active supporter of horticultural causes. He sponsored free fruit tree and seed distributions and fruit-growing contests through the *Guide*.[23] These journals had a decidedly rural audience and the garden content reflected this bias, but it did not preclude reports on city beautification or railway gardening.

Specialty magazines were also sources for the avid gardener. For example, the *Canadian Municipal Journal* published articles on important garden movements such as street tree planting. The two major railway companies published magazines for their employees. The *CPR Staff Bulletin* and the *Canadian National Railways Magazine* contained many articles on individual railway gardens, garden tips, and philosophical garden articles. Professional gardeners and florists had their own publication. *The Canadian Florist* (1905-1960) published articles on landscape gardening, new plant introductions, and cultivation tips, in addition to news of the profession.

NEWSPAPERS

The Canadian gardener could also obtain garden information from a number of other sources — some widely available, others privately published; the daily newspaper was one of the most popular sources. By 1900, the Canadian newspaper industry was flourishing, and newspapers were commonplace in many homes.[24] The recognition of the power of the press and its usefulness in disseminating information was soon applied in horticultural circles:

> The press is one of the great channels through which a taste and love for horticulture and forestry may be spread. In the absence of any periodical especially devoted to these arts, there is much need for the information that may be given through the agricultural press and local papers. It is very important that sound and reliable information should be given — information that will be adapted to the needs of the locality where published.[25]

Praise was extravagant for those horticulturists who used this medium: they were characterized as thoughtful people who were doing a "most important and valuable work."[26] Enlightened editors were also praised when they printed garden articles. For example, a group of prairie newspapers in 1905 issued as special printings, illustrated editions devoted to peonies: "the attention of the public has been called to these flowers as never before."[27]

Some newspaper columns highlighted specific garden topics, others focused on readers' inquiries. Annie Jack, who wrote a column for the *Montreal Daily Witness*, combined both styles. Her column, "Garden Talks," usually began with a short essay on a garden topic, or a general observation on life, religion or manners, followed by four or five answers to readers' questions. Her advice was always detailed and to the point.

Some horticultural society members actively promoted aggressive press campaigns to "spread the word" of civic beautification and home gardening and urged members in other cities to do the same:

> Just as dew fulfils its mission in relation to living vegetation, reviving and refreshing, so the drops from the ink wells, if the thoughts prepared for the press are really vital ones, will not fail in their function; but, if otherwise, the crop of thoughts harvested will not result in life-giving principles to a dozen, and certainly not to the thousand or million readers.[28]

The newspaper was also seen as one of the best media for reaching all classes of Canadian gardeners in lieu of a substantial Canadian garden literature. One commentator felt that many people were intimidated by technical lectures and articles in speciality journals: "to be of real use to a large proportion of citizens much of our garden literature must be of a more simple type, and in a form easily available, and the readers must be led up step by step as children are at school."[29]

The newspaper article was seen as the answer to that problem — especially for the working classes: "The newspaper is the poor man's library, and it should be our concern to help him obtain the literature he requires in a form which he can enjoy and use, at a price not beyond his ability."[30]

GOVERNMENT PUBLICATIONS

The provincial and federal governments also reacted to the problem of disseminating horticultural information. Various departments of agriculture responded to the public need by instituting agricultural and horticultural publications. Manitoba, Ontario and the Central Experimental Farm were the most vigorous publishers, printing quantities of pamphlets, bulletins and circulars. These publications covered a wide range of topics, from cooking to dairy management to injurious insects. The main pre-occupation of most series was economic — crops, agricultural techniques and stock breeds were among the most popular subjects. But there were occasional horticultural bulletins and circulars.

The Central Experimental Farm led in the diversity of its horticultural publications. Leading staff members published booklets on hardy plant material, roses, rock gardening, and even a booklet on home landscaping. In 1915, the Farm established the Division of Extension and Publicity because "some definite connecting link between the Experimental Farms and the farmers was needed, and . . . a systematic effort to disseminate this knowledge should be organized."[31]

One of the main projects of the division was to secure and distribute press articles regularly to newspapers. Often these articles (which appeared also in journals such as the *Canadian Horticulturist* or the *Canadian Florist*) were printed under the heading "Experimental Farm Notes."

The division also supervised the printing and distribution of "Seasonable Hints," published three times a year. In 1923, 300 000 were distributed on a regular mailing list and 63 000 were sent to rural banks which co-operated in distributing them to the public.[32]

The Publications Branch of the Canadian Experimental Farm was formed in 1910 to oversee the printing and dissemination of annual reports and special publications to all who requested them. At the same time, publications were announced to the public in a press notice. This generated a large demand for the free publications.[33]

The provincial governments and the agricultural colleges also issued their own free publications, obviously written for more local audiences. For example, the Manitoba Department of Agriculture in 1916 began publishing bulletins and circulars in a series called the Manitoba Farmers' Library in conjunction with the Manitoba Agricultural College:

> Every farmer in Manitoba should possess himself of a good library of Agricultural Bulletins written by the members of the Manitoba Agricultural College staff and other Agricultural authorities. This is the very best possible class of Agricultural literature. The bulletins are concise; they deal with practical questions; their authors know Manitoba conditions at first hand; they present the most advanced information on the subjects discussed.[34]

In 1918, the Manitoba Department of Agriculture published *Trees, Flowers and Fruit for Manitoba* which was one of the first comprehensive handbooks on prairie ornamental gardening. Basic methods of gardening and extensive lists of the hardiest varieties were given.

Two other provinces published their own periodicals. The Quebec Ministry of Agriculture published a monthly *Journal of*

Horticulture and Agriculture (and a French edition, *Journal d'agriculture et d'horticulture*) and distributed it by subscription at one dollar annually. The *Journal*, which had much the same format as the popular agricultural magazines, informed the Quebec rural population of the latest news: home landscaping, school gardening, beautification, as well as technical gardening articles. The British Columbia Department of Agriculture also had its own monthly journal — *Agricultural Journal of British Columbia*. It survived from 1916 to 1925 and was intended to supply information similar to the federal *Agricultural Gazette of Canada*. In addition to the provincial journals, interested gardeners could obtain information from the annual reports of the agricultural departments, or correspond with government horticulturists.

Another way in which provincial and federal departments tried to help the rural, as well as urban, gardener was by printing extensive book lists. For example, Bulletin 259 published jointly in 1918 by the Ontario Department of Agriculture and the Ontario Agricultural College was eleven pages of annotated "Books on Agriculture" with a section on garden books. The Manitoba Department of Agriculture in 1919 published a similar bulletin (#39) called "Books for Farm and Home." Usually the departments offered to order the books for the reader.

HORTICULTURAL SOCIETY REPORTS

Gardeners could also find massive amounts of information in horticultural society annual reports. Some societies published small annual reports, but the large umbrella organizations published the most consistent and comprehensive reports. The Western Horticultural Society (formerly the Manitoba Horticultural and Forestry Association) published informative reports from 1888/1889 up to the present. The issues before World War I were embued with a pioneering, missionary spirit as the members attempted to understand and extend the province's horticultural possibilities. The annual report of the Horticultural Societies of Ontario dated from 1906. Like the Manitoba report, it was distributed free to all members.

Both reports detailed the activities of member societies. Talks by individuals, slide shows, and discussions at the annual meeting were recorded. Topics ranged from fruit to flowers and vegetables, with the emphasis on ornamentals. The major gardening movements were written about, illustrated, and promoted. Canadian, British and American experts and horticultural activists were often invited to speak at the annual conventions — which were yet another way for gardeners to keep in touch with horticultural events.

In 1919, a member of the Ontario society did a survey to see

1 SARRACENIA PURPUREA
(Side-saddle Flower)
(Pitcher Plant)

what value the reports had for the members. The overwhelming consensus Mr. Baker received was one of strong support and interest:

> They are read by the members with interest, as the matter contained in them is not only interesting but of a readable nature, as well as containing invaluable information for all lovers of horticulture. The numerous beautiful photo scenes of lawns, shrubs, flower beds, and flower gardens, shown in the reports from year to year, are much admired and found exceedingly instructive.[35]

The reports were so popular that many members wanted to extend their influence beyond the circle of members, by sending the reports to every town council in the province.[36]

By 1930, our horticultural press was well-established, providing many informative alternatives. There were still gaps (no one had written anything extensive on Canadian garden history)[37] and there was still a continuing inflow of British and American publications. However, horticultural writing was influential enough to support and promote Canadian gardening. And it also enhanced the progress of plant breeding in Canada, as will be shown in the next chapter.

(Opposite)
An illustration from Canadian Wild Flowers — *Canada's first "coffee-table book." Agnes Fitzgibbon published the first all-Canadian book of wildflower paintings in 1868. Canada boasts an extensive range of florals (wild flower books) by amateur and professional botanists. Botanizing was a favourite pursuit and hobby from the Victorian era until World War I. Some writers attempted to promote wild flower gardening, but it was not a major component of the home landscape before 1930.*

8 A More Perfect Rose:

Plant Breeding in Canada

HYBRIDIZING: "A GAME OF CHANCE BETWEEN MEN AND PLANTS."[1]

Educated Canadians likely were aware of the nineteenth-century British interest in plant breeding. The British tradition dated from the late 1700s, when Payne Knight pursued the first systematic plant crossings.[2] Plant breeding in the Victorian era had been included in the general upsurge of interest in science, a time when large numbers of scientific amateurs and the few major scientific figures joined together in learned societies. (Membership in a learned society was also the mark of a gentleman.)[3]

The flood of horticultural material arriving in Britain from all parts of the Empire and the world aided the burgeoning interest in plant breeding (or hybridization as it later became known). In 1899, the Royal Horticultural Society held the first International Hybridization conference, attended by scientists as well as practical plant breeders, to discuss the problems of theory and practice in this new science.[4]

British hybridization knowledge certainly had some influence in Canadian horticultural circles, but Canadian activity in the early years before 1900 was quite informal. There were undoubtedly dabblers in scientific plant breeding, but the usual

(Opposite)
A cross between a red and a white poppy, 1919. The science of plant breeding received more general notice in the 1900s, generating activity by professionals and amateurs alike.

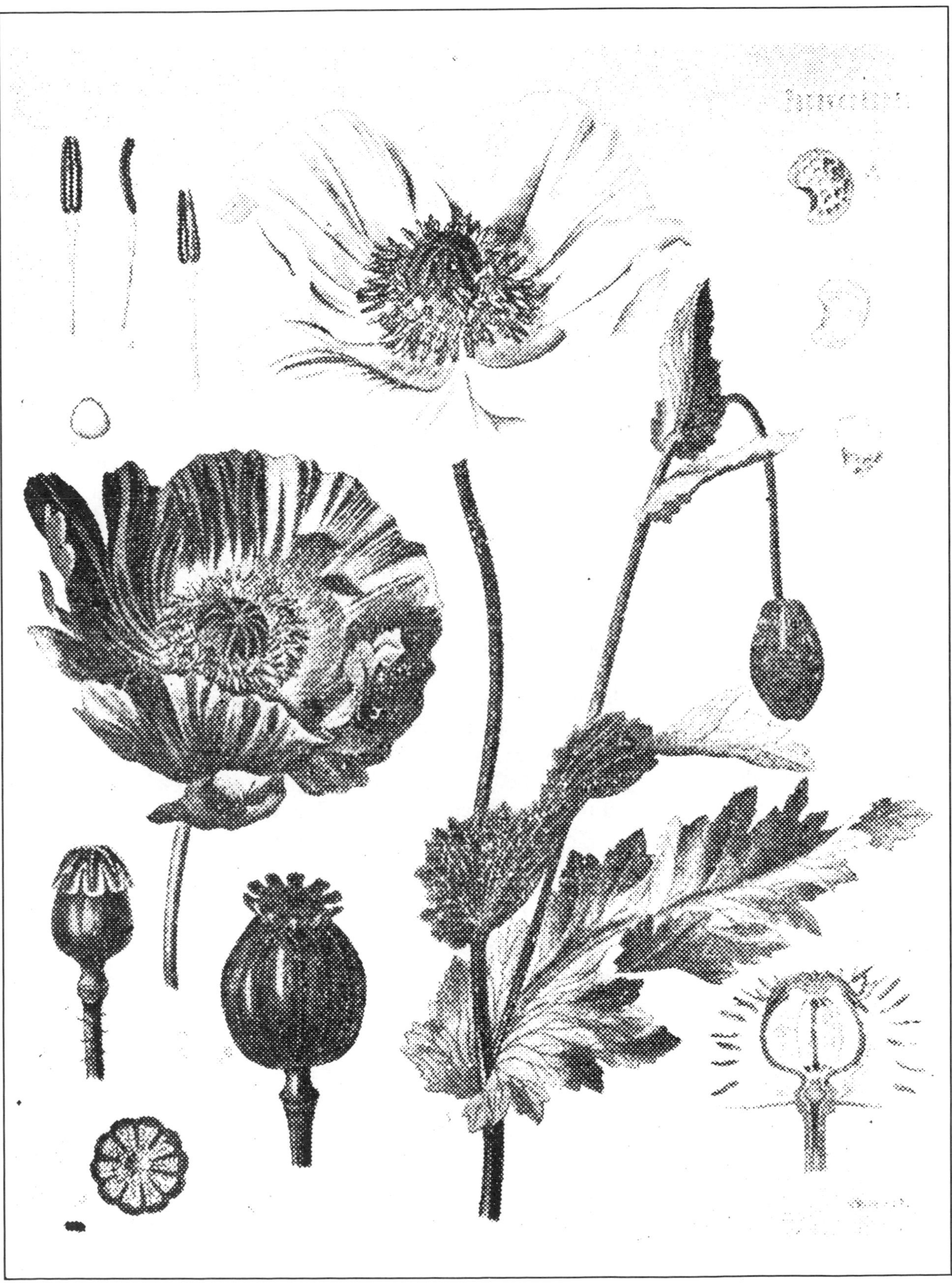

experiments centred around plant introductions.* This type of experiment was pursued by a broad range of enthusiastic gardeners and settlers who brought plants and seeds with them from their home countries and provinces. Some early agricultural and horticultural organizations offered to their members foreign plants for trial. Through published reports, word-of-mouth, and concerned nurserymen's efforts, a list of reliable plant material, although quite limited at first, was collected. Many of these horticultural "trail blazers" remain nameless.

THE RUSSIAN INFLUENCE

In the late 1870s interest in North American horticultural circles had quickened over the suitability of Russian, especially Siberian, and Northern Asian, notably Manchurian, plant material for our colder regions. Joseph L. Budd, professor of horticulture at the Iowa Agricultural College, was a pioneer experimenter in this area. By 1878 he had accumulated propagating material for nearly two hundred varieties of Russian apples and other fruit.[5] In 1882 he and Charles Gibb, a Quebec fruit enthusiast, undertook a trip through northern Europe and Russia at their own expense. Ten years before this trip, Gibb had bought a large tract of land in Abbotsford, Quebec "where he had planted extensive orchards, had prepared testing grounds for exotic trees and shrubs, and had made his home the meeting place for his many friends with common interests."[6] His Russian trip provided the seeds, not only for his own fruit experiments, but also for the foundation of the newly formed Central Experimental Farm orchard test plots.[7]

Jaroslav Niemetz in 1897. Niemetz was a Russian horticulturist who corresponded with William Saunders and sent many seed samples to Canada.

Another source of Russian information appeared in a series of letters ("Letters from Russia") written to the *Canadian Horticulturist*. Translated from the French, they contained detailed information on Russian fruits and ornamentals written by Jaroslav Niemetz of the Royal College of Winnitza. Niemetz also sent seeds and propagating material from promising stock to William Saunders at the Canadian Experimental Farm.

William Saunders was also in contact with personnel at the Imperial Botanic Gardens in St. Petersburg. By 1887, he had arranged, as head of the Experimental Farms System, for the Imperial Botanic Gardens, as well as Kew Gardens in England and the Imperial College in Japan, to send tree and shrub material to Canada.[8] One of the early Russian imports was the *Caragana arborescens* (Siberian Pea tree) which became one of the most popular trees in the West, and an indispensable part of shelter belt

---

*Plant introduction — the testing of foreign species to see if they would thrive in a different environment or climate — often existed side-by-side with hybridizing.

systems.* The early interest in Russian material, while admittedly centred on economic plants, also furthered future significant experiments with Russian and Asiatic ornamental material.[9]

EARLY HYBRIDIZING EFFORTS: "THIS IS AN AGE OF HYBRIDS . . ."[10]

By the late 1800s, ornamental, rather than economic, experiments were increasingly pursued. One of our early hybridists who concentrated solely on flowering plants was Henry H. Groff of Simcoe, Ontario. At various times in his career he was called "a wizard of horticulture," "the banker-florist," and "the Luther Burbank of Ontario."† His horticultural fame stemmed from the improvement and hybridizing of one plant — the gladiolus.[11] Basically he took a despised semi-tropical plant with insignificant flowers and developed it into a magnificent flowering plant, (1.2 metres to 1.5 metres tall; some with "waxy blossoms as wide as a man's hand"), a plant which could adapt itself to almost any climate or soil — a tremendous achievement according to his contemporaries.[12] Groff's hybridizing work (which many described as a hobby) was actually a very lucrative commercial venture which eventually made him a wealthy man.

Groff annually cultivated one and a half hectares of gladioli, retaining ten to fifteen labourers in the busy season and three permanent staff. He handled up to 50 000 seedlings in a season, and ultimately produced over one million different hybrid gladioli, although he only listed 1600 varieties.[13] During the busy season Groff spent ten hours a day supervising plantings, making crosses, and selecting promising mature plants. These ten hours excluded his normal working day as a bank manager, a job he held until retirement.

Groff did not sell directly to the public, but had agents handle the retailing, confining himself exclusively to plant experiments. He never moved from Simcoe, although at one point he supervised trial plots in California, a climate producing two gladioli crops annually. In the off-season he was busy with classification of new varieties, preparations for the next season, general administration, scientific correspondence, and writings for various publications.[14]

By 1914, after twenty-four years of effort, Groff seemed to

---

*Some writers credit William Saunders with its introduction, while others say the Mennonites brought it with them from their Russian homeland.[15]

†Luther Burbank (1849-1926): the most famous American plant hybridist of his time, known especially for his work on fruit and flowers, as well as vegetables.

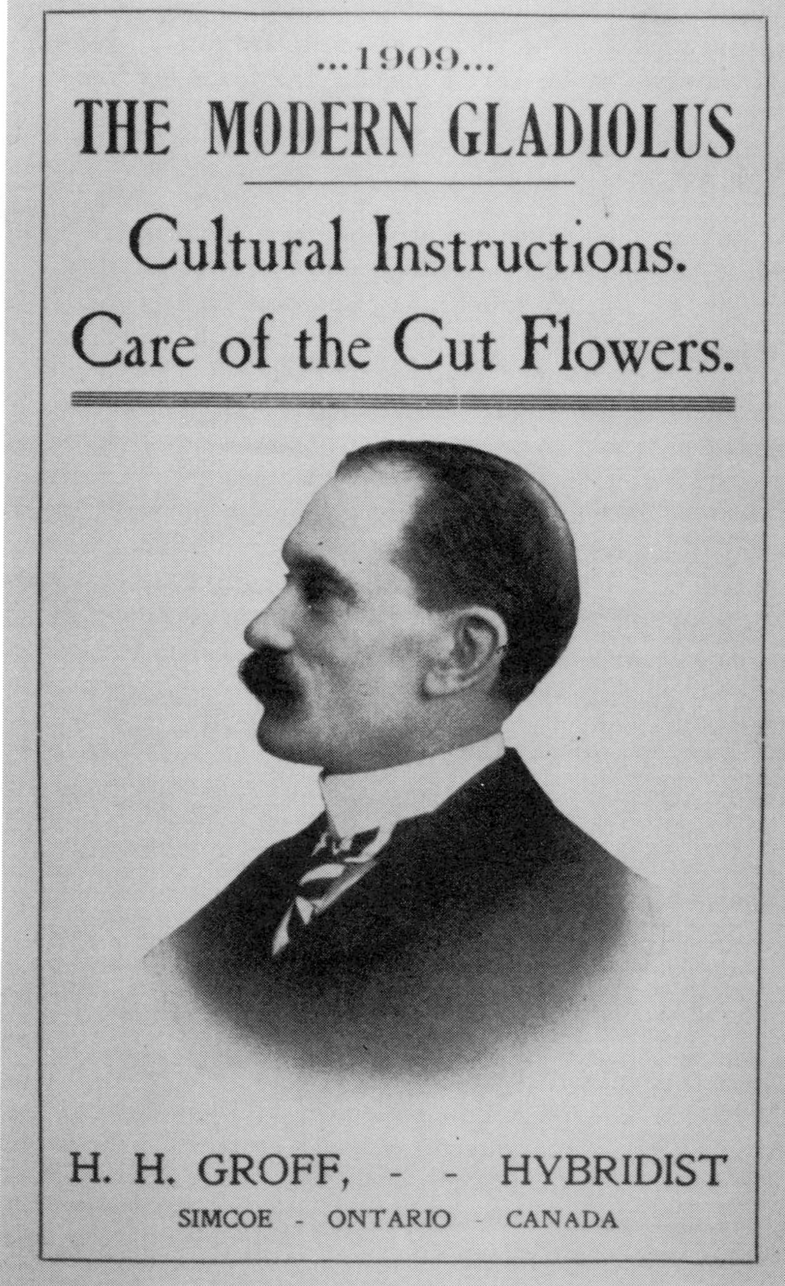

Henry H. Groff (1853-1933). He was characterized in the Farmer's Advocate *in 1908 as "a man of tremendous energy and initiative, keen of observation, and quick of movement."*

have reached the end of his interest in gladioli. In that year he sold off his entire gladiolus collection, and began working with iris and sweet corn.

Groff worked steadily at his plant breeding until his death in 1933 at the age of 81. That he found his two careers to be deeply satisfying was evident in his reflections in 1910 at the age of fifty-seven:

> The influence of an agreeable and successful diversion is most beneficial, both mentally and physically, fitting a man

> better for the duties of his trade or profession. . . You see with a clearer mental vision, you stand closer to the infinite.[16]

Before the first decade of the twentieth century had passed, hybridization theory and technique had become quite sophisticated. Standards had been fixed, co-ordination and co-operation increased, and writings on hybridizing found a wider circulation. A small army of amateur and professional hybridists had appeared: armed with the tools of the trade — tweezers, scissors, magnifying glass, small paper bags (for protecting the pollinated flower from insect interference), plant labels, notebook and pen.

To insure greater success, hybridists became more systematic and specialized by working on a particular line: disease resistant wheat, hardy hybrid tea roses, red gladiolus and so on. Information expanded on how and when to effect successful crosses, how to select the most promising seedlings, how to test under different conditions, and how to record the results. The importance of maintaining a varied botanical collection to insure a large gene pool for plant experiments was increasingly recognized. Surely, this was one of the reasons for the expansion of arboretums and botanical gardens. This also reinforced the importance of importing foreign plant material. For example, Groff decided at one point he wanted to breed the perfect yellow gladiolus, not being satisfied with the yellow colours in his collection. When he heard of a wild gladiolus of an unusual yellow colour in central Africa, he immediately contacted various sources which might supply it. By a very circuitous route he finally secured the corms from the chief engineer of a crew who were building a cantilevered bridge over the Zambesi River.[17]

PRAIRIE EFFORTS

Many early Canadian hybridizers, especially those on the prairies, did not pursue exotic species; their efforts focused on utilitarian plants. In the early days there was some amateur experimentation on the smaller ornamentals — perennials, shrubs and climbing vines.

On one level was the traditional trade in cuttings and plants between farm wives with word-of-mouth recommendations on culture and hardiness. Other gardeners ordered plant material from nurseries in Minnesota, New York, and northern Ontario. Added to this material were plants distributed by horticultural societies: in 1902 the Western Horticultural Society distributed peonies, *Hydrangea paniculata* and two varieties of lilac.[18] Experiences were shared in an informal way between these amateur experimenters — sometimes by letter, sometimes at horticultural society meetings. These introductions and hybrids had to meet exacting requirements. Not only would the severe cold kill plants; drying winds, low soil temperature, low moisture retentiveness and a high alkaline content of the soil also took a toll. For amateur and professional plant breeders, western conditions were challenging. Not only had environmental factors to be overcome, but also colour considerations, tolerance to different soil types, and disease and insect resistance had to be considered.[19] Early efforts were vitalized not only by a sense of mission, but also by the knowledge that there were really no boundaries, limitations, or terminal points in attempts to extend the boundaries of hardy plants.[20]

As the number of hardy plants grew, more efforts were made to acquaint westerners with the varieties available. In 1905, one prairie commentator noted that peonies were quite hardy in the west, a fact he felt more settlers should take advantage of. Fifty years before, he said, peonies numbered only twenty-five types, but by 1905, peony lovers could choose among 2000 varieties, ". . .and the number is constantly increasing."[21]

EFFORTS AFTER WORLD WAR I

World War I naturally caused a reduction in ornamentals research. Many plant breeders concentrated on hybridizing improved vegetable strains that would be faster ripening, hardier and resistant to disease and insects. But after the war, interest in ornamentals in the private as well as governmental sectors was revived. As noted in Chapter Six, nurseries experienced a similar boost due to more settled and prosperous conditions. Coupled with this revived interest in and expansion of ornamental plants was a call for new varieties, colours and forms to enhance our gardens.

The Dominion Experimental Farms System was a leader in the resurgence of ornamentals research and breeding. The early influence of the system under William Saunders and its role in public information have been noted, but in the 1920s intensive research and the testing and hybridizing of ornamentals was one of the system's priorities, and it played a major role in the expansion of hybridizing.

Before World War I, many Farms and Stations had perennial borders, annual flower beds, shrub and tree collections. Not all engaged in the work of hybridizing, but rather tested introduced varieties for their hardiness. The Lacombe, Alberta Experimental Station's progress in ornamental culture was typical of western Stations.

> When the Station was started [1907], avenues and shelter belts of elm, ash and Manitoba maple were planted, and, around the gardens, hedges of laurel-leaved willow and caragana. On the main lawn, some seventy different kinds of

> ornamental trees and shrubs were set out in small clumps. In the sixteen intervening years these have grown well, and now with the borders of perennial and annual flowers which have since been added, make the grounds a beautiful sight, well worthy of a visit . . . The arboretum contains the oldest and largest collection of trees and shrubs north of Calgary, and an effort is being made to test all of the annual and perennial flowers suitable to northern conditions.[22]

As the years progressed, federal advice was freely given, lectures were sponsored and the gardens promoted as visual "object lessons" for all interested gardeners. These protected prairie gardens became symbols of western fertility and a promise of prosperity and cultural advancement, as well as promotional material for rural beautification programs.

The Station at Morden, Manitoba, established in 1915, in time became the centre for research and development of ornamentals for the prairies. The Station early on conducted experiments with annuals, perennials and ornamental shrubs. By 1921 attention focused on rose culture and breeding.[23] However, systematic breeding of ornamentals by the Experimental Farms System really centred in Ottawa at the Central Experimental Farm.

W. T. Macoun (1869-1933). As Dominion Horticulturist he was instrumental in directing the Experimental Farm System's horticultural programs into more intensive research in ornamentals.

Here, the Horticultural Division was led by William T. Macoun who began working at the Central Experimental Farm in 1898 as curator of the Arboretum and Botanic Garden. He was the son of John Macoun, a famous self-taught botanist, who conducted botanical surveys for the CPR when they were plotting future western lines. By 1910, he had become the Dominion Horticulturist, overseeing the work of the twenty-four Farms and Stations in the system. In addition to his administrative duties, he carried on extensive breeding programs in apples and potatoes.

Macoun was involved in most of the horticultural movements of his time: he tirelessly promoted school gardening, served on local beautification committees, led production campaigns during the war, judged flower, fruit and garden competitions, held office in a great number of horticultural organizations, wrote articles and lectured across the country and in the United States on a variety of horticultural and agricultural topics. He was characterized as a tireless worker for the betterment of gardening.

After the war, Macoun responded to the call for an expanded range of ornamentals suited to our climatic vagaries by searching for someone to undertake the experimental work. In 1920, the successful applicant was Isabella Preston. This shy Englishwoman, in just eight years, had progressed from star pupil under J.W. Crow at the Ontario Agricultural College to one of the top hybridists in Canada. Her achievements were all the more remarkable as she was a woman in a traditionally male occupation.

Siberian iris hybridized by Isabella Preston. She named this series of iris after Canadian rivers.

She had come to Canada after her parents had died and her sister had accepted a position as a music teacher in Guelph, Ontario. She enrolled in the Ontario Agricultural College in 1912 against one friend's advice: "If you *have* to do something agricultural, why not take up poultry?"[24]

Thirty-year-old Miss Preston was soon hard at work, absorbing as much as she could under the tutelage of J.W. Crow, professor of botany. She was involved in his breeding projects, as well as the normal class work and field projects. Up to this time, the only horticultural training she had had were a few courses at the Women's Horticultural College in Swanley, Kent. Professor Crow encouraged her, guided her, and most importantly began teaching her the science and practice of hybridizing. According to an autobiographical fragment, Miss Preston remarked that from that point she began devouring all the horticultural books in the college library.[25]

Although Miss Preston did not finish her course at the college, she continued working for Professor Crow. She was given wide-ranging responsibilities in the greenhouses and trial gardens, and in 1916, she successfully crossed two species of lily, before thought to be impossible. This was a very important event. The result was the spectacular "George Creelman" lily: stately (.6 to 1.8 metres tall), strong of stem, and very floriferous — a horticultural coup. (This lily was used as breeding material for a range of new trumpet lily hybrids up into the 1960s.)[26] This breakthrough, as well as the solid work she had done for Crow and her obvious talent for ornamental breeding, brought her to Macoun's attention. Miss Preston described her transition from self-taught researcher to centre-stage hybridist quite simply:

> Dr. Macoun was looking for someone to do breeding work with ornamental plants so I applied for the position. I wanted to discontinue working with vegetables which I had to do during the war. Dr. Macoun gave me a list of plants and told me to see what I could do with them.[27]

This modest statement hides the fact that Macoun suggested she work on six different genera, genera which were less likely to duplicate the efforts of other plant breeders. The genera were: lily, rose, lilac, Siberian iris, columbine and flowering crabapple — quite a challenging range.[28] Most breeders would specialize in one or perhaps two genera, since the work involved and the knowledge of timing, technique and cultivation could be enough for one person's lifetime.

Miss Preston, who remained "Specialist in Ornamental Horticulture" for the rest of her twenty-six years at the Central Experimental Farm, set to work immediately, crossing hundreds of species with her unique talent and informed choice of compatible partents. And she was very systematic, a "stickler for detail" according to one colleague.[29] For example, she made an extensive study of the possible crosses in the lily genus, noting what did not produce results. Often she could not understand why a certain promising cross would not work — this was before plant cytologists could demonstrate the relation between chromosome counts and breeding compatibilites.[30]

However, by using all the current knowledge of hybridizing, Miss Preston began a program which produced named introductions up into the 1950s. From crosses she made in 1920 came a group of lilacs (Prestonia lilacs) which were widely recognized as important additions to this family. The Prestonia lilacs were bred for prairie conditions, so they were extremely hardy, and as an extra benefit bloomed nearly two weeks later than other varieties.[31] The colour range progressed from pink through to violet red. In all there were eighty named varieties, mostly named after Shakespearean heroines.[32] In later years some authorities chided her for naming so many of her seedlings — sometimes the differences were so minute that even she could not distinguish one hybrid from another.[33]

The lilacs were only the beginning of a long and illustrious career. Roses, Siberian iris, crabapples and lilies (her favourite flower) were crossed and tested, named and written about. Miss

Isabella Preston (1881-1965) with lilacs at the Central Experimental Farm, Ottawa. Today she is not well known beyond speciality horticulturists; many Canadians do not realize the contribution she made to our gardens.

Frank L. Skinner (1882-1967). Unable to travel to Asia himself, Skinner still managed to introduce numerous varieties from this region into our gardens by propagating samples sent from botanical gardens.

Preston, in addition to her horticultural duties, wrote extensively: two books on lilies, many booklets on ornamentals, reams of articles, and later even radio talks. Her correspondence was staggering. One day's journal entry recorded her dictating sixty letters in answer to gardening questions from the public.[34] She was also required to show visiting dignitaries around the gardens and even advise the prime minister on garden problems. By the end of her life, Miss Preston had accumulated an impressive array of awards for individual hybrids, as well as general awards including the British Veitch Memorial Medal and the Canadian Macoun Memorial Medal.

The Experimental Farms System continued to influence trends in public and private breeding programs up into the 1960s. However, a number of private hybridizers were also active in the 1920s and they too contributed significantly to the Canadian garden. One of these private breeders was Frank Skinner of Dropmore, Manitoba.

A contemporary of Isabella Preston's, Frank Skinner was born in Scotland in 1882. His family emigrated to Canada in 1895 when he was thirteen, settling near Dropmore, north of Winnipeg. Ill-health curtailed his farming duties, limiting Skinner to herding cows on horseback and studying the local flora.[35]

Skinner began to teach himself the rudiments of botany and horticulture. For some years, his only sources were Anderson's *Practical Gardener*, John Macoun's catalogue of Canadian native plants, and the annual reports of the Experimental Farms.[36] In 1909 he joined the Manitoba Horticultural Society, and began corresponding with leading horticulturists.[37] By 1911 he had given a paper at the Manitoba Horticultural Society annual meeting and had begun his first formal plant collecting.

An accident, which was to be a turning point in his career, forced him to spend the winter of 1911 in Victoria. This focused his horticultural ambitions. Impelled by memories of roses and honeysuckle from his childhood home and the knowledge of the harsh conditions of the west, Skinner decided to devote as much of his time as possible (he was still farming) to the horticultural betterment of the prairies. To this end he began reading all the horticultural, historical and scientific literature he could find in Victoria. Books on the geography, exploration, climate and flora of Northern Asia reinforced his belief that there were "many trees and shrubs in this part of the world that would be of both ornamental and economic value to the Canadian prairies."[38]

His ambition was fired:

> All about him was parent material for an unlimited extension of this line of breeding. His plow horses trod under foot every day roses hardy as the toughest Russian apple. Old World rose bowers would provide him with marriageable mates for them. About him the prairie carpet was thick inlaid with

> orange lily cups — bright gold in the hands of the plant breeder who could blend their vigor with the beauty of tender exotics. The wilds were full of plums and other fruits that could be coaxed to confer their birthright on a hybrid generation surpassing them in flavor and size.[39]

During World War I Skinner devoted himself to farming, and only returned to significant horticultural pursuits after the war. In 1918 he visited the Central Experimental Farm where Macoun taught him the latest plant breeding methods, and the Arnold Arboretum in Boston where he began a lifelong contact and exchange of material.[40]

By 1920, his nursery garden had greatly expanded. Evidently Macoun visited him after hiring Miss Preston, and in the course of the visit, told Skinner the lines she would be working along, and suggested he might follow some of them. According to a colleague, she was "hopping mad."[41] This began a covert, but basically friendly rivalry between the two.

They both began working with lilacs (identical species) at this time:

> Miss Isabella Preston and I started to work with *S. reflexa* at the same time but she was able to go to Boston for fresh pollen [he had to work with dry, shipped pollen] with the result that she succeeded in raising hybrids either two or three years before I did. The pollen sent to me from the Arnold Arboretum must have been collected from a different bush than that from which Miss Preston secured hers, for while her hybrids have all long loose panicles mine are much narrower and compact and have more red in their colour.[42]

This informal competition did not seem to deter the sharing of information and plant material. In 1922 Miss Preston wrote, thanking him for some lily bulbs, and ended with the poignant "I have a great desire to have a garden of lilies of my own."[43]

By 1924, Skinner felt encouraged enough to commercialize his horticultural hobby and Skinner's Hardy Plant Nursery began its long, influential career. He continued to grow wheat to support the family, but his greatest efforts were now directed to the nursery. This venture was never a great financial success, but it did support his breeding experiments.[44]

He, like Miss Preston, experimented on a wide range of ornamentals. In 1926, he was awarded the British Royal Horticultural Society's award of merit for a lily hybrid. By 1930, he had a number of introductions to his credit. His nursery was visited by many noted horticulturists, and he was also contacted at this time by A.E. Woeikoff, director of the experimental station in Echo, Manchuria. Woeikoff suggested a plant exchange, another fortunate event in Skinner's career.[45]

Through his writings and talks, Skinner began to be better known to the general public, and by the 1930s, articles were being written about him. (In this way he differed from Miss Preston. While she was said to be able to "talk your ear off" on her plant enthusiasms, there were two things she intensely disliked: speech-making and publicity.[46]) An extremely active man, Skinner did his own plant collecting in Europe, Canada and the northern United States. By the time he died in the 1960s, he had become one of the most famous plant breeders to work in Canada.

In addition to the prominent and professional hybridizers, the number of amateur plant breeders and experimenters had increased since the war. Many of them had turned their hobbies into commercial ventures, with gladioli breeders in the majority. Groff had sold off his collection in 1914, leaving the field open.

Mary Eliza Blacklock began her business in a small way in Toronto. She sold plants out of her urban garden (perennials, five or ten cents; shrubs, twenty-five cents) to make money for her favourite charity: the building fund of St. Anne's Anglican Church.[47] In 1914 she toured England and France, visiting hundreds of nurseries, collecting interesting plant material and seeds. When she returned she bought five acres outside Toronto. Rowancroft Gardens specialized in lilacs and peonies, but Miss Blacklock did not confine her offerings to these two families. By continual experimenting she introduced many previously unfamiliar plants into the Canadian garden.

James Crow, Miss Preston's mentor, after fifteen years at the Ontario Agricultural College, began his own business, specializing in gladioli, lilies, roses and iris. He was a very active lecturer, writer and public-spirited citizen. His hybridizing goals were quite specific; for example, his specifications in 1926 offered a thousand dollars for any new rose of Canadian origin which met his criteria in any of these three classes:

> Class 1 — a hardy climber, reasonably free from disease with flowers of or approaching hybrid-tea quality,
>
> Class 2 — a bush rose as hardy as the old H.P.'s [Hybrid Perpetuals] and with the free recurrent-blooming habit of the modern hybrid-teas. This rose must be meritorious in all aspects.
>
> Class 3 — a recurrent-blooming bush rose of reasonable all-round merit and with pronounced resistance to both mildew and black spot.[48]

His untimely death in 1933 stopped a promising private career.

In addition to the commercial hybridists, there were countless, unnamed amateur plant breeders experimenting on favourite plants in their back-yards. Enthusiasts did not need to be wealthy, they only needed patience, time and some extra space in the garden. Many never published their results, nor registered their hybrids — they just enjoyed the unending fun and surprise

J. W. Crow was professor of horticulture at the Ontario Agricultural College until 1924, when he resigned to conduct his own nursery and hybridizing business in Simcoe, Ontario.

of plant breeding. One amateur, F. Cleveland Morgan (of rock garden fame), enjoyed writing about his iris experiments as well as registering promising hybrids. In 1926, one of his hybrids, "Mount Royal," was said to be the "richest and most distinguished" in his garden.[49] It was also awarded a medal by W.T. Macoun in the Ottawa Iris Show for the best seedling exhibited.[50] Morgan obviously enjoyed hybridizing enough to influence others to try it: "do not be discouraged by seeming failure, there is always a chance of a surprise around the corner, the ten thousandth part of a chance that pays so handsomely for all the other failures."[51]

The threat of failure did not seem to deter the growing interest in plant breeding. Horticultural publications and societies continued to print articles and sponsor competitions concerning hybridization.

PLANT REGISTRATION

By the 1920s the proliferation of hybridists and the resulting multiplication of new varieties of shrubs, plants, and trees caused some concern in the industry. Not only did chaos reign in maintaining records of new varieties so as to prevent duplication of names and products, but the lack of protection of hybridists' labour was also appalling:

> Last week a thief visited a trial plot of the writer and lifted several large flowered petunias, the seed of one, a beautiful semi-double with reflected petals (a type quite unique) with flowers measuring five and one inches across, alone being worth $1,000. The writer cannot ever claim priority, and should he recognize his plant on the market, his word is only as good as that of the thief.[52]

Plant breeding was an expensive, time-consuming venture, a business which could be made even less lucrative by plant theft and underselling. Because plants at that time could not be patented, other growers could obtain material, propagate it, then sell it (even under the breeder's name) at very low prices without any remuneration to the originator.[53] This was one of the reasons plant breeders, such as Skinner, ran their own commercial nurseries — they needed financial support for their breeding work.

In 1914, Henry J. Moore, superintendent of Victoria Park in Niagara Falls, Ontario, began a campaign to gain support for a national system of plant registration. Many prominent horticulturists were behind the proposal, but the war diverted attention from it.

In 1922 the Ontario Horticultural Association formally endorsed the proposal, followed by the Canadian Horticultural Council's endorsement. In 1923, the Council approached W.R. Motherwell, Minister of Agriculture, who then lobbied the government. By the end of the year, the plant registration program was granted $10 000.[54]

The basics of the program were well organized by 1929. Registration was confined only to plants propagated vegetatively.[55] Those produced from seed were excluded because of the difficulties of producing and obtaining pure stock, and the resulting varietal changes. To register a plant, the breeder had to submit, along with a five dollar fee: the full name of the plant breeder; the name of the new plant; a brief description of the new plant; and the conditions under which the breeder wanted to sell or distribute the new plant.[56]

The provincial representative, before sending the application on to the central bureau, certified that the application covered a new variety, and had the plant properly tested to insure that it was of really "outstanding merit."[57] After acceptance, the variety was listed in official bureau files to avoid duplication of names and duplication of plant material. The first to record a duplication would be declared the original breeder. The index also tried to insure that whenever a registered plant was sold, the name of the originator would be recognized.[58]

The Canadian Horticultural Council felt the program promoted quality horticulture in Canada as well as insuring a fair monetary reward for hybridists' labours and an inducement to continue. Plant registration was also seen as a protection for the consumer. The buyer would have a greater assurance that a named plant (which sometimes could be quite costly) would indeed be the true variety.[59]

Coinciding with the protectionist tendencies of the plant registration movement was an increasing call for support of the Canadian horticultural industry against encroaching foreign imports. Up into the 1800s, American and European nurseries and seed houses were the only source for private gardeners and early commercial nurserymen. The first importations, for that matter, were the plants and seeds tucked into settlers' baggage. This inflow from succeeding waves of immigrants, packages from the home country and active solicitation of foreign nursery agents continued up into the early 1900s. A body of Canadian producers who could provide the thousands of "starters" needed by Canadian nurserymen did not exist. In 1904, the manager of Morris and Wellington nurseries in Ontario noted: "This year we found it necessary, in order to fill the demand for rare shrubs, to make a special importation from Holland. Most of our seedlings are purchased from France, which in this line supplies the world."[60]

Holland also supplied millions of bulbs. The United States supplied mainly fruit tree stock and some ornamentals and vegetable seeds, as well as some flower seeds. British seed houses also supplied great amounts of flower seed. World War I effectively demonstrated how much Canadian horticulture depended on foreign markets and the need to develop a larger supply industry of our own: "Are we satisfied with our status in the horticultural world? Emphatically we are not, and while . . . we have made decided progress the past 25 years or more, we have not kept up to the mark, as in keeping with our increase in strength and importance as a country."[61]

Some prominent horticulturists felt we had been too dependent on foreign markets and did not encourage our own development. The home gardener usually did not have much choice if he or she wanted plants that deviated from the usual varieties sold in Canada. Some thought it was all to the good if local nurserymen knew they were ordering from foreign catalogues. They felt it might spur on the local industry to carry more varieties.[62] Others cited the now commonplace adage: that nearly fifty per cent of imported stock was worthless in Canadian conditions.[63]

World War I also had the effect of heightening Canadian nationalism, which extended into the 1920s. This burgeoning nationalism was reflected in the "Buy Canadian" promotions:

> There is a growing sentiment in Canada in favour of Canadian things. We are becoming more proud of our country every year, and are looking for an individuality that will stand for Canada. One of the best ways we can impress our individuality on other countries and our own is by making Canadian trees, shrubs and herbaceous plants a prominent feature of our landscapes . . . too much attention has been given to imported species and the native material has been neglected.[64]

The promoters of this movement to encourage a national horticultural industry not only chided nurserymen and home gardeners against buying foreign material, but also shook an ad-

An Ontario gladiolus breeder, 1919. Years of work to perfect hybrids often yielded little financial reward.

monishing finger at the many horticultural societies which ordered foreign material for their plant distribution premiums.[65]

Our educational system was also cited as a factor which retarded the development of the horticultural industry. Many professional horticulturists felt there was a real need for an accredited program to train a new generation of Canadian gardeners and horticulturists. It was generally agreed that public opinion needed to be instructed. Too often professional gardeners were regarded as menials, deserving of little pay or recognition for their years of study and experience. For this reason, many promising young gardeners were leaving the trade for more lucrative employment. Nor could the horticultural community depend on trained European horticulturists to fill the gap as they had prior to World War I; they just were not immigrating to Canada in the numbers they had in former years.[66]

In addition to a system of horticultural education, and an increased awareness of the possibilities of native Canadian material, horticulturists wanted to enlist government support to raise the duties on imported plants, bulbs and seeds. For example, in 1926, Dutch rose growers exported over one million rose bushes into Canada. Labour was cheaper in Holland, so the cost of a bush was about five cents, compared to about twenty-five cents for a bush produced in British Columbia.[67] Many Canadian producers also resented foreign companies using Canada as a dumping ground for excess plant material.

In an appeal to nurserymen, horticultural society officials and home gardeners, C.K. Baillie (the first Secretary-Treasurer of the Eastern Canadian Nurserymen's Association) argued for increased support of Canadian-grown stock. In an informal survey of major Ontario growers in 1926, he discovered that a gardener could order from Canadian sources over 116 varieties of ornamental trees, 229 varieties of shrubs, 30 varieties of climbing vines, 310 types of roses and 1014 different perennials; in short, practically everything needed ". . . for home, park or street beautification."[68]

The benefits of ordering Canadian grown stock included:

- hardier, acclimatized material that was more likely to thrive: "The hardiness of varieties has been tested over a number of years, whereas many kinds imported into this country have no chance."
- less travel distance, and hence a greater guarantee of good condition on arrival: "Stock coming over the ocean is stored away in the hold of vessels without regard to its susceptibility to cold and heat and arrives in a dried up or moulded condition."
- Canadian stock was well inspected to insure that infested material is not distributed: "All kinds of injurious pests and diseases have been brought to this continent through incoming stock."

(Opposite)
A bulb farm in British Columbia in the 1920s.

- stock could be ordered and delivered on short notice without the lengthy delays caused by customs and fumigation — procedures which could take up to weeks.
- Canadian nursery firms guaranteed money back which foreign firms did not, and their price did not include extras for packing and shipping.[69]

By 1930, there were signs that the public was heeding the nurserymen and hybridizers. Statistics published in 1930 demonstrated that there was a lessening of imports and an increase in Canadian-grown stock being sold.[70] Production was up, packing and shipping procedures were refined and improved, and a greater number of varieties were being offered. In British Columbia especially, steps were taken to establish seed and bulb nurseries. One seedsman on Vancouver Island had twenty-four hectares devoted to flower seed production — his principal crops were sweet peas, pansies and antirrhinums.[71] In four years he expanded the area devoted to seed raising to over a hundred hectares. Bulb production also was on the rise. In British Columbia there were eighty firms specializing in bulbs for the retail market in 1930: on Vancouver Island alone, 200 varieties of tulips, 150 types of narcissi, and 50 types of hyacinths were being produced.[72]

By the 1930s, the Canadian garden had come of age. The amount of new plant material created by hybridists and introduced by experimenters had expanded colour and hardiness ranges. The Canadian gardener could now design gardens of greater sophistication and variety — supported by knowledge gained in the horticultural press, by improved nursery stock and distribution, and by public approval of beautification efforts. This thirty-year period was transitional for Canadian gardening. We were emerging out of a pioneering, clearing-the-land phase and into a garden-as-art or at least a garden-as-socially-relevant-art period.

The garden has long been characterized as a refuge from the world, a re-creation of paradise. But twentieth-century garden promoters created rather public refuges, noisy with rhetoric. This is not to disparage their contribution, for their enthusiasm did influence the development of horticulture in this country, and did place trowels in more Canadian hands. But their legacy today lies not in righteous horticulture, but rather in a persistance of gardening, supported by an increasing horticultural industry and press. The social movements of beautification may have expired, but our acceptances of park beautification or street planters or even petunias in the front garden continues. We may have lost a vitalizing dimension to our gardening, but we have won a belief in the possibilities and promise of the Canadian garden.

Afterword

The Preservation of Historic Gardens in Canada

Until recently garden preservation was virtually unrecognized in Canada. When Upper Canada Village was being planned in the 1950s, in the face of flooding for the St. Lawrence Seaway, it was realized that the rescued houses could not stand alone but would require a town plan and a complementary environment to lend understanding and appreciation of their meaning to the visitor. There were, however, no known surviving late eighteenth- and early nineteenth-century gardens in Canada to which the Village's organizers could refer.

They turned instead to the most likely appropriate models, American ones, for approaches. In addition, Jeanne Minhinnick, who was responsible for furnishing, and architect Peter John Stokes scoured the countryside for remnants of past landscapes. Combining the results of these searches with their findings from widely scattered documentary and pictorial sources, they planted relic materials, nursery stock and seeds in traditional layouts to complement the period houses at the site. Fifteen years later Upper Canada Village had the look of a comfortable, prosperous colonial settlement, and its gardens contributed an essential character to this perception.

Since then a number of historic villages — including Louisbourg in Nova Scotia, King's Landing and Village Acadien Historique in New Brunswick, Black Creek Village and Old Fort William in Ontario, and the Ukrainian Cultural Heritage Village in Alberta — have recognized and applied, with varying degrees of research and success, the concept of establishing an appropriate period landscape to accompany their selected buildings. It is ironic that the usual experience of Canadians in viewing historic gardens is based on recreated gardens which individually never existed!

In the 1970s Canadians took an active part in the newly

emerging North American interest in historic landscape preservation, through the publications and conferences of the Ottawa-based international Association for Preservation Technology, the 1975 New Harmony (Indiana) Conference and subsequent formation there of the Alliance for Historic Landscape Preservation, and publications such as John J. Stewart's *Historic Landscapes and Gardens: Procedures for Restoration.*[1] New directions in the preservation movement gave focus to the role of historic districts and environments, including gardens, rather than primarily to individual architectural monuments. Also in 1975, with adoption by the Historic Sites and Monuments Board of Canada of criteria for recognizing historic gardens and landscapes, the federal government through Parks Canada acknowledged the importance of past gardens. Four sites have subsequently been declared as having national historic significance: the grounds of Parliament Hill by noted designer Calvert Vaux; the surviving eighteenth-century monastic garden of the Sulpician Seminary on Rue Nôtre-Dame in Montreal; two late nineteenth-century country villa estates, Lakehurst and Beechcroft, at Roches Point, Ontario; and the Halifax Public Gardens, a late nineteenth-century Victorian park of remarkable integrity.[2]

Despite our renowned cold climate, gardening has formed part of the Canadian experience since the early days of European settlement. Yet, garden history has gone unstudied in Canada.[3] Such studies tell us much about past behaviour — about man's attitudes toward nature, about design choices, about aspirations and beliefs, about constraints, then and now. For preservation purposes, they give us information about former fashions, designs, materials and preferences upon which the identification, analysis and protection of historic gardens must be based.

Yet knowledge of the past is but one component of preservation action. Enabling legislation, clearly defined practical guidelines, and awareness of the nature and extent of the surviving historic resource are other critical factors. Current Canadian legislation does not make specific provision for historic gardens, such as that in the British National Heritage Act (1983) or the proposed Olmsted Historic Landscapes Act in the United States. Nevertheless, in addition to the federal statutes under which Parks Canada operates, provincial heritage, planning and environmental assessment legislation provides general authority for recognizing historic sites, among which historic gardens may seemingly be included. This legislation is, however, usually enabling rather than demanding, and its application to historic gardens has not been widely used.

More important than improving legislative facility for historic gardens is obtaining greater awareness and more committed support within government and private agencies for heritage, planning, and environmental assessment as well as among the public at large. Guidelines such as those prepared by the Ontario Ministry of Culture and Recreation for environmental assessments need wider recognition and application elsewhere. As yet, Canada lacks an inventory of historic gardens such as the Canadian Inventory of Historic Buildings provides for structures. Inventory involves the on-site investigation of gardens themselves, the recording of observable features, and the assessment of data compiled. It makes the garden itself the critical source. Several local inventories of historic gardens have been compiled in Canada, but the most extensive initiative to date was undertaken in 1983 by the Royal Botanical Gardens at Hamilton. Through a paper survey this program undertook to acquire data on origin, ownership, design, changes and condition of all surviving, restored or reconstructed pre-1920 gardens in Canada. This is an important effort and a clear step towards the identification of historic gardens at a scale where comparison of design, features and integrity becomes a possibility. It needs energetic follow-up from garden owners and garden lovers.

The identification and assessment of historic gardens face problems relatively unknown in the evaluation of buildings. Because gardens are comprised substantially of living material, they change naturally over time. Unless organic growth is restrained by regular maintenance, the form and character of gardens may be transformed beyond recognition, the strongest vegetation taking over the site.[5] Alternatively, plant material, circulation patterns or architectural features may be deliberately changed to reflect new fashions, interests or circumstances. Unlike buildings, where such replacements have often left physical traces, such alterations in gardens may leave only a documentary or pictorial record. Before photography became prevalent in the late nineteenth century, such records are very meagre. Prior to that period, we can often only hypothesize as to what specific gardens actually looked like or what plants they contained. What historical research tells us is whether drawings, paintings, plans or descriptions of specific gardens exist and what information they contain. Where the site has been relatively undisturbed, archaeology may locate such evidences of past layouts as paths, fence post holes and foundations of structures. Because excavation is expensive and destroys evidence as it proceeds, it has not been widely used in the study of Canadian gardens.

Besides lack of knowledge about past gardens and consequent failure to recognize their surviving remnants, other threats to historic gardens exist. They may be partially or totally destroyed by putting land they occupy to new uses, as the recent preservation struggle over the Sulpician Gardens on Rue Sherbrooke in Montreal has demonstrated.[6] Changing environments in the vicinity of historic gardens may also threaten survival of distinctive or characteristic plant material by transforming their established ecosystem, as the debate over proposed construction near the Halifax Public Gardens has noted.[7]

Despite these dangers, historic gardens have been preserved in Canada. Some, like the grounds of the Government Houses at St. John's and Ottawa and the Legislative Buildings at Winnipeg and Regina, have been preserved because of the symbolic roles their buildings have played. Others, like Butchart Gardens in Victoria and R.S. McLaughlin's elaborate Italianate gardens at Parkwood, which began in the social consciences of their owners, preserve a memory and a spectacular garden achievement. Still others, such as the Halifax Public Gardens, Mount Royal Park, and the Queen Victoria Gardens at Niagara Falls, have been sustained as public parks by the warm appreciation of their many visitors.

Some gardens have been restored as part of recognized historic sites. The surviving 1930s garden of the Prescott House at Starr's Point, Nova Scotia, for example, celebrates the tradition of the site's original resident, horticulturist Charles R. Prescott. The gardens complementing the Italianate-style Bellevue House in Kingston and the Palladian-style Grange in Toronto have been restored to historic periods. W.R. Motherwell's restored prairie homestead, including its gardens, near Abernethy, Saskatchewan, reflects the period 1910-12. Finally, private historic gardens have been preserved by the personal recognition, appreciation and care of owners. Most remain generally unknown but exceptional examples like the Fairfield House garden near Kingston, the walled "Maple Lawn" garden in Ottawa and the cottage garden at Inge-va in Perth, Ontario tell us of the importance of recognizing and protecting the small number of those whose integrity remains.

Historic garden preservation is obviously tied to the larger dimensions and momentum of the heritage preservation movement in Canada. At the same time, it is in its infancy compared to architectural preservation which, in the past decade, has gained widespread public recognition and acceptance. Historical studies, inventories and sound practical expertise in the technical aspects of garden preservation are needed in conjunction with wide public appreciation of the significance and pleasure of historic gardens in today's society if gardens are to be preserved to fulfill their role in Canada's built environment.

Susan Buggey
Chief, Historical Research
Prairie Region
Parks Canada

Picture Credits

Principal sources are credited under the following abbreviations:

CN	Canadian National Photographs
CPCA	Canadian Pacific Corporate Archives
MA	Manitoba Archives
NL	National Library of Canada
OA	Archives of Ontario
PAC	Public Archives of Canada
	Journals/Periodicals All photographs under these headings were taken by Bryan Evans
AGC	Agricultural Gazette of Canada
CF	Canadian Florist
CHG	Canadian Homes and Gardens
CH	Canadian Horticulturist
CLA	Country Life in America
FA	Farmer's Advocate
FW	The Farming World
QQ	Queen's Quarterly
RHSO	Annual Report of the Horticultural Societies of Ontario
WGPJ	Western Gardener and Poultry Journal

Half title Armand Dubé/Ministère du Loisir, de la Chasse et de la Pêche, Québec; 3 RHSO; 4 C117333/PAC; 5 Ph/340/Montreal/1760/PAC National Map Collection, by permission of the British Library; 6 left C23287/PAC, right C23553/PAC; 7 C26474/PAC; 8 C40792/PAC; 10 PA43301/PAC; 15 1491/CPCA; 16 above by permission of Vivian Hysop, below L12398/NL; 18 CH; 20 A1221/CPCA; 21 PA122675/PAC; 23 C8955/PAC; 24 PA66539/PAC; 26 13001/CPCA; 29 15380-58/OA; 31 50363-2/CN; 32 X38725-1/CN; 35 C30942/PAC; 38 CH; 39 both CH; 40 above FW, below PA136874/PAC; 41 S14672/OA; 43 QQ; 47 PA20924/PAC; 48 RHSO; 49 Ontario Department of Education, Bulletin #2, 1913; 50 Department of Agriculture, Pamphlet #4, 1917; 52 British Columbia Department of Education, Sessional Reports; 53 Quebec Department of Agriculture, Sessional Reports 1920; 55 top AGC, bottom Quebec Department of Agriculture, Sessional Reports 1915; 58 top AGC, bottom Quebec Department of Agriculture, Sessional Reports 1915; 59 *Rural Canada*; 60 AGC; 62 both AGC; 63 AGC; 67 Winnipeg Public Parks Board Annual Report, 1916; 68 PA9466/PAC; 69 CH; 70 PA87231/PAC; 72 PA32280/PAC; 73 top PA46142/PAC, bottom C30110/PAC; 75 RHSO; 76 PA48667/PAC; 78 top CH, bottom Quebec Department of Agriculture, Sessional Reports 1925; 79 AGC; 80 CH; 81 top PA40840/PAC, bottom CH; 83 C17797/PAC; 84 H2/340/Montreal/1905/PAC National Map Collection; 85 C70904/PAC; 86 PA9476/PAC; 87 left C30991/PAC, right RHSO; 88 PA31552/PAC; 89 CH; 90 PA9943/PAC; 91 AGC; 92 AGC; 93 AGC; 95 WGPJ; 97 AGC; 99 PA121666/PAC; 100 PA11360/PAC; 101 PA45895/PAC; 102 CH; 103 C1264/PAC; 104 PA86856/PAC; 107 RHSO; 109 top left CH, top right PA40463/PAC, bottom PA42808/PAC; 112 Canada, Department of Agriculture, Circular #40, 1916; 113 PA46073/PAC; 114 RHSO; 115 top CHG, bottom PA136937/PAC; 116 CLA; 117 CLA; 118 PA44684/PAC; 119 top RHSO, bottom CH; 121 CHG; 122 CHG; 123 PA9593/PAC; 124 top PA32168/PAC, bottom PA32173/PAC; 129 FA; 130 Belleville Nurseries catalogue; 131 Belleville Nurseries catalogue; 133 top WGPJ, bottom CH; 134 WGPJ; 136 PA136872/Ron Best/PAC; 137 PA136939/PAC; 138 Belleville Nurseries catalogue; 139 PA40948/PAC; 140 PA9903/PAC; 143 bottom CH; 145 Standard Cyclopaedia of Horticulture, vol. III; 149 CH; 150 CH; 151 CH; 156 C30043/PAC; 159 CF; 160 CH; 162 Pleasance Crawford, Royal Botanical Gardens collection; 165 PA136873/M.B. Davis/PAC; 166 PA137935/PAC; 167 PA136942/PAC; 168 MA; 170 OAC Review; 173 RHSO; 175 PA40949/PAC.

Bibliography

Selected Readings

Periodicals

In the course of the research for this book, a great variety of periodicals were consulted. Instead of listing all the articles consulted (which in many cases would constitute a lengthy index to the volumes), I will only note the titles of the most useful periodicals. Agricultural: *Agricultural Gazette of Canada; Canadian Countryman; Country Guide; Farmer's Advocate; Farmer's Magazine; Grain Growers' Guide; Journal of Agriculture and Horticulture,* Quebec; *Journal of Agriculture and Horticulture,* British Columbia; *Nor'West Farmer; Western Gardener and Beekeeper; Western Gardener and Poultry Journal.* Educational: *Rural Education Monthly,* New Brunswick; *Rural Education Monthly,* Saskatchewan. Gardening/Horticultural: *Annual Reports of the Horticultural Societies of Ontario; Canadian Florist; Canadian Homes and Gardens; Canadian Horticulturist; Canadian Horticultural Magazine; The Garden Beautiful Magazine; Gardening in British Columbia; Manitoba Horticulturist; Western Horticultural Society Reports.* Government: Sessional reports of the provincial agricultural and educational departments are extremely informative. Miscellaneous: *Canadian Municipal Journal; Canadian National Railways Magazine; Canadian Pacific Staff Bulletin; Maclean's; Queen's Quarterly.*

Books, Articles, Theses

Abel, P.M., "The Wildwood Was His Home," *Country Guide,* Feb. 1933, pp. 5, 25.

Allen, Richard, *The Social Passion: Religion and Social Reform in Canada 1914-28,* University of Toronto Press, Toronto, 1971.

Almey, R.J., "Annuals in Railway Gardens," *The Winnipeg Flower Garden,* Winnipeg Horticultural Society, Winnipeg, 1946, pp. 23-26.

Anderson, J.T.M., *The Education of the New Canadian,* J.M. Dent & Sons, Ltd., Toronto, 1918.

Appleton, Frank M., "The Butchart Gardens," *Horticulture,* April 1980, pp. 35-43.

Archer, John, comp., *Historic Saskatoon 1882-1947,* Junior Chamber of Commerce, Saskatoon, 1947.

Artibise, Alan F.J., *Winnipeg: A Social History of Urban Growth, 1874-1914,* McGill-Queen's University Press, Montreal, 1975.

Bailey, L.H., *The Nature Study Idea,* Doubleday and Page, New York, 1903.

——, *Standard Cyclopaedia of Horticulture,* Vol III, The Macmillan Co., New York, 1922.

Bassett, Thomas J., "Reaping on the Margins: A Century of Community Gardening in America," *Landscape,* 1981, pp. 1-8.

Baillie, C.K., "Canadian Grown Nursery Stock," *Annual Report of the Horticultural Societies of Ontario,* Toronto, 1926, pp. 42-45.

Beadle, Delos W., *Canadian Fruit, Flower and Kitchen Gardener . . .,* James Campbell and Son, Toronto, 1872.

Berral, Julia, *The Garden,* Penguin Books, London, 1966.

Bohi, Charles, *Canadian National's Western Depots: The Country Stations in Western Canada,* Railfare Enterprises Ltd., Toronto, 1977.

Bolduc, N.G., "The Waterloo Horticultural Society," *26th Annual Report of the Waterloo Historical Society, 1938,* Kitchener, 1939, pp. 12-16.

Boyd, F. Arthur W., *Railway Gardening on the Prairies: As Carried on by the*

Canadian Pacific Railway Company, B.A. Thesis, Ontario Agricultural College, Guelph, 1912.

Brittain, John, *Elementary Agriculture and Nature Study*, (New Brunswick edition), The Educational Book Co. Ltd., Toronto, 1909.

Brockway, Lucile H., *Science and Colonial Expansion: The Role of the British Royal Botanic Gardens*, Academic Press, New York, 1979.

Brodrick, F.W., *Trees, Flowers and Fruits for Manitoba*, Manitoba Farmer's Library, Extension Bulletin No. 29, Manitoba Department of Agriculture and Immigration, Winnipeg, 1918.

Brown, H.W., "History of the Kitchener Horticultural Society," *26th Annual Report of the Waterloo Horticultural Society, 1938*, Kitchener, 1939, pp. 6-12.

Brown, Robert Craig and Ramsay Cook, *Canada 1896-1921: A Nation Transformed*, McClelland and Stewart, Toronto, 1974.

Buck, F.E., *Beautified Homes and How the Farmer May Make Them*, Circular No. 40, Dominion Experimental Farms, Ottawa, 1916.

——, *Planning the Home Lot*, Circular No. 39, Dominion Experimental Farms, Ottawa, 1916.

Chadwick, George F., *The Park and the Town: Public Landscape in the 19th and 20th Centuries*, The Architectural Press, London, 1966.

Chalmers, John W., *Schools of the Foothills Province*, University of Toronto Press, Toronto, 1967.

Chicanot, E.L., "Beautifying a Railroad System," *Landscape Architecture*, April 1925, pp. 185-194.

Children's Gardening, Circular No. 13A, Ontario Department of Education, Toronto, 1913.

Chochla, Mark, "Port Arthur's Waverly Park: An Attempt at City Beautification," *Papers and Records*, Thunder Bay Historical Museum Society, 1977, pp. 24-31.

The City Improvement League of Montreal, *The First Year's Work*, Montreal, 1910.

The City of Winnipeg, Parks and Recreation Dept., *The History and Development of Assiniboine Park and Zoo in Winnipeg, Manitoba, Canada*, Winnipeg, 1972.

Clark, Samuel D., J. Paul Grayson and Linda Grayson, eds., *Prophecy and Protest: Social Movements in Twentieth-Century Canada*, Gage Educational Press, Ltd., Toronto, 1975.

Cochrane, Jean, *The One-Room School in Canada*, Fitzhenry & Whiteside, Toronto, 1981.

Collins, Louis, "A Dream of Beauty: The Halifax Public Gardens," *Canadian Antiques and Art Review*, June 1980, pp. 21-25.

Constantine, Stephen, "Amateur Gardening and Popular Recreation in the 19th and 20th Centuries," *Journal of Social History*, Spring 1981, pp. 387-406.

Cormack, Barbara Villy, *Perennials and Politics; the Life Story of Hon. Irene Parlby, LL.D.*, Professional Print., Sherwood Park, Alberta, 1968.

Cowley, R.H., "The Macdonald School Gardens," *Queen's Quarterly*, April 1905, pp. 391-419.

Craig, J.M., "Municipal Nurseries," *Second Annual Report of the Director of Agricultural Extension on the Work of the Horticultural Society of Saskatchewan, 1930*, Regina, 1930, pp. 56-58.

Cranz, Galen, *The Politics of Park Design: A History of Urban Parks in America*, MIT Press, Cambridge, Mass., 1982.

Crawford, Pleasance, *The Ontario Home Landscape: 1890-1914*, report prepared for the Department of Landscape Architecture, University of Toronto, Toronto, 1982.

——, "Some Early Niagara Peninsula Nurserymen," prepared for the Fifth Annual Niagara Peninsula History Conference, Brock University, St. Catharines, Ontario, April 16-17, 1983.

Cullen, Mary K., "The Late Nineteenth Century Development of the Queen Square Gardens, Charlottetown, Prince Edward Island," *APT Journal*, No. 3, 1977, pp. 1-20.

Cummings, H.R. and W.T. MacSkimming, *The City of Ottawa Public Schools: A Brief History*, Ottawa Board of Education, Ottawa, 1971.

Department of Education, British Columbia, *Instructions to Teachers and School Boards with Reference to School and Home Gardening*, Circular No. 4, Department of Education, Victoria, 1917.

——, *School Supervised Home-gardening and Home-project Work*, Circular No. 8, Victoria, 1921.

Derek, Clifford, *A History of Garden Design*, Faber and Faber, London, 1962.

de Wet, J.P., *A Hundred Years of Horticulture*, unpublished manuscript, ca. 1974/76.

Dodds, Philip F. and H.E. Markle, *The Story of Ontario Horticultural Societies, 1854-1973*, Picton Gazette Publishing Co., Picton, Ont., 1973.

Dominion Experimental Farm, *Fifty Years of Progress on Dominion Experimental Farms, 1886-1936*, Department of Agriculture, Ottawa, 1939.

Drysdale, Art, ed., *Canadian Nurseryman Centennial Yearbook*, Canadian Nurseryman, Ontario Nursery Trade Assoc., Burlington, Ont., 1967.

Report on the Agricultural Instruction Act, 1919-20, King's Printer, Ottawa, 1920.

Englehardt, H.A., *The Beauties of Nature Combined with Art*, John Lovell, Montreal, 1872.

Favretti, Rudy and Joy Putman Favretti, *Landscapes and Gardens for Historic Buildings: A Handbook for Reproducing and Creating Authenic Landscape Settings*, American Association for State and Local History, Nashville, 1978.

Fewster, Ernest P., *My Garden Dreams*, The Graphic Publishers, Ltd., Ottawa, 1926.

Fletcher, James, "The Value of Nature Study in Education," *Transactions of the Royal Society of Canada*, Second Series, Vol. VII, Section IV, Copp-Clark, Toronto, 1901, pp. 151-59.

Garland, Aileen, "Gardens Along the Right of Way," *Manitoba Pageant*, Winter 1977, pp. 5-7.

Gayman, Harvey M., comp., *Rittenhouse School and Gardens*, Jordan Harbour, Lincoln County, Ontario, William Briggs, Toronto, 1911.

Gibson, Edward M.W., *The Impact of Social Belief on Landscape Change . . .,"* Ph.D. Thesis, University of British Columbia, Vancouver, 1971.

Gorer, Richard, *The Flower Garden in England*, B.T. Batsford Ltd., London, 1975.

Granatstein, J.L., Irving M. Abella, David J. Bercuson, R. Craig Brown, and H. Blair Neatby, *Twentieth Century Canada*, McGraw-Hill Ryerson Ltd., Toronto, 1983.

Green, M. Louise, *Among School Gardens*, Charities Publications Committee, New York, 1910.

Hagedoorn, A.L., *Plant Breeding*, Crosby Lockwood & Son Ltd., London, 1950.

Harper, J. Russell, "Loyalist Gardens," *The Maritime Advocate and Busy East*, Feb. 1955, pp. 5-10.

Harvey, Robert, *Pioneers of Manitoba*, Prairie Publishing Co., Winnipeg, 1970.

Howitt, M.H., *Beautifying the Home Grounds of Canada*, published jointly by Department of Agriculture, Ottawa and the Canadian Horticultural Council, Ottawa, 1930.

Hutt, H.L., "The Civic Improvement Movement in Ontario," *Canadian Horticulturist*, Dec. 1908, pp. 261-62 and Jan. 1909, p. 5.

Huxley, Anthony, *An Illustrated History of Gardening*, Paddington Press Ltd., New York and London, 1978.

Jack, Annie, *The Canadian Garden: A Pocket Help for the Amateur*, Musson, Toronto, 1910.

Kerr, Don and Stan Hanson, *Saskatoon: The First Half-Century*, NeWest, Edmonton, 1982.

Lawr, Douglas, *Development of Agricultural Education in Ontario, 1870-1910*, Ph.D. Thesis, University of Toronto, Toronto, 1972.

LeMoine, James M., *Maple Leaves: Canadian History and Quebec Scenery*, Series 3, Quebec, 1865.

Lochhead, William, *Outlines of Nature Studies*, Bulletin No. 142, Ontario Agricultural College and Experimental Farm, Macdonald Institute, Guelph, 1905.

Lowenthal, David and Hugh C. Prince, "English Landscape Tastes," *Geographical Review*, April 1965, pp. 186-222.

McCready, S.B., *Gardening for Schools*, Bulletin No. 152, Ontario Department of Agriculture, Ontario Agricultural College, Macdonald Institute, Guelph, 1906.

——, "Report of the Director of Elementary Agriculture for Ontario: A Survey of the Work Carried on in Ontario in 1911," *The Report of the Department of Education, Sessional Papers of the Province of Ontario*, Vol. XLV, Part VI, Toronto, 1913, pp. 226-40.

——, "Rural Education in Ontario," *The Canadian Forum*, July 1933, pp. 376-78.

——, "Adventures of a Schoolmaster," *Western Ontario Historical Notes*, Dec. 1951, pp. 130-41.

MacGregor, James G., *Edmonton: A History*, M.G. Hurtig Publishers, Edmonton, 1967.

McIntyre, A., "The Decoration of School Grounds," *Report of the Fifth Annual Meeting 1902*, Western Horticultural Society, Winnipeg, 1902. pp. 91-100.

MacKee, William C., *The History of the Vancouver Parks System 1886-1929*, M.A. Thesis, University of Victoria, 1972.

McNeil, Robert, *Practical Tests on Gardening for Manitoba and North-West Territories*, Wilson Brothers, Winnipeg, 1884.

Macoun, W.T., "Experiences of Horticultural Research in Canada — Centralized," *Proceedings of the First Imperial Horticultural Conference*, London, 1930, pp. 19-23.

——, *Garden Making on Vacant Lots and the Home Vegetable Garden*, Circular No. 13, Department of Agriculture, Ottawa, 1917.

——, "Plant Breeding in Canada," *The Journal of Heredity*, Sept. 1915, pp. 398-403.

Madill, A.J., *History of Agricultural Education in Ontario*, University of Toronto Press, Toronto, 1930.

Major, Marjorie, *From the Ground . . . The Story of Planting in Nova Scotia*, Petheric Press, Ltd., Halifax, 1981.

Martin, Linda and Kerry Segrave, *City Parks of Canada*, Mosaic Press, Oakville, Ont., 1983.

Mawson, Thomas H., *The Life and Work of an English Landscape Architect: The Autobiography of Thomas H. Mawson*, Charles Schribners, New York, 1927.

Meek, M.A., *The History of the City Beautiful Movement in Canada 1890-1930*, M.A. Thesis, University of British Columbia, Vancouver, 1979.

Miller, James Collins, *Rural Schools in Canada: Their Organization, Administration and Supervision*, Teachers College, Columbia University, New York, 1913.

Minhinnick, Jeanne, *At Home in Upper Canada*, Clarke, Irwin & Co. Ltd., Toronto, 1970.

Moore, George, *Semi-Tropical Bedding and Carpet Gardening*, Montreal, 1888.

Morgan, F. Cleveland, "Rock Gardening in the Province of Quebec," *Report of the Conference Held by the Royal Horticultural Society and the Alpine Garden Society*, London, 1936.

Murray, A.L., "Frederick Law Olmsted and the Design of Mount Royal Park, Montreal," *Journal of the Society of Architectural Historians*, Oct. 1967, pp. 167-71.

Newton, Norman T., *Design on the Land: The Development of Landscape Architecture*, Harvard University Press, Cambridge, Mass., 1971.

Niven, Frederick J., *A Lady in the Wilderness, A Tale of the Yukon . . .*, reprinted from the *Canadian Home Journal*, printed by Farwest, 1930/31.

The Organization, Achievements and Present Work of the Experimental Farms, Department of Agriculture, Ottawa, 1924.

Ottawa Horticultural Society, *Ottawa, A City of Gardens*, prepared by R.B. Whyte, W.T. Macoun, F.E. Buck, J.B. Spencer, Ottawa, 1916.

Patmore, H.L., "The Nursery Trade, Its Supply and Requirements," *Manitoba Horticulturist*, July 1915, pp. 52-55.

Patterson, R.S., J. Chalmers and J. Friesen, *Profiles of Canadian Education*, D.C. Heath Canada Ltd. 1974.

Perkins, Dorothy, *Canadian Garden Book*, Thomas Allen Publishers, Toronto, 1918.

Pomeroy, Elsie, *William Saunders and His Five Sons*, Ryerson Press, Toronto, 1956.

Prentice, Alison, *The School Promoters: Education and Social Class in Mid-Nineteenth Century Upper Canada*, McClelland and Stewart, Toronto, 1977.

Rawlings, W.S., comp., *Handbook of Parks, Playgrounds and Bathing Beaches*, Board of Park Commissioners, Vancouver, 1925.

Roadhouse, W.B., *Rural School Fairs*, Reprinted from the *Annual Report of the Ontario Experimental Union*, Guelph, 1916.

Robertson, James W., "Education for Agriculture," Address delivered before the Members of the Legislature of New Brunswick, Fredericton, May 1908, Department of Agriculture, Bulletin No. 1, New Brunswick, 1908.

Rutherford, Paul, *The Making of the Canadian Media*, McGraw-Hill Ryerson Ltd., Toronto, 1978.

——, ed., *Saving the Canadian City: The First Phase 1880-1920*, University of Toronto Press, Toronto, 1974.

——, "Tomorrow's Metropolis: The Urban Reform Movement in Canada, 1880-1920," *The Canadian City: Essays in Urban History*, Gilbert A. Stelter and Alan F.J. Artibise, eds., Macmillan of Canada, Toronto, 1979, pp. 368-92.

——, *A Victorian Authority: The Daily Press in Late Nineteenth-Century Canada*, University of Toronto Press, Toronto, 1982.

Saskatchewan Department of Education, *The School Garden*, Circular No. 6, Regina, 1916.

——, *Seed Catalogue for School Gardens*, Circular No. 4, Regina, 1915.

Saunders, R.M., "The First Introduction of European Plants and Animals in Canada," *Canadian Historical Review*, Dec. 1935, pp. 388-406.

Schmitt, Peter J., *Back to Nature: The Arcadian Myth in Urban America, 1900-1930*, Oxford University Press, New York, 1969.

Seaton, Beverly, "The Garden Autobiography," *Garden History*, Spring 1979.

Shortt, S.E.D., *The Search for an Ideal: Six Canadian Intellectuals and Their Convictions in an Age of Transition 1890-1930*, University of Toronto Press, Toronto, 1976.

Skinner, Frank L., *Horticultural Horizons: Plant Breeding and Introducing at Dropmore, Manitoba*, Manitoba Department of Agriculture, Winnipeg, ca. 1967.

Slate, George L. and D.F. Cameron, "Isabella Preston, 1881-1965," *The Lily Yearbook*, North American Lily Society, New York, 1966, pp. 106-110.

Sloane, Susan, "Le Park de Métis," *Horticulture*, June 1979, pp. 40-45.

Snell, John Ferguson, *Macdonald College of McGill University, A History from 1904-1955*, McGill University Press, Montreal, 1963.

Spencer, J.B. ed., *The School Garden as Regarded and Carried on in the Different Provinces*, Pamphlet No. 4, Department of Agriculture, Ottawa, 1916.

——, ed., *Vacant Lot Gardening in 1917*, Pamphlet No. 6, Department of Agriculture, Ottawa, 1917.

Stamp, Robert M., *The Schools of Ontario*, 1876-1976, University of Toronto Press, Toronto, 1982.

Steeves, R.P., *The School Garden — Its Purpose — Its Care During Vacation*, New Brunswick, Department of Agriculture, ca. 1917.

Stelter, Gilbert and Alan F.J. Artibise, eds., *The Canadian City: Essays in Urban History*, Macmillan of Canada, Toronto, 1979.

Stewart, John, "Canada's Landscape Heritage," *Landscape Planning*, 1979, pp. 205-24.

—— and Susan Buggey, "Canada's Living Past — Historic Landscapes and Gardens," *Ontario Association of Landscape Architects Review*, Aug. 1976, pp. 6-13.

Stilgoe, John R., "The Railroad Beautiful: Landscape Architecture and the Railroad Gardening Movement, 1867-1930," Landscape Journal, Fall 1982, pp. 57-66.

Stothers, Robert, *A Biographical Memorial to Robert Henry Cowley, 1859-1927*, Thomas Nelson & Sons, Ltd., Toronto, 1935.

Sutherland, Neil, *Children in English-Canadian Society: Framing the Twentieth-Century Consensus*, University of Toronto Press, Toronto, 1976.

Van Nus, Walter, "The Fate of City Beautiful in Canada, 1893-1930," *The Canadian City: Essays in Urban History*, Gilbert A. Stelter and Alan F.J. Artibise, eds., Macmillan of Canada, Toronto, 1979, pp. 162-85.

Van Ravensway, Charles, *A Nineteenth-Century Garden*, Universe Books, New York, 1977.

Vaughan, Walter, *The Life and Work of Sir William Van Horne*, The Century Co., New York, 1920.

von Baeyer, Edwinna, *A Preliminary Bibliography for Garden History in Canada*, Parks Canada, Ottawa, 1983.

Vrugtman, Ina, "Preliminary Listing of 19th Century Canadian Nurseries, Seed Businesses and Florists," Royal Botanical Gardens, Hamilton, 1981.

Walker, John, "The Canadian Pacific Railway Company," *Development of Horticulture on the Canadian Prairies, A Historical Review*, Western Canadian Society for Horticulture, 1956.

Warren, W.H., "Paradise: The Butchart Gardens," *Garden*, July/Aug. 1978, pp. 14-15.

Way, Ronald W., *Ontario's Niagara Parks: A History*, Niagara Parks Commission, Niagara, 1946.

Weaver, John C., "The Modern City Realized: Toronto Civic Affairs, 1880-1915," *The Usable Urban Past: Planning and Politics in the Modern Canadian City*, Stelter, Gilbert A., and Alan F.J. Artibise, eds., Macmillan of Canada, Toronto, 1979, pp. 39-72.

——, " 'Tomorrow's Metropolis' Revisited: A Critical Assessment of Urban Reform in Canada, 1890-1920," *The Canadian City: Essays in Urban History*,

Gilbert A. Stelter and Alan F.J. Artibise, eds., Macmillan of Canada, Toronto, 1979, pp. 393-418.

Western Canadian Society for Horticulture, comp., *Development of Horticulture on the Canadian Prairies: A Historical Review*, 1956.

Wilson, J. Donald, Robert M. Stamp, Louis-Phillipe Audet, eds., *Canadian Education: A History*, Prentice-Hall of Canada, Scarborough, Ont., 1970.

Winslow, R.M., *Hints on Caring for School Gardens*, Circular No. 4, B.C. Department of Agriculture, Victoria, 1913.

Yates, Mary, "Informal Planting of the Home Grounds," *Annual Report of the Horticultural Societies of Ontario*, Toronto, 1915, pp. 29-35.

Unpublished sources

Isabella Preston's papers, Royal Botanical Gardens Library, Hamilton, Ont.

Interviews: A.R. Buckley, D.F. Cameron, Marjorie Nazer and David Myles.

Agricultural Instruction Act papers, PAC, RG 17.

Endnotes

Chapter One

[1]R.M. Saunders, "The First Introduction of European Plants and Animals in Canada," *Canadian Historical Review*, Dec. 1935, p. 339.
[2]Ibid., p.402.
[3]Ibid., p. 402.
[4]John Stewart, "Canada's Landscape Heritage, "*Landscape Planning*, Aug. 1979, p. 213; N. Metzler, *Illustrated Halifax*, John McConniff, Montreal, 1891, p. 67.
[5]J.M. LeMoine, *Maple Leaves: Canadian History and Quebec Scenery*, Hunter, Rose and Co., Quebec, 1965, pp. 64-136.
[6]Ibid., p. 94.
[7]Jean Minhinnick, *At Home in Upper Canada*, Clarke, Irwin and Co., Toronto, 1970, p. 2.
[8]Ibid., p. 15.
[9]John Stewart and Susan Buggey, "Canada's Living Past," *Ontario Association of Landscape Architects Review*, Aug. 1976, p. 9.
[10]Minhinnick, p. 14.
[11]Robert Brown and Ramsay Cook, *Canada 1896-1921: A Nation Transformed*, McClelland and Stewart, Toronto, 1974, pp. 3-4.
[12]Ibid., p. 2.
[13]Paul Rutherford, "Tomorrow's Metropolis: the Urban Reform Movement in Canada, 1880-1920," in G. Stelter and A. Artibise, *The Canadian City: Essays in Urban History*, Macmillan, Toronto, 1975, p. 39.
[14]S. Clark, J. Grayson, and L. Grayson, eds., *Prophecy and Protest: Social Movements in Twentieth-Century Canada*, Gage Educational Press, Toronto, 1975, p. 39.
[15]Ibid., pp. 40-43.
[16]Paul Rutherford, ed., *Saving the Canadian City: the First Phase 1880-1920*, University of Toronto Press, Toronto, 1974, p. xi. In 1913, *The Canadian Municipal Journal* listed 90 civic organizations which were directly or indirectly involved in programs of "civic uplift."
[17]Rutherford, "Tomorrow's Metropolis. . .," p. 382.

Chapter Two

[1]Robert Harvey, *Pioneers of Manitoba*, Prairie Publishing Co., Winnipeg, 1970, pp. 11-12.
[2]Aileen Garland, "Gardens Along the Right of Way," *Manitoba Pageant*, Winter 1977, pp. 6-7.
[3]H.J. Morgan, *The Canadian Men and Women of the Time: A Handbook of Canadian Biography of Living Characters*, Second Edition, William Briggs, Toronto, 1912, p. 355.
[4]An article in the May 1908 *Canadian Municipal Journal* claims Dunlop began his seed distribution in 1897, while later accounts in the *CPR Staff Bulletin* in 1925 state that distribution began in 1890.
[5]E.L. Chicanot, "Beautifying a Railroad System," *Landscape Architecture*, April 1925, p. 187.
[6]"The Flower Man," *Canadian Municipal Journal*, June 1922, p. 109.
[7]"A Railway Floral Department," *Canadian Municipal Journal*, May 1908, p. 187.
[8]Ibid., p. 187.
[9]Ibid., p. 187.
[10]Ibid., p. 187.
[11]Ibid., p. 186.
[12]Ibid., p. 186.
[13]Ibid., p. 186.
[14]Ibid., pp. 186-87.
[15]Chicanot, p. 190.
[16]F. Arthur Boyd, *Railway Gardening on the Prairie: As Carried on by the Canadian Pacific Railway Company*, B.A. Thesis, Ontario Agricultural College, Guelph, 1912, p. 4.
[17]*Railway and Shipping World*, Dec. 1900, pp. 383-84.
[18]"Civic Improvement," *Canadian Horticulturist*, May 1903, pp. 188-90.
[19]"Civic Improvement," p. 190, and Boyd, p. 12.
[20]"Railway Floral Department," p. 187.
[21]Boyd, pp. 12-13.
[22]"Station Grounds that Serve as City Parks," *Park and Cemetery and Landscape Gardening*, April 1912, p. 45, 46.
[23]Ibid., p. 45, 46.
[24]Boyd, p. 13.
[25]John Walker, "The Canadian Pacific Railway Company," *Development of Horticulture on the Canadian Prairies, a Historical Review*, Western Canadian Society for Horticulture, 1956, p. 49.
[26]Boyd, pp. 4-6.
[27]Plant distribution — verified plant lists of material used until 1917 (collected from various sources, including Boyd). Deciduous trees: Manitoba maple, cottonwood, Russian poplar, balsam poplar, Russian golden willow, Russian red willow, laurel leafed willow, acute leafed willow, American elm, native ash. Coniferous trees: native white spruce, Colorado blue spruce, Scotch pine. Ornamental shrubs: lilac, caragana, flowering currant, honeysuckle, spirea, dogwood, sand cherry, western or ornamental crab, ginnale maple, buffalo berry, golden leafed elder. Annuals: cannas, alternanthera, coleus, salvia, castor bean plant, caladium, alyssum, celosia, petunia, aster, pansy, marigold, poppy, geranium.
[28]Boyd, p. 25.
[29]"How the C.P.R. Helps Beautify Canada," *The Garden Beautiful Magazine*, July 1938, p. 7.
[30]"Railway Floral Department,' p. 186.

[31]"Report of the London Society for 1908," *Annual Report of the Horticultural Societies of Ontario*, Toronto, 1908, p. 112.
[32]"Echoes of the Horticultural Society's Convention," *Farmer's Advocate*, March 26, 1914, p. 599.
[33]Boyd, p. 22.
[34]Ibid., p. 21.
[35]"Landscape Work at C.P.R. Stations," *Canadian Florist*, June 29, 1917, p. 110.
[36]G.C. Bramhill, "C.P.R. Station Gardens," *OAC Review*, March 1913, p. 29.
[37]"How the C.P.R. . . .," p. 6.
[38]*CPR Staff Bulletin*, Feb. 1922, p. 8.
[39]"Floral Supplies," *CPR Staff Bulletin*, March 1917, p. 6.
[40]B.M. Winegar, "Railways and Horticulture," *Annual Report of the Horticultural Societies of Ontario*, Toronto, 1921, p. 20.
[41]"Floral Supplies," p. 6.
[42]G.A.B. Krook, "A Few Hints to Canadian Pacific Amateur Gardeners," *CPR Staff Bulletin*, April 1918, p. 8.
[43]"How the C.P.R. . . .," p. 6.
[44]"A Prize Winning Garden," *Canadian Horticulturist*, May 1918, p. 118.
[45]*CPR Staff Bulletin*, July 1924, p. 14.
[46]"How the C.P.R. . . .," p. 8.
[47]J.R. Almey, "Annuals in Railway Gardens," *The Winnipeg Flower Garden*, Winnipeg Horticultural Society, Winnipeg, 1946, p. 23.
[48]*Montreal Star*, April 28, 1921.
[49]*CPR Staff Bulletin*, May 1940.
[50]Ibid.
[51]Winegar, p. 19.
[52]*CPR Staff Bulletin*, June 1921, p. 10.
[53]Post 1917 list of plant material, seeds and bulbs compiled from agent's reports in the *CPR Staff Bulletin* and articles written by the Floral Committee. Trees: ash, beech, Carolina, Russian and Lombardy poplars, catalpa, cedar, dogwood, elm, hard, soft and Manitoba maples, jack pine, laurel, locust, Norway spruce, red pine, Scotch pine, sumac. Shrubs: *Berberis purpurea*, *Berberis thunbergi*, bush honeysuckle, carragana, deutzia, golden elder, hydrangea, Japanese rose, Japanese tamarac, lilac, *Philadelphus coronarius*, rose hybrids, *Rosa rugosa*, silver elder, *Spirea opulifolia aurea*, *Spirea van Houtii*, sweet briar, viburnum, *Wiegelia rosea*, willows. Perennials: achillea, aquilegia, bleeding heart, *Campanula carpatica*, campanula medium, clematis, delphinium, English daisy, forget-me-not, foxglove, gaillardia, golden glow, gypsophylla, hollyhock, hops, iris, larkspur, lychnis, peony, phlox, pinks/sweet William, poppy, shasta daisy, tiger lily, Virginia creeper, wild cucumber vine. Bulbs: tulips. Annuals: achyranthes, African daisy, antirrhinum, aster, balsam, begonia, calendula, California poppy, candytuft, canna, carnation, castor oil plant, chrysanthemum, clarkia, coleus, cornflower, cosmos, dahlia, dracaena, dusty miller, everlasting, four o'clock, geranium, gladiolus, helianthus, heliotrope, kochia, lavatera, lobelia, marigold, mignonette, morning glory, nasturtium, pansy, portulaca, saleroi, salpiglossis, salvia, scabiosa, stock, sunflower, sweet alyssum, sweet pea, verbena, zinnia.

Chapter Three

[1]Douglas Lawr, *Development of Agricultural Education in Ontario, 1870-1910*, Ph.D. Thesis, University of Toronto, 1972; or John MacDougall, *Rural Life in Canada*, Westminster Co., Toronto, 1913.
[2]S.E.D. Shortt, *The Search for an Ideal: Six Canadian Intellectuals and Their Convictions in an Age of Transition 1890-1930*, University of Toronto Press, Toronto, 1976; see the Introduction.
[3]Paul Rutherford, "Tomorrow's Metropolis: the Urban Reform Movement in Canada, 1880-1920," in G. Stelter and A. Artibise, eds., *The Canadian City: Essays in Urban History*, Macmillan, Toronto, 1979, p. 371.
[4]Neil Sutherland, *Children in English-Canadian Society: Framing the Twentieth-Century Consensus*, University of Toronto Press, Toronto, 1976, p. 156.
[5]Robert M. Stamp, *The Schools of Ontario, 1876-1976*, University of Toronto Press, Toronto, 1982, p. 53.
[6]L.H. Bailey, *The Nature Study Idea*, Doubleday and Page, New York, 1903, and Peter J. Schmitt, *Back to Nature: The Arcadian Myth in Urban America, 1900-1930*, Oxford University Press, New York, 1969.
[7]R.H. Cowley, "The Macdonald School Gardens," *Queen's Quarterly*, April 1905, pp. 393-97.
[8]S.B. McCready, *Gardening for Schools*, Ontario Agricultural College, Macdonald Institute, Guelph, Dec. 1906, p. 23.
[9]William Lochhead, "School Gardens," *Canadian Horticulturist*, July 1903, p. 276.
[10]McCready, p. 4.
[11]*The Canadian Horticultural Magazine*, Jan. 1898, p. 299.
[12]G.R. Patullo, "Beautifying School Grounds," *Canadian Horticulturist*, Jan. 1903, p. 39.
[13]"Notes from Horticultural Societies: Paris, Ontario," *Canadian Horticulturist*, Feb. 1903, p. 81.
[14]Cowley, pp. 400-02, 415-18.
[15]Ibid., p. 403, 410-15.
[16]Ibid., p. 401.
[17]Ibid., p. 416.
[18]Ibid., p. 416.
[19]Ibid., p. 401.
[20]See discussions in Cowley.
[21]M. Louise Green, *Among School Gardens*, Charities Publications Committee, New York, 1910, p. 326.
[22]Cowley, p. 399.
[23]J.W. Robertson, in Green, p. 335.
[24]Cowley, p. 406.
[25]Ibid., p. 406.
[26]Ibid., p. 408.
[27]R.B. Whyte, "Interest the Child in Horticulture," *Canadian Horticulturist*, Jan. 1907, p. 6.
[28]*Elementary Agriculture and Horticulture and School Gardens in Village and Rural Schools — Explanatory and Descriptive Circular*, Circular 13, Ontario Department of Education, Toronto, 1907, p. 179.
[29]Ibid., p. 182.
[30]Ibid., pp. 182-83.
[31]Ibid., p. 177.
[32]Ibid., p. 17.
[33]McCready, p. 3.
[34]Harvey M. Gayman, comp., *Rittenhouse School and Gardens*, Jordan Harbor, Lincoln County, Ontario, William Briggs, Toronto, 1911, p. 32.
[35]Ibid., p. 41.
[36]Circular 13, 1913, pp. 6-9.
[37]Stamp, p. 71.
[38]Mrs. R.B. Potts, "School Children and Horticulture," *Annual Report of the Horticultural Societies of Ontario*, Toronto, 1915, p. 55.
[39]*The Agricultural Instruction Act*, Department of Agriculture, Ottawa, 1913, p. 7.
[40]Ibid., p. 10.
[41]Letter from James Duff to Martin Burrell, May 29, 1913, PAC, RG 17,

Vol. 2779, File 229666A.

[42]Robert C. Brown and Ramsay Cook, *Canada 1896-1921: A Nation Transformed*, McClelland and Stewart, Toronto, 1974, pp. 198-99.

[43]O.J. Stevenson, *Country Life Reader*, George J. McLeod, Toronto, 1924, p. 56.

[44]John W. Chalmers, *Schools of the Foothills Province*, University of Toronto Press, Toronto, 1967, p. 133.

[45]"School Gardening: Manitoba," *Agricultural Gazette of Canada*, Jan. 1915, p. 56.

[46]"The Variation in Elementary Courses in Agriculture," *Agricultural Gazette of Canada*, April 1918, p. 376.

[47]Ibid., p. 376.

[48]S.B. McCready, "Report of the Director of Elementary Agriculture for Ontario: A Survey of the Work Carried on in Ontario in 1911," *The Report of the Department of Education, Sessional Papers of the Province of Ontario*, Vol. XLV, Part VI, Toronto, 1913, p. 236.

[49]"Farmers and Education," *Rural Education Monthly*, Sussex, New Brunswick, April 1918, p. 3.

[50]*Rural Education Monthly*, Sussex, New Brunswick, June 1917, p. 1.

[51]Lawr, pp. 1, 241.

[52]Ibid., pp. 1, 241.

[53]Ibid., p. 149.

[54]"Rural School Fairs: South Saskatchewan," *Agricultural Gazette of Canada*, Jan. 1918, p. 69.

[55]W.B. Roadhouse, *Rural School Fairs*, reprinted from the *Annual Report of the Ontario Experimental Union*, Guelph, 1916, p. 6.

[56]"Agriculture in Schools: Quebec," *Agricultural Gazette of Canada*, Feb. 1915, p. 142.

[57]Jean Cochrane, *The One-Room School in Canada*, Fitzhenry and Whiteside, Toronto, 1981, p. 98.

[58]"Home and School Gardening," *Agricultural Gazette of Canada*, March 1917, p. 230.

[59]See discussion in *Instructions to Teachers and School Boards with Reference to School and Home Gardening*, Circular No. 4, B.C. Department of Education, Victoria, 1917.

[60]"Patriotism and Production," *Rural Education Monthly*, Nov. 1917, p. 1.

[61]S.B. McCready, "Horticulture in Our Schools," *Annual Report of the Horticultural Societies of Ontario*, Toronto, 1919, p. 56.

[62]"Report of the Horticulturist," *Report of the Department of Agriculture for the Year of 1920*, Quebec, 1921, p. 133.

[63]"Agricultural Instruction in Elementary Schools," *Agricultural Gazette of Canada*, Nov.-Dec. 1922, p. 522.

[64]See discussion in Brown and Cook, Chapters 15 and 16.

[65]See summation in Richard Allen, *The Social Passion: Religion and Social Reform in Canada, 1914-28*, University of Toronto Press, Toronto, 1971.

[66]Letter from Minister of Agriculture to R.W. Neely, Secretary of the Canadian Society of Technical Agriculturists, Feb. 12, 1924, PAC, RG 17, Vol. 2896, File 18-1 part 1.

[67]Sutherland, pp. 221-22.

Chapter Four

[1]George Champion, "What Horticulture Means to Winnipeg," *Manitoba Horticulturist*, May 1915, p. 35.

[2]Norman T. Newton, *Design on the Land: The Development of Landscape Architecture*, Harvard University Press, Cambridge, 1971, p. 367.

[3]Walter Van Nus, "The Fate of City Beautiful in Canada, 1893-1930," in G. Stelter and A. Artibise, eds., *The Canadian City: Essays in Urban History*, Macmillan, Toronto, 1977, p. 165.

[4]Newton, p. 415.

[5]Van Nus, p. 165.

[6]Don Kerr and Stan Hanson, *Saskatoon: The First Half Century*, NeWest, Edmonton, 1982, p. 36.

[7]Paul Rutherford, "Tomorrow's Metropolis: The Urban Reform Movement in Canada, 1880-1920," in Stelter and Artibise, p. 373.

[8]Van Nus, p. 166.

[9]Ibid., p. 166.

[10]See M.A. Meek, *The History of the City Beautiful Movement in Canada, 1890-1930*, M.A. Thesis, University of British Columbia, 1979, and the Van Nus article for a general discussion of City Beautiful history and thought.

[11]H.J. Snelgrove, "President's Address," *Annual Report of the Horticultural Societies of Ontario*, Toronto, 1909, p. 12.

[12]T.H. Race, "The Horticultural Society," *Canadian Horticulturist*, May 1904, p. 190.

[13]H.L. Hutt, "The Civic Improvement Movement in Ontario," *Canadian Horticulturist*, Jan. 1909, p. 5.

[14]Ibid., p. 5.

[15]Ibid., p. 5.

[16]H.L. Hutt, "How to Make Work of Horticultural Societies Effective," *Canadian Horticulturist*, Dec. 1909, p. 264.

[17]The City Improvement League of Montreal, *The First Year's Work*, Montreal, 1910, p. 21.

[18]"Work of the Hamilton City Improvement Society," *Canadian Horticulturist*, April 1903, p. 157.

[19]Eben E. Rexford, "Our Village Improvement Society: A Hint for Our Horticultural Societies," *Canadian Horticulturist*, Oct. 1901, pp. 435-6.

[20]H.L. Hutt, "The Civic Improvement Movement in Ontario," *Canadian Horticulturist*, Dec. 1908, p. 55.

[21]Jane Walker, "Trade Talk," *The Commentator*, Saskatoon, April 7, 1982. p. 2.

[22]George Champion, "Street Tree Planting and Boulevarding in Winnipeg," *Canadian Horticulturist*, Feb. 1910, p. 31.

[23]Ibid., p. 32.

[24]Ibid., p. 31.

[25]"City Street Shade Trees," *Canadian Horticulturist*, April 1901, p. 43.

[26]D.P. Penhallow, "Shade Trees for Our Cities, *Canadian Horticulturist*, April 1907, p. 86.

[27]Ibid., p. 86-7.

[28]Champion, "What Horticulture means. . .," p. 36.

[29]J.B. Spencer, "Street Trees and Their Relation to Horticulture," *Annual Report of the Horticultural Societies of Ontario*, Toronto 1923, p. 14.

[30]Ibid., p. 14.

[31]"Street Trees — How Citizens Can Help," *Canadian Municipal Journal*, Sept. 1921, p. 237.

[32]Henry J. Moore, "Report of the Committee on Tree Planting," *Annual Report of the Horticultural Societies of Ontario*, Toronto, 1928, p. 9.

[33]Charles Chambers, "Address," *Annual Report of the Horticultural Societies of Ontario*, Toronto, 1929, pp. 51-2.

[34]Frank Bennett, "How the St. Thomas Horticultural Society Became the Largest in the Province," *Annual Report of the Horticultural Societies of Ontario*,

Toronto, 1913, p. 117.
[35]*Annual Report of the Horticultural Societies of Ontario*, Toronto, 1913, p. 18.
[36]*Annual Report of the Horticultural Societies of Ontario*, Toronto, 1915, p. 22.
[37]"Eyesores Give Way to Beauty Spots," *Annual Report of the Horticultural Societies of Ontario*, Toronto, 1926, p. 56.
[38]Bennett, p. 118.
[39]"The Little Gardeners of Hamilton," *Canadian Horticulturist*, Nov. 1902, p. 472.
[40]"Beautifying the Church Grounds with Gardens," *Western Gardener and Poultry Journal*, Aug. 1920, p. 324.
[41]Frank Bennett, "Another Pioneer Horticultural Society," *Western Gardener and Poultry Journal*, Jan. 1921, p. 6.
[42]A. McIntyre, "The Decoration of School Grounds," *Report of the Fifth Annual Meeting, 1902, of the Western Horticultural Society*, Winnipeg, 1902, p. 91.
[43]G.R. Patullo, "Beautifying School Grounds," *Canadian Horticulturist*, Jan. 1903, p. 39.
[44]*Canadian Horticulturist*, May 1904, p. 218.
[45]"Arbor Day Observance," *Rural Education Monthly*, New Brunswick, April 1916, pp. 203.
[46]"A Few Interesting Experiences," *The Saskatchewan Rural Education Monthly*, Nov. 1917, p. 4.
[47]J. MacKay, "Beautification of Rural Schools," *Agricultural Gazette of Canada*, March 1916, p. 271.
[48]Adrian Desautels, "Beautifying the Rural School," *Journal of Agriculture and Horticulture*, March 1928, p. 131.
[49]*Rural Education Monthly*, New Brunswick, Nov. 1925, p. 1.
[50]W.S. Dinnick, "Town and City Back Yard Development," *Annual Report of the Horticultural Societies of Ontario*, Toronto, 1914, p. 117.
[51]A.B. Warburton, "Tree Planting in Charlottetown, P.E.I.," *Canadian Horticulturist*, Feb. 1910, p. 38.
[52]Hutt, "The Civic. . .," p. 212.
[53]"The Back Yard Beautiful," *Canadian Horticulturist*, June 1903, p. 150.
[54]E.T. Cook, "Beauty and Economy in Home Surroundings," *Annual Report of the Horticultural Societies of Ontario*, Toronto, 1914, p. 66.
[55]Dinnick, p. 66.
[56]Bennett, "Another. . .," p. 7.
[57]"Corner Rockeries in Cities," *Canadian Horticulturist*, June, 1905, pp. 264-5.
[58]"Work of the Civic Improvement Society of Hamilton," *Canadian Horticulturist*, Dec. 1903, p. 326.
[59]S. Short, "The Ottawa Garden Competitions," *Canadian Horticulturist*, Jan. 1907, p. 18.
[60]R.B. Whyte, "President's Address," *Annual Report of the Horticultural Societies of Ontario*, Toronto, 1912, p. 8.
[61]John Taylor, "A Capitalist Plans the Capitol," paper read at the Canadian Historical Association annual meeting, Ottawa, June 1982, p. 5.
[62]George F. Chadwick, *The Park and the Town: Public Landscape in the 19th and 20th Centuries*, The Architectural Press, London, 1966, p. 19.
[63]Ibid., p. 19.
[64]Newton, p. 268.
[65]Ibid., p. 267.
[66]A.L. Murray, "Frederick Law Olmsted and the Design of Mount Royal Park, Montreal," *Journal of the Society of Architectural Historians*, Oct. 1967, p. 164.
[67]Ibid., p. 163.
[68]Ibid., p. 163.
[69]John Stewart, "Canada's Landscape Heritage," *Landscape Planning*, Aug. 1979, p. 219.
[70]John Steward and Susan Buggey, "Canada's Living Past — Historic Landscapes and Gardens," *Ontario Association of Landscape Architects Review*, Aug. 1976, p. 9.
[71]Warburton, p. 38.
[72]Mary K. Cullen, "The Late Nineteenth Century Development of the Queen Square Gardens, Charlottetown, Prince Edward Island," *Association of Preservation Technology Bulletin*, 1977, p. 7.
[73]William C. MacKee, *The History of the Vancouver Parks System, 1886-1929*, M.A. Thesis, University of Victoria, Victoria, 1972, p. 11.
[74]Alan F.J. Artibise, *Winnipeg: A Social History of Urban Growth, 1874-1914*, McGill-Queen's University Press, Montreal, 1975, p. 267.
[75]Ibid., p. 268.
[76]Ibid., p. 268.
[77]"The Village Park and Cemetery," *Canadian Horticulturist*, Jan. 1903, p. 30.
[78]Ibid, p. 30.
[79]Ibid., p. 30.
[80]MacKee, p. 12.
[81]"Brampton's New Park," *Canadian Horticulturist*, Aug. 1903, p. 325.
[82]Thomas Mawson, *The Life and Work of an English Landscape Architect: The Autobiography of Thomas H. Mawson*, Charles Schribners, New York, 1927, pp. 191-205.
[83]City of Winnipeg, Parks and Recreation Department, *The History and Development of Assiniboine Park and Zoo in Winnipeg, Manitoba, Canada*, Winnipeg, 1972, p. 5, 12, 33.
[84]J.P. Jaffray, "Galt Civic Improvement," *Annual Report of the Horticultural Societies of Ontario*, Toronto, 1908, p. 71, and Hutt, "The Civic. . .," p. 262.
[85]Jaffray, p. 71.
[86]"London Parks," *Canadian Horticulturist*, Aug. 1905, p. 308.
[87]Arthur Sharpe, "Trees and Shrubs for Small Parks," *Annual Report of the Horticultural Societies of Ontario*, Toronto, 1918, pp. 131-9.
[88]"Children's Parks as Peace Memorials," *Manitoba Horticulturist*, May 1919, p. 47.
[89]Edward Odling, "Arnold Park, Davidson," *2nd Annual Report of the Director of Agricultural Extension, on the Work of the Horticultural Societies of Saskatchewan*, Regina, 1930, pp. 54-6.
[90]George Baldwin, "Vacant Lot Gardening," *Annual Report of the Horticultural Societies of Ontario*, Toronto, 1916, p. 104.
[91]J.L. Wilson, "Report," *Annual Report of the Horticultural Societies of Ontario*, Toronto, 1912, p. 12.
[92]*Canadian Horticulturist*, March 1918, p. xiii.
[93]"Vacant Lots as Gardens," *Conservation*. Aug. 1913, p. 2.
[94]Chester Walters, "A Garden Club in Hamilton," *Canadian Municipal Journal*, Dec. 1915, p. 433.
[95]Irene Wilson, "Solving the Problem of the Unemployed Women," *Farm and Ranch Review*, April 1915, p. 224.
[96]"Growing Food on Vacant Lots," *Agricultural Gazette of Canada*, Feb. 1915, p. 183.
[97]"Rotary Gardens in Toronto Help Canada's Food Production," *The Toronto Sunday World*, Sept. 8, 1918, p. 8.
[98]"Vacant Lot Gardening," *Agricultural Gazette of Canada*, Dec. 1915, pp. 1198-1202.
[99]G.H.M. Baker, "Allotments and Home Gardens," *Annual Report of the Horticultural Societies of Ontario*, Toronto, 1918, pp. 17-18.

[100]"The Toronto Vacant Lot Association Annual Report, 1918," Typewritten copy, p. 2.
[101]W.G. McKendrick, "Flowers at the Front," *Canadian Horticulturist*, Jan. 1918, p. 11.
[102]Canadian Food Bulletin, "Home Garden Campaign in Various Parts of Canada," *Manitoba Horticulturist*, March 1918, p. 29.
[103]J.B. Spencer, ed., *Vacant Lot Gardening in 1917*, Department of Agriculture, Ottawa, 1917, p. 14.
[104]S.E. McLellan, "Vacant Lot Gardening: Medicine Hat, Alberta," *Agricultural Gazette of Canada*, Dec. 1915, p. 1200.
[105]J.L. Wilson, "Report," *Annual Report of the Horticultural Societies of Ontario*, Toronto, 1916, p. 16.
[106]A.J. Cowling, "How I Won the First Prizė in the Calgary Vacant Lot Competition," *Western Gardener and Poultry Journal*, May 1921, p. 217.
[107]Thomas Dockray, "Vacant Lot Gardening," *Annual Report of the Horticultural Societies of Ontario*, Toronto, 1918, pp. 43-44.
[108]"Garden Lots," *Canadian Municipal Journal*, Aug. 1917, p. 347.
[109]Spencer, p. 15.
[110]Dockray, p. 40.
[111]"Vacant Lot Gardening," *Agricultural Gazette of Canada*, Dec. 1917, p. 1094.
[112]*Canadian Horticulturist*, Oct. 1918, p. 238.
[113]John Barnecut, "Calgary Vacant Lots Garden Club Hold Their Sixth Annual Meeting," *Western Gardener and Poultry Journal*, Dec. 1920, p. 83.
[114]G.A.T. Mason, "The Ninth Annual Meeting of the Calgary Vacant Lots Garden Club," *Western Gardener and Beekeeper*, Jan. 1924, p. 81.

Chapter Five

[1]John Hughes, "Partners with God," *Report of the Horticultural Societies of Ontario*, Toronto, 1916, p. 66.
[2]G.A.T. Mason, "The Ninth Annual Meeting of the Calgary Vacant Lots Garden Club," *The Western Gardener and Beekeeper*, Jan. 1924, p. 75.
[3]Hughes, p. 66.
[4]R.B. Whyte, W.T. Macoun, F.E. Buck, and J.B. Spencer, *Ottawa, a City of Gardens; a Guide for the Improvement of the Lawns and Gardens in Ottawa*, Ottawa Horticultural Society, Ottawa, 1916, p. 5.
[5]Julia Berral, *The Garden*, Penguin Books, London, 1966, p. 277.
[6]Derek Clifford, *A History of Garden Design*, Faber and Faber, London, 1962, p. 208.
[7]Richard Gorer, *The Flower Garden in England*, B.T. Batsford Ltd., London, 1975, p. 139.
[8]Frederick Todd, "Landscape Architecture," *The Canadian Architect and Builder*, 1901, p. 77.
[9]Ibid., p. 77.
[10]H.B. Dunington-Grubb, "Beyond Four Walls," *Royal Architectural Institute of Canada Journal*, July 1932, p. 220.
[11]H.W. Brown, "History of the Kitchener Horticultural Society," Waterloo Historical Society, *26th Annual Report*, 1938, p. 9.
[12]H.J. Moore, "Distinctive Gardening," *Canadian Florist*, May 30, 1919, p. 104.
[13]George Moore, *Semi-Tropical Bedding and Carpet Gardening*, Montreal, 1888, p. 1.
[14]J.A. Ellis, "How to Make the City Grounds Attractive," *Canadian Horticulturist*, June 1905, p. 229.
[15]E. Byfield, "Herbaceous Borders that Bloom for Seven Months," *Canadian Horticulturist*, May 1907, p. 112.
[16]H.M. Speechly, "Perennials: The Backbone of Manitoba Gardens," *Canadian Horticulturist*, Aug. 1907, p. 189.
[17]H.M. Speechly, "Good Taste in Gardening," *Canadian Horticulturist*, April 1908, p. 78.
[18]Mary Eliza Blacklock, "The Arrangement of a Flower Garden," *Canadian Horticulturist*, Dec. 1909, p. 267.
[19]W.R. Reader, "Landscape Gardening," *The Western Gardener and Poultryman*, Jan. 1922, p. 146.
[20]Mrs. Walter Parlby, "The Woman's Garden," *Grain Growers' Guide*, April 7, 1920, p. 81.
[21]Dorothy Perkins, *Canadian Garden Book*, Thomas Allen Publishers, Toronto, 1918, pp. 46-7.
[22]W.E. Groves, "Beautifying the Home," *Canadian Horticulturist*, Floral Edition, April 1921, p. 51.
[23]Mrs. Annie Jack, *The Canadian Garden. A Pocket Help for the Amateur*, Musson, Toronto, 1910, p. 40.
[24]W.H. Hutt, "Beautifying the Home Grounds," *Canadian Horticulturist*, Jan. 1904, p. 41.
[25]Pleasance Crawford, *The Ontario Home Landscape: 1890-1914*, Report prepared for the Department of Landscape Architecture, University of Toronto, Toronto, 1982, p. 19.
[26]Frank J. Scott, *Victorian Gardens: The Art of Beautifying Suburban Home Grounds*, D. Appleton and Co., New York, 1870, p. 51.
[27]M.H. Howitt, *Beautifying the Home Grounds of Canada*, published jointly by the Department of Agriculture, Ottawa and the Canadian Horticultural Council, Ottawa, 1930, pp. 12-13.
[28]Crawford, p. 28.
[29]"The Pergola for Shade and Ornament," *Canadian Florist*, May 11, 1922, p. 128.
[30]Crawford, p. 27.
[31]Ibid., p. 27.
[32]C.E. Woolverton, "The Home and Its Environment," *Canadian Horticulturist*, May 1900, p. 180.
[33]Mrs. Walter Parlby, p. 81.
[34]Barbara Villy Cormack, *Perennials and Politics; The Life Story of Hon. Irene Parlby, LL.D.*, Professional Print., Sherwood Park, Alberta, 1968, p. 84.
[35]G.A.B. Krook, "Increasing Farm Values," *Nor'West Farmer*, Dec. 1923, p. 1197.
[36]Mrs. John J. Funk, "The Farm Garden," *Western Gardener and Poultryman Journal*, Feb. 1920, p. 65.
[37]W.R. Leslie, "Adorning the Farmstead," *Nor'West Farmer*, March 1930, p. 7.
[38]Dorothy Perkins, "The Rockery and Japanese Garden at Villa Fiora," *Canadian Homes and Gardens*, May 1927, p. 36.
[39]Ibid., p. 37.
[40]Ibid., p. 37, 60.
[41]Gorer, p. 144.
[42]Anthony Huxley, *An Illustrated History of Gardening*, Paddington Press Ltd., New York and London, 1978, p. 309.
[43]Miles Hadfield, *A History of British Gardening*, John Murray, London, 1979, p. 418.
[44]"Discussion Period," *11th Annual Report of the Western Horticultural Society*, Winnipeg, 1908, p. 31.
[45]John Hutchinson, "Beautiful Rock Gardens May be Found About Victoria," *Country Life in B.C.*, April 1926, p. 28.
[46]Keith Dixon, *Vancouver Island Rock and Alpine Garden Society 1921-1971*, 1971, pp. 2-3.

[47]F. Cleveland Morgan, "Rock Gardening in the Province of Quebec," *Report of the Conference Held by the Royal Horticultural Society and the Alpine Garden Society*, London, 1936, p. 21.
[48]Ibid., p. 27.
[49]Alice MacKay, "Lady Byng's *Au Revoir* to Canadian Horticulture," *Canadian Homes and Gardens*, Nov. 1926, p. 99.
[50]"An Amateur's Famous Half Acre Garden," *Canadian Horticulturist*, July 1911, p. 163.
[51]"The Home of a Horticultural Enthusiast," *Canadian Horticulturist*, March 1905, p. 105.
[52]Dr. H.M. Speechly, "A Westerner in the Gardens of Toronto," *Manitoba Horticulturist*, Nov. 1915, p. 79.
[53]"Rosemary and Lavender," *Canadian Magazine*, 1926, p. 176.
[54]Susan Sloane, "Le Parc de Métis," *Horticulture*, June 1979, p. 44.
[55]Ibid., pp. 40-5.
[56]Ibid., p. 44.
[57]Ibid., p. 44.
[58]Walter Vaughan, *The Life and Work of Sir William Van Horne*, The Century Co., New York, 1920, p. 265.
[59]Ibid., p. 63.
[60]Conversation with David Myles, 1982.
[61]Graham Spry, "Country Homes Around Lower Fort Garry," *Western Gardener and Poultry Journal*, Aug. 1920, pp. 336-7.
[62]Julia W. Henshaw, "Wonder Gardens of the Canadian West," *Country Life in America*, Jan. 1923, p. 45.
[63]Frederick J. Niven, *A Lady in the Wilderness, a Tale of the Yukon. . .*, reprinted from the *Canadian Home Journal*, Farwest, 1930 or 1931, pp. 6, 7.
[64]Pam Hobbs, "Victoria's Garden Spots," *Globe and Mail*, May 1, 1982, p. 10.
[65]Frank M. Appleton, "The Butchart Gardens, *Horticulture*, April 1980, p. 38.
[66]L. Dean-Hatch, "The Sunken Gardens of Victoria," *The Canadian Magazine*, May 1925, p. 117.
[67]Appleton, p. 38.
[68]Dean-Hatch, p. 117.
[69]W.H. Warren, "Paradise: The Butchart Gardens," *Garden*, July-Aug. 1978, p. 14.
[70]Dean-Hatch, p. 118.

Chapter Six

[1]Marjorie Major, *From the Ground. . .the Story of Planting in Nova Scotia*, Petheric Press Ltd., Halifax, 1981, p. 96.
[2]Ina Vrugtman, "Preliminary Listing of 19th Century Canadian Nurseries, Seed Business and Florists," March 1981.
[3]J. Russell Harper, "Loyalist Gardens," *The Maritime Advocate and Busy East*, Feb. 1955, p. 10.
[4]Pleasance Crawford, "Some Early Niagara Peninsula Nurserymen," *Agriculture and Farm Life in the Niagara Peninsula: Proceedings, Fifth Annual Niagara Peninsula History Conference*, Brock University, St. Catharines, 1983, p. 1.
[5]Ibid., p. 7.
[6]Ibid., p. 8.
[7]Ibid., p. 8.
[8]Ibid., p. 11.
[9]Ibid., pp. 5-6.
[10]Ibid., pp. 12-16.
[11]"Nurseries Which are a Credit to Canada," *Canadian Horticulturist*, Nov. 1904, p. 463.
[12]Ibid., p. 465.
[13]"One of Canada's Leading Nurseries," *Canadian Horticulturist*, Sept. 1904, p. 380.
[14]Ibid., pp. 378-9.
[15]Ibid., p. 378.
[16]Dr. H.M. Speechly, "An Appreciation of A.P. Stevenson," *Western Gardener and Poultry Journal*, Jan. 1923, p. 111.
[17]Ibid., p. 107.
[18]"A Visit to Patmores," *Western Gardener and Poultry Journal*, Aug. 1921, p. 315.
[19]H.L. Patmore, "The Nursery Trade, Its Supply and Requirements," *Manitoba Horticulturist*, July 1915, p. 52.
[20]Ibid., p. 52.
[21]John George, "Eastern Nursery Stock," *Western Horticultural Society Annual Report*, Winnipeg, 1900, p. 13.
[22]Ibid., p. 14.
[23]Cynthia Westcott, *The Gardener's Bug Book*, The American Garden Guild and Doubleday and Co., New York, 1946, p. 359.
[24]*The Organization, Achievements and Present Work of the Experimental Farms*, Dept. of Agriculture, Ottawa, 1924, p. 11.
[25]*Fifty Years of Progress on Dominion Experimental Farms 1886-1936*, Dept. of Agriculture, Ottawa, 1939, pp. 19, 20.
[26]*The Organization. . .*, p. 11.
[27]Elsie Pomeroy, *William Saunders and His Five Sons*, Ryerson Press, Toronto, 1956, p. 31.
[28]*The Organization. . .*, p. 12.
[29]Ibid., p. 7.
[30]J.P. de Wet, *A Hundred Years of Horticulture*, unpublished manuscript, ca., 1974/76, p. 16.
[31]Ibid., p. 17.
[32]Ibid., p. 20.
[33]Speechly, p. 137.
[34]Crawford, p. 4.
[35]Ibid., p. 4.
[36]William Scott, "Ornamental Shrubs and Hardy Perennial Plants," *Western Horticultural Society Annual Report*, Winnipeg, 1898, p. 22.
[37]Patmore, p. 54.
[38]Crawford, p. 4.
[39]Patmore, p. 54.
[40]W.A. Macleod, "A Saskatchewan Nursery," *Western Gardener and Poultryman*, Dec. 1931, p. 81.
[41]"Patmore Co. Pioneers in Nursery Field," *Canadian Florist*, Oct. 26, 1926, p. 327.
[42]"Dahlia, Perennial and Plant Specialists," *Canadian Florist*, Oct. 22, 1928, p. 466.
[43]"Statistics in Canadian Floriculture," *Canadian Florist*, July 29, 1930, p. 373.

Chapter Seven

[1]Correspondence with Pleasance Crawford.
[2]John Stewart and Susan Buggey, "Canada's Living Past — Historic Landscapes and Gardens," *Ontario Association of Landscape Architects Review*, Aug. 1976, p. 7.
[3]Ibid., p. 12.
[4]Ibid., p. 12.
[5]Delos W. Beadle, *Canadian Fruit, Flower, and Kitchen Gardener. A Guide in All Matters Relating to the Cultivation of Fruits, Flowers and Vegetables, and Their Value for Cultivation in This Climate*, James Campbell and Son, Toronto, 1872, pp. 270-1.
[6]Ibid., p. 271.
[7]Robert McNeil, *Practical Tests on Gardening for Manitoba and North-West Territories*, Wilson Brothers, Winnipeg, 1884, p. 31.

[8]Henry James Morgan, ed., *The Canadian Men and Women of the Time: A Hand-book of Canadian Biography*, D. and J. Sadlier and Co., Montreal, 1898, p. 496.
[9]Ibid., p. 496.
[10]*Garden Magazine*, Feb. 1905, p. 17.
[11]Pleasance Crawford, "The Canadian Garden of Annie Jack," Hortulus catalogue, Oct. 1981.
[12]Annie Jack, *The Canadian Garden. A Pocket Help for the Amateur*, Musson, Toronto, p. 1910. p. 98.
[13]Ibid., p. 99.
[14]Dorothy Perkins, *Canadian Garden Book*, Thomas Allen Publishers, Toronto, 1918, p. 36-7.
[15]Charles G.D. Roberts and Arthur L. Tornnel, eds., *Standard Dictionary of Canadian Biography*, Vol. II, Trans Canada Press, Toronto, 1938, p. 19.
[16]Perkins, pp. 101-2.
[17]Ibid., p. 17.
[18]Beverley Seaton, "The Garden Autobiography," *Garden History*, Spring 1979, p. 101.
[19]E.P. Fewster, *My Garden Dreams*, The Graphic Publishers, Ltd., Ottawa, 1926, p. 116.
[20]Ray Desmond, "Victorian Gardening Magazines," *Garden History*, Winter 1977, p. 47.
[21]Paul Rutherford, *The Making of the Canadian Media*, McGraw-Hill Ryerson Ltd., Toronto, 1978, p. 46.
[22]"The Past, Present and Future of the *Canadian Horticulturist*" *Canadian Horticulturist*, April 1904, p. 144.
[23]J.P. de Wet, *A Hundred Years of Horticulture*, unpublished manuscript, ca. 1974/76, p. 14.
[24]Paul Rutherford, *A Victorian Authority: The Daily Press in Late Nineteenth Century Canada*, University of Toronto Press, Toronto, 1982, see Chapter One.
[25]Peter Middleton, "The Evolution of Horticulture," *Western Horticultural Society Annual Report*, Winnipeg, 1905, p. 102.
[26]"Mr. W.T. Macoun, Canada's Leading Horticulturist," *Canadian Horticulturist*, May 1907, p. 125.
[27]C.S. Harrison, "The Paeony — the Flower for Manitoba," *Western Horticultural Society Annual Report*, Winnipeg, 1905, p. 98.
[28]Mrs. R.B. Potts, "Press Work in Relation to Horticulture," *Annual Report of the Horticultural Societies of Ontario*, Toronto, 1916, p. 89.
[29]Ibid., p. 91.
[30]Ibid., p. 91.
[31]*The Organization, Achievements and Present Work of the Experimental Farms*, Department of Agriculture, Ottawa, 1924, p. 143.
[32]Ibid., p. 144.
[33]"The Publications Branch," *Agricultural Gazette of Canada*, Jan. 1914, p. 27.
[34]*Country Life in Canada*, Aug. 1916, end page.
[35]G.H.M. Baker, "Are Our Annual Reports Interesting and Valuable to Our Horticultural Societies?," *Annual Report of the Horticultural Societies of Ontario*, Toronto, 1919, p. 43.
[36]Ibid., p. 43.
[37]For an extensive review of Canadian gardening literature see Edwinna von Baeyer, *A Preliminary Bibliography for Garden History in Canada*, Parks Canada, Ottawa, 1983.

Chapter Eight

[1]Harry Brown, "Suggestions for the Improvement of Our Horticultural Products by Cross-Fertilization or Hybridization," *Annual Report of the Western Horticultural Society*, Winnipeg, 1904, p. 58.
[2]Miles Hadfield, *A History of British Gardening*, John Murray, London, 1979, p. 272.
[3]Lucile H. Brockway, *Science and Colonial Expansion: The Role of the British Royal Botanic Gardens*, Academic Press, New York, 1979, p. 63.
[4]Hadfield, pp. 394-5.
[5]W.H. Alderman, *Development of Horticulture on the Northern Great Plains*, Great Plains Region, American Society for Horticultural Science, 1962, p. 55.
[6]J.P. de Wet, *A Hundred Years of Horticulture*, unpublished manuscript, ca. 1974/76, p. 1.
[7]Ibid., p. 2.
[8]Elsie Pomeroy, *William Saunders and His Five Sons*, Ryerson Press, Toronto, 1956, pp. 46-47.
[9]Western Canadian Society for Horticulture, comp., *Development of Horticulture on the Canadian Prairies: An Historical Review*, 1956, p. 54.
[10]H.H. Groff, "The Science of Plant Breeding," *Annual Report of the Horticultural Societies of Ontario*, Toronto, 1908, p. 78.
[11]W.A. Craick, "The Banker with the Gladiolus Hobby," *Biographical Scrapbook*, Metropolitan Toronto Library Board, Vol. 1, pp. 440-2.
[12]Ibid., pp. 440-2.
[13]*Toronto Star*, Oct. 1933.
[14]Craick, pp. 440-2.
[15]Discussed in Pomeroy, *William Saunders and His Five Sons*, and *Development of Horticulture on the Canadian Prairies*.
[16]Craick, pp. 440-2.
[17]Ibid., pp. 440-42.
[18]*Development of Horticulture on the Canadian. . .*, p. 25.
[19]de Wet, p. 2.
[20]Ibid., p. 2.
[21]C.S. Harrison, "The Paeony — the Flower for Manitoba," *Annual Report of the Western Horticultural Society*, Winnipeg, 1905, p. 97.
[22]*The Organization, Achievements and Present Work of the Experimental Farms*, Dept. of Agriculture, Ottawa, 1924, pp. 272-3.
[23]Ibid., p. 224.
[24]Bob Collins, "Canada's Lady of the Lilies," *Canadian Homes and Gardens*, July 1953, p. 47.
[25]Handwritten manuscript, 195?, Royal Botanical Garden Archives, Hamilton, Ontario.
[26]George L. Slate and D.F. Cameron, "Isabella Preston, 1881-1965," *The Lily Yearbook*, North American Lily Society, New York, 1966, p. 108.
[27]Note sent from Isabella Preston to Charles M. Curtis, 1956, Royal Botanical Gardens Archives, Hamilton, Ontario.
[28]"Isabella Preston" Mimeograph, Central Experimental Farm, Ornamentals Division, Ottawa.
[29]Interview with D.F. Cameron, Oct. 12, 1982.
[30]Ibid.
[31]Donald Wyman, "The Preston Lilacs," *American Nurseryman*, Dec. 1, 1970, p. 11.
[32]Ibid., p. 11.
[33]Interview with D.F. Cameron.
[34]Isabella Preston's work journals, Royal Botanical Gardens Archives.
[35]F.L. Skinner, *Horticultural Horizons: Plant Breeding and Introducing at Dropmore, Manitoba*, Manitoba Department of Agriculture, Winnipeg, 1967, p. 9.
[36]P.M. Abel, "The Wildwood Was His School," *Country Guide*, Feb. 1933, p. 5.
[37]"Dr. Frank Leith Skinner," Manitoba Department of Cultural Affairs and Historical Resource, Winnipeg, 1981, p. 1.

[38]Skinner, p. 12.
[39]Abel, p. 5.
[40]"Dr. Frank Leith Skinner," p. 1.
[41]Interview with A.R. Buckley, Oct. 25, 1982.
[42]Skinner, p. 107.
[43]Letter from Isabella Preston to Frank Skinner, Oct. 12, 1922, Manitoba Archives, MG 14, C 45.
[44]"Dr. Frank Leith Skinner," p. 2.
[45]Skinner, p. 24.
[46]Rosa Shaw, "She Creates Beauty," *Chatelaine*, Oct. 1943, p. 84.
[47]Art Drysdale, ed., *Canadian Nurseryman Centennial Yearbook*, 1967, p. 24.
[48]J.W. Crow, "Hybridizing for Amateurs," *Annual Report of the Horticultural Societies of Ontario*, Toronto, 1927, p. 27.
[49]F. Cleveland Morgan, "Notes on Hybridizing Iris," *Canadian Homes and Gardens*, Oct. 1926, p. 56.
[50]Ibid., p. 56.
[51]Ibid., p. 56.
[52]H.J. Moore, "Plant Registration," *Canadian Florist*, Sept. 5, 1919, p. 203.
[53]"Dr. Frank Leith Skinner," p. 6.
[54]H.J. Moore, "Plant Registration," *Canadian Horticulturist*, Nov. 1923, p. 253.
[55]W.T. Macoun, "Plant Registration in Canada," *Canadian Florist*, Oct. 22, 1929, p. 474.
[56]"Canadian Horticultural Council Plant Registration Bureau," *Agricultural Gazette of Canada*, Jan./Feb. 1923, p. 65.
[57]Ibid., p. 64.
[58]Ibid., p. 66.
[59]Moore, 1923, p. 253.
[60]"Nurseries Which Are a Credit to Canada," *Canadian Horticulturist*, Nov. 1904, p. 465.
[61]W.J. Potter, "Canadian Horticulture: Past, Present and Future," *Canadian Florist*, Oct. 1 and 15, 1920, p. 287.
[62]Dr. H.M. Speechly, "Perennials: The Backbone of Manitoba Gardens," *Canadian Horticulturist*, Aug. 1908, p. 190.
[63]W.J. Potter, "Developing Horticulture in Canada," *Canadian Florist*, Oct. 15, 1920, p. 287.
[64]W.T. Macoun, "The Best Native Trees and Shrubs," *Canadian Florist*, March 30, 1922, p. 91.
[65]C.K. Baillie, "Canadian Grown Nursery Stock," *Annual Report of the Horticultural Societies of Ontario*, Toronto, 1926, p. 45.
[66]Potter, "Canadian Horticulture. . .," p. 288.
[67]C.A. Allen-Heeney, "Foreign Nursery Stock Floods British Columbia," *Country Life in B.C.*, Nov. 1926, p. 12.
[68]Baillie, p. 43.
[69]Ibid., pp. 44-5.
[70]"Statistics on Canadian Floriculture," *Canadian Florist*, July 29, 1930, pp. 373-4.
[71]C.A. Robinson, "Seed Growing in British Columbia," *Canadian Florist*, Nov. 8, 1927, p. 431.
[72]Reece H. Hague, "Commercial Bulb and Seed Growing in B.C.," *Canadian Florist*, Feb. 25, 1930, p. 87.

Afterword

[1]American Society for State and Local History, Technical Leaflet No. 80 1974.
[2]John J. Stewart, "Notes on Calvert Vaux's 1873 design for the Public Grounds of the Parliament Buildings in Ottawa," APT *Bulletin*, No. 1, 1976, 1-27; Susan Buggey and John J. Stewart, "Lakehurst and Beechcroft: Roches Point, Ontario, Canada," *Journal of Garden History*, No. 2, 1981, 147-66; Alex Wilson, "The Public Gardens of Halifax, Nova Scotia," *Journal of Garden History*, No. 3, 1983.
[3]See Edwinna von Baeyer, *A Preliminary Bibliography for Garden History in Canada*, Parks Canada, Ottawa, 1983; and most recently "Historical Perspectives," *Landscape Architectural Review*; "*Gardens*"; *Canada Century Home*; and APT *Bulletin*, No. 4, 1983.
[4]*Guidelines for the Man-Made Heritage Component of Environmental Assessments*, 1981.
[5]For a vivid description of the problem, see Lois Lister and Victoria Lister Carley, "Love at Second Sight: An Urban Villa in Toronto," *Garden Design*, No. 3, 1983, 30-35.
[6]Gilles Roy, "Le Jardin des Sulpiciens Une Richesse Délaissée," *Continuité*, hiver, 1984, 44-45.
[7]*The Globe and Mail*, May 8, 1984; "Halifax's High-rise War," *Maclean's*, May 14, 1984.

Index